International Studies of the

Committee on International Relations

University of Notre Dame

GIUSEPPE MAMMARELLA

ITALY AFTER FASCISM

A POLITICAL HISTORY
1943–1965

UNIVERSITY OF NOTRE DAME PRESS
1966

FOREWORD

The history of Italy after the fall of Fascism is mainly the history of the attempts made to change the country's political and social structures and to solve its age-old and lingering historical problems. In the twenty or more years since the restoration of political democracy, these efforts have failed to produce tangible results. Yet, in this period the Italian people have given convincing proof of their vitality and their will to proceed on the road toward political progress. The country has been reconstructed at a faster rate than could have been expected after a war that left it physically devastated and in a state of profound moral prostration. Since the work of reconstruction has been completed, Italy has achieved such a remarkable level of economic development that it has become known as the Italian economic miracle. The postwar constitution assures the widest possible representation of the popular will; and although not fully implemented, its provisions have never been altered or violated. Despite these positive achievements, however, the main goal of Italian democracy after the fall of Mussolini — the creation of a fully integrated society — has not yet been attained.

This goal has been the basic historical objective of all the regimes that have succeeded one another from the time of the country's unification in 1861. While the Risorgimento achieved territorial unity, it left unsolved the problem of creating a common national conscience. The cultural and economic divisions between South and North, and the gap which separated the working classes from the rest of the political community were never bridged by the ruling class which emerged out of the Risorgimento and governed the country until 1922. The Fascist regime sought to achieve unification by pursuing a policy of national expansion aimed at resolving Italy's internal problems by adventures abroad. The total failure of this policy brought the Italian nation to the verge of ruin.

Since World War II, although many concrete efforts have been made to eradicate the most striking social and economic inequalities, the problem of national unification remains. Two ideologies, each representing a different political *Veltanschauung*, have divided the country into opposing camps: Communism, whose aim is a radical change in the existing social and political system, and Christian Democracy, which has as its goal a gradual modification of this system. The clash between these mass parties, each with its political allies, has deepened the historical divisions and has rendered the process of unification even more difficult. The postwar political history of Italy is the history of the struggle between these two forces, and their allies and of the shifts in alignments on which the achievement of unification or its indefinite postponement will ultimately depend.

Some of the episodes in this complicated process might be difficult for foreign observers to understand. For those accustomed to a more pragmatic approach to politics, certain aspects of the Italian political system might appear needlessly cumbersome. The purpose of this book is not only to give a chronological account of the political events of the period 1949-1965, with an indispensable reference to earlier periods, but also to clarify the basic issues around which the political debate has developed and to show how certain apparently doctrinaire questions were closely connected with practical problems and real situations.

Born out of lectures given in my course on Italian politics at Stanford-in-Italy, this history has been constantly reshaped. I owe my students a debt of gratitude for their comments, questions and discussions. I also want to thank Betty and Victor Velen for their most valuable assistance in revising the English manuscript and for their excellent suggestions.

G. M.

Stanford University
Florence, January 1966.

CONTENTS

PART THREE

THE YEARS OF QUADRIPARTITE GOVERNMENT, 1948-1953

PART ONE

The war 1939-1945
and the end of Fascism

CHAPTER 1

MUSSOLINI'S FALL

Late in the evening of July 25, 1943, the Italian people were struck by this dramatic announcement: Benito Mussolini had been dismissed as head of the government,[1] King Vittorio Emanuele III had taken over the supreme command of all fighting forces and had appointed Marshal Pietro Badoglio as the new Prime Minister. After almost twenty-one years, Fascist rule had come to an end, and all political power had been transferred to the Italian monarch. The former dictator, "taken into custody" by order of the King, was placed under the guard of the faithful *Carabinieri Reali* on the small island of Ponza off the Neapolitan coast, where, during his rule, the "Duce" had isolated his political opponents.

From the moment Italy entered the war, on June 11, 1940, forces were set in motion that were to bring about Mussolini's downfall a short but historic three years later. The groundwork, however, had been laid earlier. At the beginning of 1938 the Fascist regime, given its military

---

[1] On October 1922, after the March on Rome, Mussolini was asked by the King to form the new cabinet following the resignation of Luigi Facta; his title was Prime Minister, Italy at the time being a parliamentary monarchy. Later, when Fascism had become established as a dictatorship, and the parliamentary system was abolished, Mussolini preferred to use the title of *Capo del governo*, which, although equivalent to that of prime minister, "sounded more Italian".

3

successes in Ethiopia and Spain together with the firm hold it maintained on the country, had reached the maximum of its international prestige.[1] Fascism and Mussolini were passively accepted by the majority of the Italians. Organized opposition to the regime was limited to a few symbolic gestures made by university student groups, anti-Fascists in exile or the sporadic activity of Communist cells organized with much effort and at great risk in some of the big factories of Northern Italy.

In less than a year, however, this situation began gradually to change. The pro-German policy adopted by Mussolini which on May 22, 1939, led to the signing of the "Pact of Steel" alienated many Italians who were sympathetic to the dictator. Memories of the First World War and the *Risorgimento* tradition, which had been anti-Germanic in spirit, were still very alive. The decline of Mussolini's still then unchallenged prestige can be dated from 1939, when a few months after the Munich Pact his intention of bringing Italy into the war on the side of Germany appeared every day clearer. The declaration of war less than a year later, apart from official manifestations of enthusiasm and self-confidence, typical of every dictatorship, created grave concern among the most conscious sections of the population. In spite of assurances by the Fascist propaganda machine that the war would be won in a few months, many Italians who had fought in the First World War and who were familiar with British determination as well as German ruthlessness looked upon Italy's future with much uncertainty.

The views of the pessimists, whom Mussolini contemptuously branded as defeatists, were soon confirmed. After an uncertain start, military operations took an unfavorable turn for Italy; there were, of course, short-lived military gains. But after the successful Italo-German drive in Egypt, in the

---

[1] The Munich Pact marked the highest point of the national and international prestige of Mussolini. Acting in the role of mediator between Germany on the one hand and France and England on the other, Mussolini was presented by skillful Fascist propaganda as having saved Europe from the impending war.

spring of 1942, which was stopped by the British forces 40 miles from Alexandria, the fortunes of war turned steadily against the Axis. The rosy predictions of the Duce had not materialized; his speeches lost their original boldness; and, more and more, he exhorted the Italians to ever new efforts and new sacrifices. But his words no longer had appeal to the population. After three years of ruthless war, fought by Italian soldiers on seven different fronts—from East Africa to Tunisia, from France to the Soviet Union—the country was exhausted. An enormous military effort had been undertaken under the worst possible conditions. Considering the lack of training, equipment, and skilled leadership, the resistance of the Italian forces lasted longer than could have been reasonably expected.

ITALY'S UNPREPAREDNESS FOR WAR

On the eve of Italy's entrance into the war the country's economy and military potential were depleted. Following the conquest of Ethiopia in 1935-1936 and the intervention in the Spanish civil war (1936-1939) in support of Franco's nationalists against the Republican coalition, both of which had used up large quantities of military equipment, the Italian army needed a long period to rebuild its effectives. Modern armaments were lacking, the military units were disorganized, and most of them were below their normal complements.[1] The military leaders, especially at the highest level, were unprepared to engage in a modern war and were divided by petty rivalries. The condition of the Air Force, to which Mussolini had dedicated considerable effort, though it was nullified by the incompetence and dishonesty of his collaborators, was no better.[2] The Navy, third largest in

---

[1] Of the 73 divisions Italy had on the eve of the war, only 19 were fully equipped. The major gaps were in artillery and means of transportation.

[2] General Valle, head of the Air Force, reported 3,000 airplanes in condition of full efficency; according to the navy's information service, there were only 982. (Ciano's Diary, April 29, 1939).

5

Europe with regard to tonnage, was well equipped, well trained and modern, although it was hampered by chronic fuel shortages.

The precarious situation of the Army made Mussolini's famous claim of "eight million bayonets" rather illusory. The dictator was either misinformed about the real strength of his forces or, openly bluffing, he boasted of Italian military power in order to give weight to Italy's international position and inspire self-confidence among the Italian people, whom he often reproached as not being warlike enough. Italy could probably have mustered eight million men under her flag, but her economy was unable to provide the weapons and services needed for a modern army. Italian war industries, which had prospered during the last thirty years, had reached a high technical level, but the raw materials for manufacturing heavy weapons were lacking. Copper, tungsten, cobalt, vanadium, basic materials for war production, could not be found in Italy at all, and the foreign currency necessary to purchase them abroad was scarce. In any case, even if the raw materials could have been provided, rearmament would have required time, at least two years according to the most optimistic estimates.

The economic and financial situation of the country was also poor.[1] Both agriculture and industry were seriously strained because of the costly policies of economic self-sufficiency (*autarchia*) that was promoted by Mussolini, partly to make the country economically independent from the rest of the world and partly to satisfy national pride. In consequence of the exceptional military expenses of the 1930's, the government deficit was to reach as high as 12 billion lire (1938); while the value of the *lira* had considerably decreased on the international market. The situation called for a period of concentrated effort to put the economy and the Army back on their feet. Finally, the people them-

---

[1] Over the last ten years—1928-38—per capita daily calories had decreased from 2806 to 2723 and the average hourly salary by 4%, while international trade was reduced in value by one third.

selves wanted peace; their spirits were low after the long period of tension provoked by the wars abroad and the push for *autarchia* at home.

Documents and memoirs published after the war provide sufficient evidence of the fact that Mussolini had a distorted picture of the country's real situation. Like all dictators he preferred to surround himself with incompetent yes-men and flatterers, who, ready as they were to please him and to pretend optimism, encouraged the adventurous trend of his policies. Count Galeazzo Ciano, then Foreign Minister and son-in-law of the Duce, reports in his Diary that as soon as the clash between Germany and the Allies appeared unavoidable, Mussolini became increasingly restless. When the war broke out, he felt he could not stay out of it; after having played a big game in international politics for several years, it was too humiliating to remain "with our hands folded while others write history." His hostile attitude toward France and Great Britain, the propaganda put forth over a period of several years, based on the claim of "a place in the sun" for Italy, plus the very nature of Fascist ideology which glorified action and violence, were all elements pushing him toward entry into the conflict.

THE "SHORT WAR"

Following the early German military successes of 1939 and 1940 in Poland, Norway and France, Mussolini became convinced that the war would be of very short duration, and that, if he acted skillfully, he might obtain great advantages at little cost. Hence, the attack on France, when that country was collapsing under the massive thrusts of the German armoured divisions, was justified by Mussolini on the grounds that "Italy needed a few hundred deaths to sit at the peace table." This blatantly cynical attitude was never shared by the Italian people; wide segments of the public who, in spite of Fascist propaganda, still felt close ties with their western neighbor, were deeply ashamed of the "stab in the back."

7

The expectations of the dictator, however, did not materialize. After the armistice with France, the anticipated fall of England did not follow. The German air offensive on Britain in the Summer of 1940 failed. The Italian attack on Greece, decided on by the Duce to match the successes of the German "Blitzkrieg," lasted over six months. At first, the Italian troops were pushed back in Albania. The whole operation was to be concluded only after much effort and with the help of German military intervention.[1] Following these developments, the internal position of Fascism and of Mussolini started weakening. The majority of Italians had accepted, somewhat meekly and without enthusiasm, Mussolini's decision to enter the war. When the main assumption on which Mussolini's decision had been taken proved wrong, when it became clear that the war would be long and hard, the attitude of the Italians turned first into one of criticism and ultimately into ill-disguised antagonism. Times became more and more bitter because of mounting losses, restrictions and the hopelessness of the struggle. For the first time, in the face of so much official optimism, the tragic facts of the war unveiled the real nature of Fascism to the Italian people. It became clear to what extent it consisted in empty rhetoric, improvisation and trickery. More light was shed on the personality of Mussolini, the myth of whose infallibility gradually gave way to recognition of the real man, a shrewd and squalid adventurer. This new awareness did not absolve the Italians of their responsibility for having all too readily accepted "Fascist truths" at their face value. But it did represent a start along a hard and long road, costly in blood and sacrifices, which was to bring the nation to a moral redemption.

The first open manifestations against the regime were the industrial strikes which broke out in Turin in March 1943 and extended in a few days to the industrial centers of

---

[1] The German Army, after the invasion of Yugoslavia at the beginning of April 1941, moved from there and from Bulgaria in a march against Greece which, attacked from all sides, collapsed and signed an armistice with both Italy and Germany (Salonika, April 24, 1941).

Northern Italy. The official justification for these strikes, the first to take place under the regime, which had abolished them peremptorily, was higher wages, but their real character was political. Although the strikes lasted only a few days, their importance was great since they marked the revival of the clandestine action of anti-Fascist opposition groups. Their re-emergence in the struggle was also to manifest itself with the increased circulation of anti-Fascist pamphlets, small newspapers and other underground publications attacking the principles of the Fascist regime, its tyranny and corruption, and above all, stressing the paramount responsibility of Mussolini and accusing him of having thrown the country into a ruinous and meaningless war.

The winter of 1942-43 had been disastrous for Italo-German forces on all fronts. The two battles of El Alamein in North Africa and of Stalingrad in the Soviet Union marked the end of the offensive capabilities of the Axis forces. From then on the military events were to take a faster turn; the Axis forces retreated on both the Russian and North African fronts. After the loss of Lybia and the American landing in Algeria (bringing the war in North Africa to an end on May 12, 1943), it became clear that the major effort of the Allies would henceforth be concentrated on the weakest and geographically closer of the two Axis powers: Italy. This was, in fact, the decision that had been taken at Casablanca in January 1943 by President Roosevelt and Prime Minister Churchill. The massive daily bombing of major Italian cities and industrial centers made this quite evident. The most responsible sectors of the Italian public realistically came to the conclusion that the war would soon be lost. Italy, they thought, should try to withdraw from the war and negotiate a separate armistice in order to avoid becoming a battlefield and to spare further destruction and losses among the civilian population.

To secure honorable peace terms from the Allies now appeared to be the most important goal; but to achieve this end a number of intermediate steps had to be taken.

Fascism and Mussolini were the main stumbling blocks in

the way of peace. Mussolini was too deeply committed with Germany to accept the idea of a separate armistice, which among other things would also have meant the end of his regime. It was reasonable to assume that the Allies, on their part, would impose much harder conditions if the Italians were to surrender with Mussolini still in power. This had been made clear on several occasions during the war. "One man and one man alone," Churchill stated in an address broadcast to the Italian people during the first months of the war, "is held responsible for Italy's participation in the war." The Allies had adopted this line in a psychological warfare campaign aimed at creating a gulf between the Fascist leaders and the population. This distinction was not made merely as a propagandistic device, however; it reflected in part the Allied position. The British, in particular, could not forget that Mussolini had made territorial claims in Africa, which menaced the British position in the Mediterranean and contributed to the political situation that brought Europe to war. The Allied powers might have been willing to help the country to redeem itself had Fascism and its leader been overthrown.

The sudden disappearance of Fascism in Italy, however, would not have solved the Italian problem, according to Allied opinion. Fascism, in the mind of certain Anglo-Saxon leaders and sections of the public, had saved Italy from Bolshevism. This essentially wrong interpretation of a political phenomenon that was much more complex, was also shared by Churchill who, on occasion before the war, had voiced his approval of Mussolini's internal policies. Since Mussolini had become an uncompromising enemy by having sided with Hitler, the only power that could save Italy from the danger of a Communist revolution after the fall of Fascism, according to the same opinion, was the monarchy. The Allied policy toward Italy should therefore aim at reinforcing the position of the King and the prestige of the Royal House. This was Churchill's personal view and it was fully endorsed by the British crown, which had no desire to see another European monarchy wiped out by a popular revolution. Several times, notably toward the end of the war, it was presented as the official policy of Great Britain toward Italy. Later, at the Quebec Conference, in August 1943, this view was communicated to Roosevelt, who, although not completely in agreement, nevertheless recognized British preeminence in decisions concerning Italy's political future. Since the Allies adopted this position then, it was clear that only the King could gain for Italy advantageous peace conditions. Hence, when the first secret moves aimed at disentangling the country from the German alliance were under way, the Royal House automatically became the center of the plot. Apart from the fact that he was favored by the Allies, the King was the most suitable person to direct such an operation since, as the supreme constitutional figure, he was the only one who could dismiss Mussolini by decree.

TOWARDS THE COUP D'ÉTAT OF JULY 25TH

To every objective observer King Vittorio Emanuele III had a major responsibility for the disastrous situation in which Italy found itself. Apart from the essential role he played in the establishment and strengthening of the Fascist regime in 1922, the King had done little to dissuade Mussolini from involving the country in the war. In spite of the fact that during the Fascist regime the King had been obliged to put up with humiliations inflicted by the dictator, he seemed to be satisfied to maintain his honorary prerogatives, while his real powers were gradually reduced by the adaptation of the Italian Constitution—a rather flexible document—to the exigencies of a dictatorship.[1]

---

[1] After 1926, when all political parties except the PNF (Partito Nazionale Fascista) were outlawed, the Italian parliamentary system ceased to function in practice. Following the 1929 and 1931 elections, only the Fascist party had representatives in the *Camera dei Deputati*, which was convened only to endorse Mussolini's decisions. The Senate equally lost most of its independence, in spite of the fact that its members were appointed for life by the King. In 1938 the *Camera dei Fasci e delle Corporazioni*, whose members were designated by Mussolini and the Fascist Party, replaced Parliament.

On several occasions, in the fall and winter of 1939-1940, the King had timidly confided to a few intimates his opposition to Italy's entrance into the war, but he did not try to take an official stand or to seriously influence the decisions of the Duce in any way, despite the fact that he was well aware of the precarious situation of the Army. He disliked the Germans, and it was known that he was fundamentally opposed to the alliance with Germany. But this attitude, fairly widespread in the country among all social classes, was considerably influenced and probably modified by the easy German victories over Poland, Norway and, above all, France, and by the exceptional efficiency shown by the German military machine. Thus, even the King, on the very eve of Italian participation in the conflict, thought as the majority of Italians did at that time that regrettable as it might be to fight on the side of Germany, it was probably the lesser evil since Germany would emerge victorious from the war.

During the war, contrary to the King's role in the first World War, King Vittorio Emanuele III did not participate actively or directly in military operations. He delegated the Supreme Command of all armed forces to Mussolini, and apart from a few short visits to the battle fronts, he followed the military developments from his royal residence.

In the winter of 1943, when it was clear that Italy faced total defeat, the King, following the advice of some court dignitaries and army generals who were particularly close to the royal family, began to think seriously of disengaging Italy from Germany. The ultimate goal of this operation was to be a separate armistice with the three major Allied powers (Great Britain, the Soviet Union and the United States).

The plan was fairly complicated. The King had a weak and irresolute character, and until the last moment he appears to have considered that the Duce might still prove, after all, the man best suited to guide Italy along the perilous road to peace. In fact, on May 15, 1943, for the first time, he communicated his concern to the dictator, writing him: "It is time to think very seriously of the necessity of disentangling Italy's destiny from that of Germany."

12

This gesture was apparently not inspired by the King's loyalty to, or confidence in, his prime minister, but rather by the fear that the country might split into two factions, one representing the die-hard Fascists who favored continuing the war to a catastrophic end, the other, conscious of impending defeat, who hoped to save what could be saved.

Equally dangerous appeared the possible reaction of Germany; if the Italians withdrew from the war, it would leave the German's southern flank exposed. The King, somewhat naively, relied very much on Mussolini's friendship with Hitler, thinking that the Italian dictator might persuade his colleague to accept Italy's justifications for abandoning the struggle. Probably, in the King's plan, Mussolini had been assigned this precise task: to bring about, in the most advantageous way, the disengagement of Italy from Germany. As soon as this should be accomplished, the King would take over the second part of the operation to negotiate an armistice with the Allies.

These assumptions of Vittorio Emanuele III were not entirely wrong. Under the psychological shock of military failures, Mussolini was also wavering. Short of a complete victory for the Axis, which at that point seemed impossible even to the most deluded minds, the dictator was thinking of ending the war with some kind of Machiavelian operation wherein diplomatic skill would make up for military failure.

MUSSOLINI'S LAST CHANCE

The dictator's morale had been deeply shaken by the war. Italian military inefficiency and the nation's poor fighting spirit had been bitter disappointments. He thought that during his twenty years of power he had built a new society patterned on Fascist principles. Instead, confronted with the hard realities of the war, everything was slowly crumbling. Many times, during the war years, he felt he had been betrayed, first by the army generals who had shown a lack of understanding and enthusiasm for Fascist aims, and

13

second by the Italian people who, in spite of all the political and ideological justifications which the dictator had presented, did not "feel" the war was their own. He also felt betrayed by the Fascist chiefs, who, although they had been subservient in peace-time when things were going well and there were privileges to share, now, when the regime began to be seriously menaced, criticized it openly. Accustomed to twenty years of flattery, the Duce found this particularly difficult to bear.

But the most damaging to Mussolini's pride were the humiliations he suffered as a result of Hitler's complete lack of consideration for his advice and the arrogance with which he was treated by the German generals and diplomats. Too many times Mussolini, whose ambition was to play the role of political primatum in his relations with his German ally, had to face a *fait accompli*, such as the sudden attack on the Soviet Union which Hitler had decided upon without either consulting or informing him.

From a position of superiority to Hitler, in the early period of Italo-German relations, Mussolini had descended to the role of a subordinate.[1] His infrequent conferences with the Führer became mere monologues by the German dictator, to whom Mussolini was obliged to listen with hardly patient resignation.

The last of these meetings, before Mussolini's fall, took place at Feltre, a small town in northern Italy, on July 19, 1943. The military situation was desperate for Italy. After the Tunisia campaign, which had cost Italy some of her best divisions, the Anglo-American forces landed in Sicily on July 10th. They met with strong resistance by the three German divisions on the island, but the more numerous although poorly equipped Italian forces were collapsing. In addition the Sicilians, and this was the hardest blow to the Italian

---

[1] In the early days of Italo-German relations in 1934-1935, at the time of Hitler's first attempts to extend Nazi-control over Austria, which Mussolini opposed, the Italian dictator riding on the wave of his success treated Hitler, still relatively unknown on the international scene, as an apprentice statesman. At the time of the first Mussolini-Hitler meeting in Venice (June 1934) Mussolini expressed to intimates his antipathy and disrespect for Hitler.

dictator, welcomed the Allied troops as liberators. In the face of such a desperate situation, pressure was put on Mussolini by the new Chief of Staff, General Vittorio Ambrosio, and by several Fascist chiefs to speak plainly to Hitler, to tell him that Italy was in no position to continue the fight. Had Mussolini taken this stand, the coup d'etat, which had not yet been definitely decided upon by the King, might not have occurred. Once again, however, confronted by Hitler's eloquence and almost hypnotic influence, Mussolini remained silent and thus let pass his last opportunity.

THE ORGANIZATION OF THE "COUP"

After this meeting, which demonstrated Mussolini's incapacity to act, the King realized that the decision could not be postponed. To wait longer might mean the loss of his throne and the end of the dynasty. The situation on the "home front" was worsening every day: the morale of the population had reached its lowest point now that the war was being fought on Italian soil. Food rations were dangerously depleted;[1] the black market was flourishing at the expense of the poor. Disinterest in the conduct of the war was widespread as a result of the severe bombing and the food shortage; survival had become the main concern of the population. In such a situation the maintenance of public order became increasingly difficult.

Among the various forces that had been soliciting royal action against Mussolini were the anti-Fascist groups. Although still acting clandestinely, they became daily more emboldened and were preparing to participate in the political life of the country as soon as Mussolini fell and political freedom was restored.

These anti-fascist groups were made up of the political

---

[1] The individual ration of bread was 200 grams a day in a country where the normal consumption per capita is around 350. All items necessary to one's diet (flour, sugar, coffee, meat, oil, fats) were strictly rationed.

parties already in existence before the Fascist takeover, as well as new political forces that had matured in exile or in the underground during the Fascist years. Some of them had a revolutionary character with programs calling for radical changes, in particular the replacement of the monarchy by a republic. King Vittorio Emanuele knew that he would have to answer to them for his long complicity with Fascism.

With the exception of the Communist Party, pre-Fascist political groups, as well as the new ones that had been formed during the Fascist regime were not yet adequately organized. Some of their former leaders had disappeared during the long reign of Fascism, while the younger ones did not yet have the necessary prestige or experience. In the winter of 1943, anti-Fascist groups, mainly through the intermediary of Ivanoe Bonomi, a Social Democratic leader and former prime minister of the pre-Fascist period, began to put pressure on the King in an effort to persuade him to act against Mussolini. On April 27, 1943, a secret committee to coordinate anti-Fascist action was created, comprising all anti-Fascist political forces from the Communists to representatives of the old conservative classes. Putting aside their strong ideological differences, they appeared ready to cooperate with the monarchy in the destruction of the Fascist regime. But the King was aware that in return for their cooperation a price would be imposed by the most progressive parties in terms of future reforms: that their alliance would be only a temporary one and that as soon as Fascism fell some would take up their next objective, the substitution of the monarchy by a republican form of government.

Vittorio Emanuele and his advisers did not need to rely on these political groups in effecting the coup d'etat; a purely military coup would bring more favorable results to them and be much less binding. On the contrary, the participation of the political parties in the plot, they thought, might even provoke a popular insurrection, which in such a precarious moment for the country, might get out of control. The King therefore put off these political groups while his advisers hurried preparations for the coup. He feared that if the anti-

Fascist parties acted first to overthrow Fascism in a popular uprising—the strikes of the previous March might well have been the forerunner of this—the monarchy's cause would have been lost. In taking the initiative against Mussolini, the King was thus mainly concerned with saving his throne, by posing before the country as the champion of political liberties against the tyrant and as the savior of the country from complete annihilation.

Hence the anti-Fascist parties, which had a greater moral right to participate in the overthrow of the dictatorship than the monarchy and the Army, had no part in the operation that brought about the end of the Fascist regime. Their absence could also be explained by their unpreparedness to exploit the situation. It was due mainly, however, to the King's unwillingness to have them as partners.

The organization of the coup was in the beginning a strictly military affair. The King could count on the complete backing of the Army, which had always remained faithful to him, the *Carabinieri* (the Italian military police) and the civil police. General Angelo Cerica, commander of the *Carabinieri*, and former police chief Carmine Senise started work on the detailed plan of the operations, keeping the Chief of Staff, General Vittorio Ambrosio, fully informed. The most important role in the plot to overthrow Mussolini, however, was unexpectedly played by some of the more prominent Fascist leaders.

Except in the early period of the Fascist movement, Mussolini had no opponents within his own party. Dino Grandi, Italo Balbo, Roberto Farinacci, all Mussolini lieutenants, had only regional following, each in his own area, and could not compete with Mussolini for the favor of the masses. After the March on Rome, which brought Fascism to power, Mussolini, as prime minister and supreme chief of the party, remained unchallenged. The Duce could not have tolerated anyone sharing the stage with him; he tended to isolate the strongest personalities in the movement. Grandi became a top diplomat; Balbo dedicated himself to the improvement of the Air Force and eventually died in an air accident in 1940. The others of the *Quadrumviri*[1] were given honors but held positions of little political responsibility. Thus Mussolini protected himself against the ambitions of his lieutenants. However, when Mussolini's prestige started to wane with the first military failures, criticism began to be expressed privately in high Fascist circles. As defeat became inevitable, the criticism turned to opposition, which, however, did not come out into the open until the coup d'etat.

Grandi, Giuseppe Bottai (former minister of education) and Ciano were well aware of the necessity of coming to terms with the Allied powers. Bottai and Ciano were strongly anti-German. In 1939, on the eve of Italy's entrance into the war, when he was ambassador to Great Britain Grandi openly favoured a deal with Great Britain which might have resulted in Italian neutrality. These men knew that opposition to the Fascist regime was mounting in the country and that they could count on the support of several members of the *Gran Consiglio del Fascismo*, the supreme body of both the state and the Fascist party, in a move against the dictator. Grandi probably had contact with the crown through Duke Pietro Acquarone, minister for the royal household and political adviser to the King. As soon as the King knew that Grandi was planning an attack on Mussolini in the next meeting of the *Gran Consiglio del Fascismo*, he suspended his own plan of action, which was to take place on July 26th. A revolt of Fascist leaders against Mussolini, like the one Grandi was preparing, would certainly make his task much easier.

On July 25th, Fascist leaders and the royal house developed what looked to be a common action, each performing its part in a perfectly synchronized operation. The common purpose was to save the country from disaster, but personal motivations were equally strong. The Fascist chiefs hoped to save their personal positions and what might possibly be salvaged of Fascism. The King was primarily concerned with

---

[1] *Quadrumviri*, a Latin word that denoted the four men who formed the general staff of the Fascist army, which on October 28, 1922, directed the march on Rome (Italo Balbo, Michele Bianchi, Emilio De Bono and Cesare Maria De Vecchi).

18

the future of his dynasty; and the Army generals, with their careers.

The operation proceeded smoothly and was so speedily accomplished that the public, faced with a fait accompli, was taken completely unaware.

JULY 25TH

The meeting of the *Gran Consiglio*, which was to put an end to more than twenty years of Fascism, began in the late afternoon of July 24th and lasted until 3 a.m. the following day. The opposition violently attacked the dictator from the outset. There were dramatic moments. Grandi went so far as to accuse Mussolini of having betrayed the country to the Germans and even dared to call him assassin for having started a war in which hundreds of thousands of people had been killed. After he had recovered from the initial shock of these attacks, the dictator counter-attacked with energy, accusing the opposition of high treason. Some members of the council, on whom the opposition counted, were wavering. They feared that the dictator might call in his personal guard and have them arrested. Finally, after much discussion, a motion presented by Grandi was voted upon. The motion called for the restoration of all military and constitutional power to the King, which was tantamount to decreeing the fall of the Fascist regime and its leader. The motion was approved by a majority of 19 to 7. Following the vote, the fate of the dictator, abandoned by the majority of his followers, rested in the hands of the King.

In the afternoon of July 25th, Mussolini went to consult the King on the situation. The dictator, still sure of his power, had not yet fully grasped the meaning and gravity of the vote against him. Vittorio Emanuele, who, that morning, had by secret decree appointed Marshall Pietro Badoglio to succeed Mussolini as prime minister, told the Duce of his decision to dismiss him. As Mussolini left the conference with the King,

19

he was arrested, for protection as he was told, by two officers of the *Carabinieri* charged with this delicate mission.

The news of Mussolini's fall and Badoglio's appointment, communicated to the Italian people on the same evening, was greeted with wildly enthusiastic demonstrations in every Italian town. The end of Fascism was closely linked, in the minds of the people, with the expectation that the war would also end. For so many years the dictator had pursued warlike policies; it was natural that the population believed his fall meant the end of the struggle. Although the new prime minister in a message addressed to the country clearly stated that "the war continues," everyone refused to believe it. In fact, the new government intended to end the war as soon as possible, but it needed time. Disengagement from Germany and the armistice with the Allies were both difficult and perilous operations for which no definite plans yet existed. The government, therefore, felt it should proceed with caution, since an open declaration of its aim would have invited immediate German retaliation and it would have put Italy in an unfavorable bargaining position with the Allies.

CHAPTER 2

ARMISTICE AND CIVIL WAR

THE ARMISTICE DEALINGS

Some of the King's advisers hoped that the complex problem of making the armistice acceptable to both the Germans and the Allies could be solved by a declaration of Italian neutrality issued right after the armistice was signed. But this soon appeared unrealistic. The Allies wanted to use the Italian air bases in order to be able to launch air attacks on German towns and factories from Italy. It was logical that the Allies would expect some military advantage from the Italian armistice at the expense of the Germans. The Italian government should have immediately realized, too, that violent German reaction to a separate Italian armistice was unavoidable and should have taken all the necessary measures to neutralize it. Though this would not have been easy, it was at least possible. German forces in Italy at the time of Mussolini's fall totaled only seven divisions, while Badoglio could count on what remained of the Italian home reserves and the support of the entire population, including the Fascists, who had not reacted to Mussolini's downfall; even the *Milizia*, the militarized Fascist body, had made no resistence to its being fully integrated into the regular Army. Instead of prompt and determined action, Badoglio delayed the start of negotiations with the Allies and gave the Germans, who with Mussolini's fall had become highly suspicious of the Italians, enough time to send more troops to Italy. By the end of August, a month after the dictator's

21

collapse, the Germans had enough forces in Italy to be able to control any move of the Italian Army.

The armistice negotiations were long and drawn-out for two reasons. First, the Anglo-Americans were unprepared for Mussolini's fall and, consequently, for the problems raised by Italy's request for an armistice; second, the Italian government was too optimistic about the terms of the armistice. The general staff, the government and also the public all expected mild conditions. This may well have been the result of Allied propaganda, which had led the Italians to believe that the fall of Mussolini would automatically change the British and American attitude toward Italy. The King and his advisers were convinced that the statement of the "Big Three," made after the meeting at Casablanca and calling for the "unconditional surrender" of the enemy, would not apply to the new Italian regime. In this belief, soon to be proved illusory, they started to make the first cautious overtures to the Allies, almost simultaneously in two cities: Lisbon (on August 4th) and Tangiers (August 5th) which, being in neutral countries, were the only possible places where contact could be made with the other party.

The two Italian plenipotentiaries, Marquis Blasco D'Ajeta, high official of the Foreign Ministry, and Consul General Alberto Berio, soon discovered that the Allied representatives did not intend to enter into diplomatic negotiations over future peace-treaty conditions; in fact they refused to discuss any guarantees with regard to the final territorial settlement, the pre-Fascist colonies, and the future size of the Italian Army, and they made it clear that the only acceptable basis for an armistice with Italy was unconditional surrender. As a consequence, all future contacts had to be made at the military level.

MISUNDERSTANDINGS AND SUSPICIONS

The military negotiations, in which the major participants were General Giuseppe Castellano for the Italians and Major

General Walter Bedell Smith for the Allied Command, lasted about twenty days. They resumed in Lisbon and in Sicily and moved slowly in an atmosphere of suspicion and misunderstanding on both sides. As they had during the early contacts on the diplomatic level, the Italian emissaries tried again to negotiate over the terms of Italian surrender. At the start the positions of the two parties were far apart. General Castellano's mandate was limited; he was instructed to negotiate only on the conditions and details of Italian participation in the war against Germany. After the hope for Italian neutrality had been dissipated, the new Italian leaders considered that changing sides was a logical sequence to Mussolini's overthrow and the only way to save Italy from the consequences of Fascist political failures. They therefore felt they could apply for Allied status; they did not expect instead the demand for unconditional surrender. This, they thought, would be imposed only on Germany.

The Italians believed their position would be supported by the promises made by the Allies on several occasions. On July 17, a few days before Mussolini's fall, these promises were repeated in a joint proclamation to the Italian people by President Roosevelt and Prime Minister Churchill: "All your interests and traditions have been betrayed by Germany and your own false and corrupt leaders; it is only by disavowing both that a reconstituted Italy can hope to occupy a respected place in the family of European nations."

Contrary to Italian hopes, the Allies took a firm stand, making clear that they would only consider surrender on their terms. The problem of Italian participation in the war against Germany would be discussed later, they affirmed, after the signing of the armistice. More specifically, in an aide-memoire (the so-called Quebec document, dated August 18), drafted by both Roosevelt and Churchill then meeting in Quebec, it was formally stated that Italian help in the war against Germany would provide the basis for any subsequent modifications of the armistice status.—"They must work their way," Churchill said.

The Rome Government realized that there was no choice

but to accept the Allied demands. The situation was becoming more serious every day; Sicily had been totally occupied by the Allied forces, which were preparing to land on the Italian mainland. The majority of the population desired an end to the war at any cost. The Italian emissaries were thus instructed to try to obtain at least certain guarantees of a military nature in order to avoid the Italian peninsula becoming a battlefield; a large-scale Allied military operation, initiated immediately after the armistice announcement, might have prevented this.

An Allied landing in force, north of Rome, could have created the conditions for a speedy occupation of the rest of Italy and would have protected the royal family and the Italian government from German retaliation. The Allies, at first, refused to venture such an operation, because of the limited forces at their disposal, and they grew suspicious that Italian insistence on this point might hide some Machiavelian deception. Precious time was, therefore, lost before the Allies realized that the Italian demand was motivated by the fact that the Italian command had little reliance in the ability of its crumbling divisions to meet the inevitable German reaction. General Dwight D. Eisenhower, Allied Commander in the Mediterranean, then decided to meet in part the Italian requests and to land troops south of Rome (the locality had not been specified to the Italians for security reasons). An American airborne division was also to be parachuted into Rome. With the help of the Italian Army, it was to defend the capital from German attack until the arrival of the troops from the southern landing point.

The Italian Government accepted this solution and on September 3, at 5 p.m., General Castellano signed the military clauses of the armistice (so-called, Short Armistice[1]) in Cassibile, a small Sicilian town near Siracusa. They provided for the immediate cessation of hostilities, the complete surrender

---

[1] Another document—the so-called "Long Armistice" which was signed on September 29th by Badoglio on the island of Malta—contained the political, economic and financial conditions for the Allied occupation of Italy.

of the Italian Army, Navy and Air Force, and for the jurisdiction of an Anglo-American military government over all Italian territory. These provisions were to be kept secret until the Allied landing and the airborne landings in Rome took place.

COLLAPSE OF THE ITALIAN GOVERNMENT AND ARMY

Unfortunately for Italy, the situation took a different turn than originally planned. The airborne operation had to be cancelled because the Italian forces that were in the Rome area could not secure control of the necessary airfields. At the same time the Italian Government discovered that the Allies planned to make the promised landing south of Naples. This meant leaving Rome, the government, the King and a large area in central and southern Italy at the mercy of the Germans. In fact, there was no time before the Allied landing and the announcement of the armistice to organize the resistance of the Italian army, and to hold such a large area until the arrival of the Allies. Therefore Badoglio proposed to postpone the announcement of the armistice until a new plan could be devised. The Allies refused and General Eisenhower threatened that if the Badoglio Government failed to meet the armistice terms and to announce it as had been agreed upon, it would lead to "the dissolution of your government and of your nation." Badoglio thus had no choice, and on the evening of September 8th in a radio message he announced the signing of the armistice to the Italian people. The proclamation ended with the order to the Italian armed forces to cease hostilities against the Allies and to be prepared "to resist any attack from any other source."

During the long and intricate armistice dealings, German forces had been pouring into Italy as a precaution against the collapse of the Italian Army, which was feared by the German command. It was hoped in Italian governmental and military circles that at the announcement of the armistice the Germans might withdraw to the Appenines and constitute a line of

25

defense there; but once again these hopes did not materialize. A few hours after Badoglio's radio broadcast, German troops were approaching Rome. They were met with little resistance, from small units of the Italian regular Army and some improvised partisan groups. On the early morning of the 9th the royal family, the government and the military authorities left the capital for Pescara on the Adriatic coast. From there they embarked on a destroyer of the Italian Navy and continued to Brindisi, a town in Apulia, well beyond the reach of the Germans.

After the flight of the King and the government, the Germans took over Rome and in a few days completed the occupation of the other Italian centers.

The Italian Army, deprived of the guidance of the high command and left without orders, completely collapsed; resistance to the German troops was organized in a few instances, but lasted only for a very short while. Almost all the military units, already disorganized and weakened by three years of war, dissolved and disbanded in complete chaos. Officers and soldiers abandoned their uniforms and their arms and went home.

The situation of the Italian troops abroad, especially those stationed in the Balkans, was even more drastic. Lacking orders and short of supplies, they found themselves caught in the middle between the local partisans and German troops. The Italian garrisons on the Greek islands of Corfú and Kephallenia were exterminated by the Germans; some units in Greece were disarmed and deported to German concentration camps. In Yugoslavia the effectives of two Italian divisions joined Tito's partisan army, forming the Garibaldi division, which fought against the Germans until the end of the war. On the whole, as a consequence of the armistice, Italy lost 40,000 men in the Balkans. Only the fleet and most of what was left of the Air Force were saved. Although with some losses, almost the entire Italian Navy, following Badoglio's instructions, and about four hundred planes, were able to join the Allied forces, reaching the harbors and airfields in northern Africa or Sicily.

Analyzing the situation that developed after the announcement of the armistice, it appears clear that the goals that Badoglio and the King had had in mind during the negotiations for the armistice were completely defeated. The Italian Government was obliged to accept unconditional surrender, while a prompt military action on the part of the Allies, which would have saved Italy from becoming a battlefield, could not be carried out. The horror and the destruction of two more years of fighting lay in prospect for the country and its people.

THE RESPONSIBILITIES FOR THE FAILURE

The disintegration of the Italian Army weakened Italy enormously in dealing with the Allies. They had made it clear that Italian collaboration in the war against Germany would be the first condition for an improvement of the military, political and economic terms imposed by the armistice, as well as by the final peace treaty. Now that Italy had lost her Army, she was deprived of her main bargaining power. For the Allies, the surrender of Italy, although important from a political point of view, was almost negligible from the military point of view. If the Allied commanders, however, had acted more quickly and with more determination, putting aside their doubts and their mistrusts, not wholly justified, they could have, in a few weeks, brought the front line much closer to the German border with incalculable consequences for the duration of the war. A long military campaign and the heavy losses in manpower could have been avoided.

However, the main responsibility for the failure of the operation rested with the King, Badoglio and the Italian High Command. The nonexistence of a plan on which to base the military, if not diplomatic, phase of disengagement from the German alliance and the lack of leadership were the two factors that, more than any other, determined the tragic situation which the Italian people now faced. Apart from all other considerations, Badoglio, the Army chiefs and King Vittorio

Emanuele cannot escape severe moral judgement for having left their posts in such a difficult moment, so concerned were they for their personal safety. It is believed that the King's decision to leave Rome the day after the armistice cost him his throne. There is no doubt that his flight weighed heavily in determining the future attitude of the Italian people toward the monarchy, whose prestige had been already considerably lowered by its involvement with Fascism and the war.

After forty-five days of the Badoglio Government, the country was in an even more difficult situation than before. The hopes for a quick Allied occupation of the peninsula had been completely shattered. The landing that had been agreed upon during the armistice negotiations was made at Salerno, seventy kilometers south of Naples, on September 9th. There the British and American forces had met with the strong resistance of German troops, which had been given time to organize. Only after hard fighting and considerable losses were the Allies able to break through the German encirclement and advance northward. In the meantime, however, German troops south of Salerno had been given the possibility of retreating northward to new fortified positions. Hence, one of the main purposes of the Allied landing, that of cutting off German troops still in Calabria and Southern Campania, was also not achieved.

On October 1st, Naples was liberated by the Allied troops. In the last five days of the German occupation the Neapolitans rose up against the Germans, and hard house-to-house fighting took place in some sections of the city. This was to be the first popular Italian participation in the Allied war effort against the German occupiers. The resistance movement, which was to symbolize the moral redemption of the Italian people from its mistakes of the Fascist period, started with the heroic "five days of Naples."

With the approach of the winter season, the Allied march was forced to stop. The front-line held fast along the river Garigliano and from the stronghold of Cassino to the Adriatic coast (the Gustav Line) until the following spring. Preparations for the opening of the second front in western France

28

weakened Allied units in Italy, and from a war of movement the Allied Command switched to a war of position in the winter of 1943-1944. The only exception was a surprise landing at Anzio on January 22, 1944, which was promptly encircled by German troops; the bridgehead constituted by the Allies remained "frozen" under naval protection until spring.

The peninsula was thus cut into two parts. The southern regions and the islands[1] were under Allied control. The Italian Government's jurisdiction remained limited to a few provinces in Apulia, given by the Allied Command to the King of Italy as a gesture of their intention to recognize the monarchy at a future date. These provinces formed what was to be somewhat ironically called the "Kingdom of the South" with Brindisi as its capital; there the King and Badoglio established the residence of the court and the government. The northern and central regions, including Rome, remained under German occupation, which was ruthless and oppressive from the beginning. Eager and subservient collaborators, the *fascisti repubblicani* were soon to be rebaptized contemptuously by the population *repubblichini*.[2]

THE "REPUBBLICA SOCIALE ITALIANA"

Immediately after the announcement of the armistice, some Fascist leaders, who after the coup d'etat of July 25th had taken refuge in Germany, issued a proclamation announcing that a new Fascist governemnt, acting in the name of Mussolini, would soon be formed. On September 12th, German parachutists in a surprise action liberated Mussolini from Campo Imperatore, a summer resort on the Gran Sasso.[3] He

---

[1] Sardinia was evacuated as being untenable by the German troops right after the announcement of the armistice.

[2] It is a game of words impossible to translate. The *fascisti repubblicani* (republican fascists) were given the nickname of *repubblichini* (little republicans).

[3] The former dictator had been transferred there at the end of August

was flown to German headquarters in eastern Prussia, where he met Hitler and started working for the reconstruction of a new Fascist regime.

On September 16th, he made his first speech after his liberation over Radio Munich, presenting the main points of his program to the Italian people. He accused the King, Badoglio and the high military circles around the royal family of having betrayed the Italian people, Fascism and the German Ally. By their defeatism and anti-German attitude, the Duce claimed they alone were responsible for the military defeats during the war. In announcing his new program, Mussolini declared that Italy would be a republican state, built on social principles, those same principles that had originated the Fascist movement. Among the first acts of the new government were the formation of a new Fascist army to continue the war until final victory on the side of Germany and Japan, and the punishment of those Fascist traitors who had collaborated with Badoglio and the King in the coup d'etat of July 25th. Mussolini also promised the destruction of the capitalist class through wide nationalizations in industry and the full reevaluation of work "as the most valid basis of the national economy."

This social program was far beyond the principles of the fascist corporative state, fulfilled only in its formal structure, during twenty years of the Fascist regime. This might be interpreted as a return for Mussolini to his socialist background and to some of the early professed Fascist aims; actually, in a political sense, it was a last minute effort to regain the favour of the Italian working class. On September 23rd, Mussolini announced his new cabinet, in which only minor figures participated. The residence of the government was established at Salò,[1] a small town on Lake Garda, well within the protection and under the watchful eye of the Germans. There until

---

after a sojourn at Ponza and subsequently at La Maddalena, a small island off the Sardinian coast.

[1] From which "The Republic of Salò" as the "Italian Social Republic" is otherwise called.

his violent end the Fascist dictator lived, a sick man plagued by bitterness. He never recovered his energy or appeal.

This attempt to rebuild a new Fascist state proved an almost complete failure. Of his announced program, Mussolini only succeeded in punishing some Fascist "traitors." On January 10, 1944, a Fascist tribunal in Verona sentenced to death all but one of the nineteen members of the Fascist *Gran Consiglio* who had voted against Mussolini in the meeting of July 24th. Only six, however, had been arrested: among them were former Foreign Minister Ciano and Marshal De Bono, one of the *quadrumviri*. They were shot on January 11th. Grandi, who had engineered the plot against Mussolini, had escaped imprisonment. After hiding out for a while in Italy, he went, as did several other former Fascist chiefs, to South America, where Fascism could still count on many sympathizers.

The rebuilding of the Fascist army was slow and difficult; the Germans, who had no confidence in Italian military collaboration, did not press the issue, preferring to use Italians as workers on their fortifications and in their factories. Some response to Mussolini's call came from the younger generation, which had been educated and formed during the Fascist period. The military usefulness of these very young recruits was, however, limited; for the most part, they were employed to keep public order and in the fight against the partisan movement, which was preparing to start offensive actions.

The new social doctrines announced by Mussolini and debated during the first Fascist Congress in Verona (November 1943)[1] were to remain almost completely unrealized. The working class first showed indifference to the new Fascism, and subsequently, with the spread of Socialist and Communist influence, became violently opposed, providing in the last year of the war in Italy the largest number of forces to the resistance movement. Even the newly reaffirmed alliance with Germany produced no results. On the contrary, ignoring Ita-

---

[1] The Congress produced the so-called *Manifesto di Verona* which remains as the basic program of the *Repubblica Sociale Italiana*.

31

lian interests, the Germans continued at an accelerated pace, between October 1943 and February 1944, the process of administrative integration of the Alto Adige, the Italian border region heavily populated with German elements, into the German state and extended their jurisdiction to several provinces of Venezia Giulia and Tridentina in a manner equivalent to annexation.[1]

The new Fascist state was an artificial creation. Its jurisdiction in Italy, occupied as it was by German troops, was quite nominal, since the real governors were the German military commanders. The very existence of a Fascist government, in the north and central part of Italy, opposed to the Badoglio government, which had an equally nominal jurisdiction over part of the south, automatically created the danger of civil war. This was to become a reality on October 13th when Badoglio declared war on Germany to express "the willingness of the new Italy to regain her place among the democratic nations."

---

[1] On October 1, 1943, the Venezia Giulia and all its provinces, including Trieste, passed under the jurisdiction of a German *Gauleiter*. German ordinances were sent to all local chiefs of the *Guardia nazionale repubblicana,* the Fascist military police, which was notified that following a direct agreement between Hitler and the Duce, the civil jurisdiction in those regions was to be taken over by the Germans. Mussolini denied the existence of any such agreement and wrote several times to Hitler protesting. At first the Führer gave military reasons as the explanation of the German takeover; he did not answer subsequent protests and Mussolini was obliged, as in the past, to accept this *fait accompli.*

CHAPTER 3

THE ITALIAN POLITICAL PARTIES

DIFFICULT BEGINNINGS

In the already liberated south the new Italian democracy was taking its first uncertain steps. This part of Italy was in an extremely critical situation, separated as it was by the front-line from the richest and most advanced regions of the country. Conditions for the development of a democratic political life were lacking: illiteracy among the half-starving population was high; the economy, mainly agricultural, was traditionally backward. There were small islands of very cultivated, intellectual elites but these had little interest in social problems, while the middle class was politically unprepared and indifferent as the result of a centuries-old history of despotism and economic depression.

Apart from these regional considerations there were other, more general problems, which weighed heavily on the country and were rooted in the years of Fascism. Twenty years of dictatorship had left an almost complete political vacuum.

In November 1926, Mussolini had deprived the representatives of all political parties of their parliamentary mandate. This act marked the end of the parliamentary system and the dissolution of all political parties. A multi-party system, in which the fundamental principles of democracy, if not rooted in a strong tradition of parliamentary life and of local autonomy, were at least respected, was transformed into a dictatorship. Mussolini, through the *Partito Nazionale Fascista* (PNF), was the only arbiter of political life.

Before its takeover, Fascism had never missed a chance to attack the institutions and principles of liberal democracy, as part of its ideological line, which was strongly influenced by Sorel and other political thinkers of the early 20th century who were opposed to parliamentary democracy. Therefore, after first suppressing all forms of democratic life (the last relatively free election in Italy was in 1924), Mussolini started to root out of Italian society the vestiges of a democratic spirit. Italian youth were given a Fascist education, which exalted violence and the cult of the strongest. In history textbooks pre-Fascist Italy was presented in an unfavorable light and Mussolini was extolled as the savior of the country from chaos and subversion. As a consequence, the names of the anti-Fascist parties meant very little to the generation formed under Fascism, and their political programs were unknown.

During twenty years of Mussolini's dictatorship the basic problems of the country had been quietly neglected. Fascism, always playing an optimistic tune and overemphasizing the importance of public works executed during the dictatorship, denied the existence of major economic problems and presented a picture of Italy as a paradise of social justice. Fascist influence on the old and new generations of Italians resulted in what might be called "de-education." Italian schools and culture were particularly affected, isolated as they were from outside influence and from reality.

It is easy to understand, therefore, how deep the disorientation was in liberated Italy just after Mussolini's fall. The only forces that could contribute to a meaningful political revival were the anti-Fascist groups that had survived the twenty years of dictatorship. Their task, however, was discouragingly large, considering the weakness of their situation. Fifteen years of inaction, of clandestine activity had gravely affected their organizations: the old cadres, whose members were forced to stop their political activity or go into exile, had lost touch with the country and with the desires of the common people, and too often in engaging in polemics among

34

themselves they became lost in abstractions. Relatively few people were in a position to give substantial help to rebuilding a state based on the genuine values of democracy. This situation was advantageous to those political extremists whose interpretation of the political struggle was more akin to the experience and frame of reference of the Fascist generation. The middle classes, which had been the most deeply affected by the Fascist experience, were reluctant to accept the new forms of political life and too often contented themselves with merely a formal adherence to "democracy," without understanding its real meaning. The situation of the prole-tariat was no better, especially in the south; during the Fascist regime, it had been completely cut off from any kind of organized political activity. Fascist corporativism[1] had been, in fact, the greatest mockery of the working classes, since it had abolished all their bargaining power with the ultimate effect of completely denaturing the function of the trade unions. Hence, in this area, too, a long process of reorgani-zation had to be initiated, but first it was necessary to regain the confidence of the workers in the democratic system, to educate them and to train them in the techniques of political struggle in a democratic society.

All these problems were of first magnitude. It would have been highly unrealistic to expect quick and valid solutions,

---

[1] The basic idea of the Fascist corporate system was that the state would act as mediator between workers and employers. Both workers and employers were organized into 22 categories (or corporations), according to the type of work; in each corporation, together with the employers and workers representatives, were also Fascist officials, mainly from the Fascist unions (the only ones allowed); their function was to settle labor disputes which might arise within the corporations. This was the Fascist solution to the class struggle; that is, to channel into a state-controlled organization all of the conflicts between the workers and the employers. In reality in this system the workers were completely deprived of their bargaining power and of their only weapon, strikes, which were outlawed. Since Fascism was tied to big business and to the great agrarian landowners, and since Fascist officials in the corporations acted according to the policies established by the Fascist Government, the interests of the workers, for whom Mussolini claimed to have the greatest regard, were sacrificed to the political exigencies of Fascism.

under the circumstances; long and sometimes painful experiences were unavoidable.

THE "COMITATI DI LIBERAZIONE NAZIONALE"

In so negative a picture, the initial willingness of the anti-Fascist parties to overcome their political differences and to cooperate in the restoration of democracy was the most important and positive sign. This willingness manifested itself in the formation of the C.L.N. ("Committees of National Liberation"). These were anti-Fascist committees that had been active underground from the beginning of 1943. Soon after Mussolini's fall, they came into the open under this name, in spite of Badoglio's official prohibition of organized political activity. Representing all political tendencies, from extreme left to extreme right, they soon engaged in a propaganda effort designed to inform and to encourage the people to participate in active political life.

After the announcement of the armistice, the CLN soon grew in number. On September 9th, the Central Committee of National Liberation was created in Rome to organize the first active resistance against the invading German troops. In the liberated south the CLN became the center of political activity, while in the central and northern part of Italy they reverted to clandestinity in order to organize the resistance movement against the German and neo-Fascist occupier. In both cases they symbolized the union of all anti-Fascist forces, different with regard to ideological background and political programs, but all equally determined to act together for the rehabilitation of Italian society from its Fascist past.

The "Committees of National Liberation" were to play a prominent role on both the social and national levels in the two years between the armistice and the end of the war in Italy. The political history of these two years is mainly the history of this movement. Six political parties were represented in the CLN of southern and central Italy (only five in the North). These parties, which resumed open political activity after twenty years of absence from the Italian scene, achieved a common front in the CLN. Their alliance, realized in spite of deep political and ideological differences, found its *raison d'être* in the attempt to provide common solutions to the basic problems of the reconstruction of Italian society and the Italian state.

From the extreme left to the right the CLN parties were the Italian Communist Party (PCI), the Italian Socialist Party (PSIUP),[1] the Action Party (PdA), the Democratic Labor Party (PDL, a small political group whose following was almost exclusively in southern Italy), Christian Democracy (DC), and the Italian Liberal Party (PLI). Except for the Partito d'Azione, which sprang up out of the resistance to Fascism, all of these political parties had existed before the Fascist period.

The oldest among them, in terms of political experience and historical tradition, was the Liberal Party (PLI). It dates back to the period of the Italian *Risorgimento*, not so much as an organized party in the modern sense but rather as a current of ideas or a political orientation.

THE LIBERAL PARTY

The political class of noble and bourgeois extraction, which united Italy and made it independent, and which from 1860 held the reins of power in the new state until the advent of Fascism, was *liberale.* This term does not correspond conceptually to that of the American "liberal"; it must be considered within the historical framework of Europe in the second half of the 19th century. Liberalism in that period meant acceptance of parliamentary democracy, *laissez faire* principles in economy, the recognition of the fundamental freedoms, tempered, however, by the necessity to safeguard and maintain a political system from which the working classes were

---

[1] PSIUP stands for Socialist Party of Proletarian Unity (*Partito Socialista di Unità Proletaria*), the official denomination of the Socialist Party from 1945 until 1947.

4.

excluded. In Italy, the Liberal Party provided the cadres for the ruling class which, having initially started from the progressive positions of the *Risorgimento* period, ended in a conservative defense of its privileges.

In the practice of government the qualification "liberal" had an ambiguous connotation; in fact, the Italian liberal government from 1861 to the First World War swung from conservative and sometimes reactionary positions (Francesco Crispi) to progressive ones (Giovanni Giolitti). During this period the popular masses and their interests were not represented in the government, which remained the monopoly of relatively small groups, closely linked together. Within the liberal party of that time were a leftist and a rightist current. But left and right were merely formal terms and did not correspond to different political positions. In fact, when, following the changes in parliamentary life, the opposition became the majority and took over, no major change in the previous political orientation followed. The former opposition transformed itself into the majority simply by adopting the program of its predecessors. This phenomenon was called "transformism"; thanks to it, Italian parliamentary life ran quite smoothly until World War I.

Lacking a strong and determined opposition, every crisis was easily solved among the parliamentary groups. No party organized in a modern sense existed; groupings, whose members were not bound by party discipline, often shifted from one political combination to the other, while a few politicians, due to their skill and personal prestige, pulled the strings in parliament.

The end of the First World War marked a crisis in this system. The popular masses, organized by the Socialist Party and by the *Partito Popolare* (the Catholic Party), started pressing for social reforms. The liberal cabinets, which succeeded one another at an accelerated rate in the period 1919-1922, were unable to hold off these demands. The adoption of universal suffrage and the proportional system, introduced in 1912 and 1919, considerably weakened the Liberal Party. They resulted in the formation of powerful

38

party machines, which diminished the importance of those political groups on which the liberal politicians had based their personal power.

When Fascism and Mussolini appeared on the political scene, the *liberali* tried to exploit "Fascist dynamism" against the socialist danger; in doing so, they loosed a force which they were unable to control, and which, in the end turned against them.

On October 28, 1922, the Fascists felt strong enough to attempt to seize power. On that date the "March on Rome," a partly political, partly military demonstration, took place. Fascist armed squads, numbering about 85,000 (some say 150,000) men, descended on Rome from all over Italy. The liberal prime minister Luigi Facta responded meekly, only at the last moment announcing a "state of siege" and calling for the intervention of regular army troops. The King, who was to sign the document declaring the state of siege, refused. With the help of the regular army he could have easily defeated the Fascists. He chose instead to give them a free hand and on the same day he dismissed Facta and appointed Mussolini to replace him as prime minister.

After the Fascist takeover, the former political class tried to come to terms with Mussolini with the intention of controlling the dictator. But the Duce showed clearly that he did not want to share his power with anyone. The former liberal leaders, including the eldest and most able of them—Giolitti—soon discovered how difficult and humiliating it was to collaborate with this apprentice dictator. After the Congress of Leghorn (October 1924) the Liberal Party became openly opposed to Fascism.

When Mussolini felt his power was secure, he abolished political liberties: in 1926 the Liberal Party, along with every other party was suppressed[1] and its leaders were put under

---

[1] From June 1924 on, the representatives of the democratic parties started to desert meetings of the Chamber to manifest their opposition to Fascism. To this opposition, the so-called *Aventino*, adhered most of the Liberals the *Partito Popolare*, the Republicans, Radicals and Socialists. On November 9, 1926, the Fascist members of the Chamber approved a law

police surveillance or persecuted in small ways. Some *liberali* then sought other means to make their opposition to Fascism known. The foremost figure among this group was Benedetto Croce, the internationally known Neapolitan philosopher whose historical analysis of Italian society in the years 1870-1915[1] constituted the Bible of the Liberals' creed. Under Fascism Croce continued to publish his *Quaderni della Critica*, a highbrow cultural journal, which the Fascist censors did not attempt to suppress, and the philosopher's house became a well-known meeting place for intellectuals opposed to the regime.

A few other members of the party ended by supporting Fascism, but the majority of the *liberali* continued to maintain a critical attitude toward the regime, without going as far as organized opposition.

In 1943, with the return to free political life, the Liberal Party, in view of its tradition and political experience, returned with great prestige to the political arena. Some of the most notable political personalities of the pre-Fascist era, still alive, reappeared in prominent positions within the party. The enormous influence of Benedetto Croce, the party's undisputed spiritual and political leader, attracted new younger elements. These brought not only fresh energy, but also revived the conflict between the progressive and the conservative interpretation of the liberal doctrine, which had grown up out of the ideological opposition to Fascism. These two different orientations were generally linked with the regional or professional backgrounds of party members, some of whom, teachers, lawyers and students, were men with a genuinely progressive ideas. They recognized the new era and were well aware of the necessity of orienting the country toward a modern and intelligent reformism; landowners, particularly from the south, and small or big businessmen made up the conservative and sometimes reactionary wing. They were in favor of the

depriving the *Aventiniani* of their parliamentary mandate. This illegal act marked the end of free political life in Italy.

[1] Benedetto Croce: *A History of Italy 1871-1915*, Oxford: The Clarendon Press, 1929.

restoration of the political and social conditions that had existed prior to Fascism. For them, the "old values," that is, the values of pre-World War I liberal society, remained unchanged. Disregarding the social and historical evolution that had taken place, they thought that a return to these values would solve the problems of the new Italian democracy. In spite of these distinctions, which continued for several years to divide the party in the post-war period, its political position at the end of the Fascist regime remained fundamentally conservative and was openly opposed to radical changes in society. Though staunch supporters of political liberty, the *liberali* failed to understand the requests for social and economic justice demanded by the working classes and soon directed their political action in the defense of the interests of the privileged bourgeosie.

THE SOCIALIST PARTY

A general socialist movement originated in Italy with Mazzini's social and political interpretation of the *Risorgimento* and with the goals he set for the new Italian society which was to emerge from it. After the decline of Mazzini's influence, the socialist cause remained alive, since it was inherent in the anarchist movement. However, neither Mazzini's teachings nor anarchist ideals resulted in any systematic political action.

The Italian Socialist Party was founded in 1892, at a time when Socialist movements had already attained important political standing in France, Germany and, with a unique character, in Britain. Modern industry, which developed slowly after the unification of Italy, and the extremely backward conditions prevalent in the country account for the late start of Italian socialism as an organized movement.

As in all other countries where socialism developed, in Italy too, the party soon divided into different currents, corresponding to different ideological positions that were destined to remain one of its characteristic features. There were two main tendencies, the extremist (*massimalismo*) and the moderates (*riformista*). The *massimalisti*, whose stronghold was Milan, based their ideology on orthodox Marxism; they were opposed to parliamentary democracy and favored revolutionary action. The *riformisti* stood for a policy of gradual social change to be realized, as long as this was possible, within the framework of the parliamentary system.

The history of Italian socialism is the history of the conflicts between maximalists and reformists, between the tradition of humanitarian socialism "à la Mazzini" and the new influence of Marxist ideas.

These ideological distinctions, however, were clear only to a small minority within the Socialist Party: the party élite, which included intellectuals of bourgeois background and groups of industrial workers of the northern industrial districts. The masses, especially in the South, did not participate in the ideological debate and were disinterested in such distinctions. It was typical of the ideological disorientation prevailing at the time in Sicily, for instance, to see carried at the head of Socialist political parades portraits of Marx together with the picture of the Madonna or Saint Joseph. The working classes in the South embraced socialism in protest against their poor living conditions, and in rebellion against the exploitation to which they were subjected. These motivations remained the basis for the success of the Communist movement after World War II.

The Socialist Party maintained a stand of uncompromising opposition to the government. It sent its representatives to Parliament in increasing numbers, especially after 1912, when universal suffrage was instituted, but it invariably abstained from participating directly in the governments, even in the most progressive cabinets. In international relations the Italian Socialists, like most other European Socialists, advocated a pacifist policy and never missed a chance to declare their uncompromising opposition to all wars, which were considered a capitalist expedient for the conquest of new markets.

In 1912, when Italy declared war on Turkey in order to

42

gain possession of Libya, the Socialists violently opposed the war, and Mussolini, then a Socialist leader, together with Pietro Nenni, then a Republican and later secretary of the Socialist Party, were arrested as organizers of pacifist demonstrations. In 1914, on the eve of World War I, Mussolini's attitude changed; he then became a fervent "interventionist." He came out in favour of Italian participation on the side of the Allied powers against Austria, the traditional enemy of Italy which still ruled the *terre irredente*.[1] For taking this position, which was contrary to the Socialist line, Mussolini was expelled from the party.

In 1915, when Italy entered the war, despite their earlier opposition and advocacy of passive resistance, the Italian Socialists, like the French and German Socialists, reversed to half-hearted cooperation in the war effort. In general, the Socialist workers responded to the draft, even though, during the conflict, a spirit of defeatism was quite widespread among them as a result of the anti-war propaganda of the extremist currents. In the most difficult moments of the war, such as the defeat of Caporetto, the government promised, in an effort to boost the morale of the troops and to induce them to fight with renewed vigor, that at the war's end a new period of social justice would begin, and that all social classes would share in its fruits. After the victory the workers went home with new expectations: the farmers looked forward to a land reform which would have made them small proprietors, and the industrial workers hopefully anticipated higher wages and a more direct participation in the management of the factories.

None of these hopes materialized, nor the promises made during the war by the government. In reaction to this, extremist currents within the party prevailed once more, incited the Socialist electorate to revolutionary action, and a

---

[1] The *terre irredente* were the territories on the eastern Italian border still under Austrian rule: the towns of Trento, Trieste, Gorizia and the Venezia Giulia region. The irredentist movement, which dates from 1876, aimed at the liberation of those territories from the Austrian yoke and their annexation to Italy.

period of social and political unrest began. In the years 1920-1921 a wave of general strikes produced chaos in the country's economic life: factories were occupied by workers in an attempt to gain control of the management, and in the country, land-hungry peasants occupied uncultivated areas.

The government did not intervene. Prime Minister Giolitti[1] was a progressive liberal, as well as one of the most complex personalities in Italian politics. Giolitti was convinced that if the police were to intervene to oust the workers from the occupied factories or lands, it would create a dangerous revolutionary atmosphere. Despite the fact that in the election of 1919 the Socialists had sent 156 (out of 535) representatives to Parliament, thus becoming the largest Italian party, Giolitti knew that the party was a colossus with feet of clay, that it lacked the leadership and organization to be a genuinely revolutionary political force. The Socialist Party split in 1921, which resulted in the formation of the Communist Party, proving the soundness of this analysis. The liberal leader, however, had not been able to foresee the reactions of the middle class to the Socialist victory. Big business, the large landowners and the propertied bourgeoisie in general had been scared by the Socialist gains in the elections of 1919 and by the strikes of 1920-1921. They feared a socialist revolution in which the Socialist Party would seize power. Their fears were unjustified, because the Socialist Party was rent by internal dissension and fundamentally weak. Nevertheless, the Russian Revolution and the revolutions in other parts of Europe (Germany, Hungary) had badly frightened the European bourgeoisie. Mussolini exploited these fears with political skill; he repudiated his progressive past and now posed as the new defender of the "old values" against Socialist and Communist subversion. His armed squads (Fascism had a strong para-military organization created with the financial subsidies of the industrialists and landowners) waged constant warfare, often under the benevolent eyes of the police, against Socialist Party local headquarters, Socialist newspapers, unions

---

[1] The Giolitti Cabinet lasted from June 1920 to June 1921.

44

and cooperatives. Mussolini's *Squadristi* killed or clubbed their political enemies or forced them to drink castor oil "so that they could purify themselves of their socialist heresy." In less that two years the Socialist Party and its trade-union organizations were in the process of disintegration. Fascism meanwhile was growing in power and gaining adherents among the middle class.

After the Fascists seized power, the conflicts between Socialism and Fascism continued in Parliament: in spite of the number of Socialist representatives (123 after the election of May 1921, compared with 35 Fascists), the Socialists alone were too weak to oppose Fascist dynamism effectively; neither could they agree with other parties on constituting a united front against the dictatorship. Exploiting basic dissensions between Socialists, Catholics and Liberals, Mussolini gained ground also in Parliament and after the successful election of 1924, which gave him control of the Chamber, he proceeded gradually to overpower and suppress the parliamentary system.

In 1924 a Socialist deputy, Giacomo Matteotti, who attacked and criticized Mussolini in the Chamber, was kidnapped and killed by Fascist squadrists. Public opinion, which was becoming aware of Mussolini's intent, was deeply shocked by this new act of Fascist violence and, for a few months, it appeared that Fascism might collapse and that Mussolini's political career might come to an end. Once again, however, dissensions among the anti-Fascist groups rendered them incapable of exploiting the crisis. Mussolini succeeded in consolidating his forces and was soon able to retake the initiative.

In 1926 all Socialist representatives were deprived of their parliamentary mandates; some were tried and imprisoned, while others escaped abroad and took refuge in Paris, which became a headquarters for anti-Fascist refugees. There, in August 1934, the Communists and the Socialists in exile concluded an agreement for common political action against Fascism: the *Patto d'Unità d'Azione* (Unity of Action Pact.) Following this agreement, whose effects were to continue after the fall of Fascism, Italian Communists and Socialists were to develop joint underground activities.

When the Spanish civil war broke out in 1936 and Mussolini sent Italian troops to help Franco, the Italian Socialists and Communists joined the Spanish Republic and fought together in the International Brigades, thus cementing the collaboration between the two parties.

Following the collapse of Fascism, when political activity resumed in Italy, the Socialist Party was one of the first to reappear, under the leadership of Pietro Nenni and Giuseppe Saragat. The latter was the leader of the party's moderate current. The traditional conflict between maximalists and reformists soon re-emerged and was complicated by the issue of collaboration with the Communists, which Saragat and his followers opposed. Post-war Italian political life has been deeply affected by this conflict, which has had a prolonged and complicated history.

THE COMMUNIST PARTY

The impact of the Russian Revolution was widespread in Europe. Almost everywhere serious crises occurred as a result of the Communist victory in the Socialist movements, reviving the old conflicts between the extremist and moderate currents.

In the Italian Socialist Party this struggle was violent. It considerably weakened the workers' movement and was partially responsible for its inability to react to the pressures and attacks of Fascism.

Most of the leading figures of Italian Socialism, Filippo Turati, Claudio Treves, Giuseppe Modigliani, who rejected revolution as a way to power were losing control of the party as a result of the disrupting activities of the extremist minority, which advocated revolutionary action. The general strikes of 1920-1921 were staged under pressure from the extremist elements. After their failure, the revolutionaries realized they would not be able to impose their program on the entire Socialist Party. They decided to break away and in Leghorn, on January 1921, founded the Italian Communist Party (P.C.I.).

The industrial town of Turin with its élite of specialized workers had been the cradle and became the stronghold of the P.C.I.; there, the news of the Russian Revolution was enthusiastically received.

The main leaders of the party in 1921 were Amadeo Bordiga, now retired from active politics; Palmiro Togliatti, the present party secretary; and Antonio Gramsci, its principal founder, and theoretician. Gramsci died after long years of imprisonment during the Fascist dictatorship; his "Letter from Jail" remains one of the most interesting documents of the anti-Fascist resistance.

From its very beginning the PCI was very closely linked with the Communist Party of the Soviet Union through membership in the Third International, which soon recognized the PCI as its Italian section. Some of the ideological clashes which took place in the Soviet Union in the late twenties and early thirties were also to develop in the PCI, which, after a number of purges, finally fully accepted the Stalinist line.

The Communist Party was not outlawed immediately after the Fascists came to power in 1922, but it soon became the main target of Fascist violence. The eighteen Communist representatives, like those of all the other anti-Fascist parties, were deprived of their parliamentary mandate in 1926. A series of anti-Communist trials followed the constitution of the "Fascist Special Tribunal for the defense of the State." Some of its leaders were arrested and spent long years in prison or in confinement, while others escaped arrest and left the country. Togliatti himself went into exile and spent most of the period in Russia, where he was made a member of the Presidium of the Comintern, from 1934 to 1943. While a member of the Comintern, Togliatti elaborated with its general secretary, Bulgarian Communist leader, Georgi

47

Dimitrov, the "Popular Front" policy,[1] which was adopted in 1935 in France and Spain. The Unity of Action Pact, signed in 1934 between the PSI and PCI in exile, falls within the framework of the "Popular Front."

Several Communist leaders, such as Luigi Longo, fought against Franco in the Spanish Civil War, acquiring military experience which proved most important in the partisan resistance in the years 1944-1945, and which eventually gave the Communist Party a considerable advantage.

During Fascism the PCI, although working in collaboration with Socialist elements, was the only political party able to maintain an underground organization, which, though limited in members, was very well prepared to take advantage of all possible situations. The strikes that broke out in the factories in Milan and Turin during March and April 1943, and which marked the first open revolt against Fascism, were organized mainly by the Communists.

After the fall of Fascism the PCI, thanks to an efficient leadership, a good organization and increasing support from the industrial working classes of the North, appeared to be gaining steadily. Its strategic aim was to become the only representative of the working classes.

THE ACTION PARTY

This was the only party to have been created in exile during the Fascist regime. It was organized in Paris where several anti-Fascist groups had found a difficult and uncertain

---

[1] The policy of forming a "Popular Front" with other democratic forces has been one of the main Communist political programs in Western Europe. Presented as an alliance against Fascist and reactionary forces, it has been in reality an attempt by the Communists to attract within their sphere of influence the parties of the democratic left (Social-Democrats, Republicans and Radicals) and to attain important power positions in government coalitions formed with these parties. "Popular Fronts" were formed in France (cabinet presided over by the Socialists Léon Blum) and in Spain (Republican coalitions during the civil war, presided over by the Socialist Largo Caballero and by the Republican Negrin).

refuge from Fascism. In 1937, Carlo Rosselli, the leader and theoretician of the party, was assassinated by the "cagoulards," French fascists who followed orders from Mussolini's political police. Rosselli had set down the ideological basis of a movement which called itself *Giustizia e Libertà.*

The "Giustizia e Libertà" group and the political party that grew out of it (the Action Party) had their ideological roots in Mazzini's aims and in the radical-democratic traditions of the *Risorgimento.* The Action Party wanted to translate into reality the social and democratic ideas which, during and after the period of the *Risorgimento*, had inspired Italian political and intellectual thought. Within the *Giustizia e Libertà* movement there were several tendencies which were later carried over into the Action Party; the main currents adhered to a concept of "Liberal Socialism," from the title of Rosselli's main work, and "Liberal Revolution," the name of a political weekly, published in Turin during the early period of the Fascist dictatorship and directed by Piero Gobetti,[1] a brilliant young political writer.

Rosselli's "Liberal Socialism" represents an attempt to formulate a theory of modern socialism free of Marxist determinism. (Rosselli strongly criticized the Marxist theory of the inevitability of the class struggle and of the final revolution.) In his writings Rosselli tried to establish a connecting link between the early liberal tradition of the *Risorgimento*, from which he adopted his ideas of freedom and political democracy, and socialist demands for the structural reform of Italian society. The result is a reformism free of Marxist formulas, a more up-to-date interpretation of socialism. Gobetti's idea of the "liberal revolution" places the emphasis on the liberal rather than socialist tradition, and on the necessity of injecting the new blood of the working class into the old body of Italian 19th-century liberalism. According to his theory, the obsolescent conservative class should make

---

[1] Gobetti, persecuted by the Fascist police, left the country and went to Paris where he died on February 16, 1926.

49

room for the new democratic forces and invite them to share government responsibilities. The main function of the intellectuals was to work in close contact with the workers with the purpose of preparing them to take on the new political tasks.

The different traditions, socialist and liberal, from which the two groups developed, proved to be a divisive force when the time for action came in 1943 and 1945. The Action Party was mainly a party of intellectuals (teachers, writers, artists, professionals), for whom certain theoretical distinctions acquired a fundamental importance. Its ambition was "to go to the masses," an aim that it was never able to carry out since it remained a party of ideas; it took an active and prominent part in the partisan movement, but failed to assert itself in post-war political life.

The contribution of the Action Party, however, was of the utmost importance. Its program took form in exile and was expounded later during the period of clandestine activity (1942 and 1943) in the columns of the newspaper *L'Italia Libera,* which was secretly published an distributed. It included many of the principles which were to be embodied in the new Constitution. This program advocated the adoption of a republican form of government, the creation of regional autonomies, antitrust laws, the nationalization of electric power, factory councils, progressive taxation, a land reform, popular education, elimination of Church privileges (most of the PdA were anti-clerical) and the development of the South.

In 1943 the PdA had great prestige but little following. Its asset was its intellectual vitality and the personal force of its leaders: most of them were outstanding figures in all fields of national life. This small party tried to communicate to the country the urgency of a fundamental change in political, social and moral life. Only such a total rebirth could provide the basis on which to build a solid and vital democracy.

The present-day DC (*Democrazia Cristiana*) is the post-war heir of the old *Partito Popolare*, founded in 1919 by a Sicilian priest, Don Luigi Sturzo.

The birth of the *Partito Popolare* officially marked the return of Italian Catholics to active political life after a long period of non-participation, dating back to 1870 when the Italian government occupied Rome. This put an end to the sovereignty of the Pope, to complete the unification of Italy.

Pope Pius IX withdrew to the Vatican palaces and assumed an openly hostile attitude toward the new Italian government. This marked the beginning of the so-called "Roman Question," which was to remain unsettled for sixty years. In 1874 the Pope issued a papal edict (Encyclical), the famous "Non Expedit," ordering Italian Catholics to abstain from active politics (*né eletti né elettori* = neither elected nor electors). This *mot d'ordre*, on the whole, was not observed by the majority of the Italians; otherwise, in view of the overwhelming percentage of citizens of Catholic faith, the life of the new state would have been paralyzed. The Catholics gradually abandoned their passive attitude and well before World War I they were taking part in the elections, both as voters and as candidates for political appointments. However, since no organized Catholic party as yet existed, Catholic candidates figured in the lists of other parties. Toward the end of the century, the position of the Pope appeared to have undergone a change. The "Rerum novarum" Encyclical, issued on May 16, 1891, which laid down the social doctrine of the Church, was interpreted as indirect encouragement to Catholics to resume political activity. In competition with the Socialist unions, such Catholics as Guido Miglioli and Romolo Murri, organized the workers in so-called "white leagues," the first Catholic trade-unions, and the sociologist Giuseppe Toniolo elaborated the ideological principles on which the *Partito Popolare* was to be based.

In January 1919, Pope Benedict XV lifted the "non

expedit" edict. Don Sturzo and his friends had been waiting for this change in the political situation: the *Partito Popolare*, the party of Catholics, was born the same year. Its program was modern and progressive. It condemned imperialism, demanded the adoption of proportional representation, the vote for women and the distribution of large uncultivated estates among peasants; complete separation of state from Church influence and an increase in local autonomy were also two important points of this program. By calling for the separation of Church and state, the new party tried to reaffirm its independence from the Church and to present itself as a genuine national party. The request for more local autonomy represented a reaction to excessive centralization which had plagued Italian political life since the very beginning of the new Italian state.

These principles were far from being accepted by everyone within the party. Side by side with progressives and socialist-oriented elements, there were moderates and conservatives. The co-existence of leftist and rightist elements within the party remained a permanent feature, first, of the *Partito Popolare*, and subsequently of the Christian Democratic Party. In spite of the frequent clashes between the opposing factions, the common Catholic faith and the influence exerted by the religious hierarchy represented a solid element of cohesion.

The electoral success of the new party was outstanding from its very beginnings. The political elections held in the year of its foundation sent 100 Catholic representatives to Parliament. This success was due to good organization and the skilled leadership of Don Sturzo. The *Partito Popolare* was in fact the first modern party with a well-organized national network of branch organizations, daily and weekly papers and important financial resources. Moreover, the party controlled a strong farmers' union, which was more powerful than the Socialist-dominated union. But the circumstances that made the *Partito Popolare* a party of a new type were the broad powers of the party secretary and the strict discipline that bound all the *popolari* representatives in Parliament to follow the policies decided on by the party's executive organ. This introduced a new element into Italian political life. The old "combinations," which up to now had been the basic feature of political life, personal agreements, and give-and-take among the few prominent leaders who commanded the votes of their respective groups, were no longer possible with the representatives of the *Partito Popolare.*

This new political situation, to which the other mass party, the PSI, had also contributed, in addition to the widespread social unrest which the government was not ready to face, brought Italian politics to a standstill and gave a free hand to the Fascists. Only a coalition between the *popolari* and the numerous currents of the *Liberali* might have mustered a strong enough majority to rule the country with authority and impede the progress of Fascism. Such an agreement was not forthcoming. First, because of a fundamental ideological conflict between the two parties: the Liberal Party was a traditionally lay party which included "free thinkers" and Masons among its prominent members; it had always stood for a state free from any clerical influence. Moreover, the "Roman Question," still unsettled, had created a huge gap between Catholics and Liberals. Therefore a political alliance was considered by both parties and by the Vatican either with hostility or reluctance. Giolitti, a master of the old political school, considered Sturzo a *parvenu* in politics and, being sure of his own power and prestige, did not make a serious attempt to reach an agreement with the *popolari.* Don Sturzo, on his part, did not look with particular favor upon Giolitti. In fact, on February 22nd, the eve of the Fascist take-over, he opposed Giolitti's return to power (he had left in June 1921); the latter was the only statesman in a position to oppose firmly the Fascist coup. Instead Sturzo preferred Facta, an almost unknown lawyer, who became the last pre-Fascist Prime Minister.

The *popolari*, although bound to respect the political decisions of their secretariat, were divided on the issue. Some of the leaders of the most conservative currents regarded Fascism, if not with favor, at least, with indulgence; others openly approved of Fascist violence against the Socialists.

53

5.

Consequently the Fascist seizure of power was the result of a series of political mistakes and indecisions for which all the major political parties shared responsibility.

The collaboration with Mussolini, attempted by Sturzo at the beginning of the regime, soon failed. In April 1923 Mussolini felt he commanded sufficient strength to oust the *popolari* ministers from his cabinet. In the action against the Catholic party, Mussolini was encouraged by the attitude of the Church. Despite his socialist past, Mussolini posed as a defender of the Catholic religion. After his successful fight against the Socialists, the Vatican considered that a Catholic party, whose birth had been justified by the necessity of counteracting the appeal of socialism, was no longer needed. The Church gradually withdrew its support from Don Sturzo, whose activities were regarded as too progressive and looked upon with little favour, if not with suspicion, in certain Vatican circles.

In 1925 Sturzo left the country, going into voluntary exile; from 1925 to 1946, the year in which he returned to Italy, he lived in the U.S.A. After Sturzo's departure, the party leadership was taken over by a young member of Parliament from the Trentino region, Alcide De Gasperi. One year later, in 1926, the *Partito Popolare* was outlawed along with the other parties. While some of its members collaborated with the Fascist government, most returned to their professional activities and abstained from active politics, maintaining a critical attitude toward Fascism and Mussolini.

Catholic opposition to Fascism gradually dissipated when a few years later, Mussolini reached a final settlement with the Vatican over the "Roman Question." This settlement represented a milestone in state-church relations and was to have considerable influence on the future of Catholic politics in Italy.

The Lateran Agreements (*Patti Lateranensi*) were signed on February 11, 1929, after long negotiations. A complete settlement, juridical, financial and political, was reached on all problems that had been pending between the Vatican and the Italian state since 1870. The Italian Government recognized the Vatican as an independent state, a large indemnity and the Vatican palaces were turned over by Italy (Arts. 3 and 27).[1] A number of privileges were granted to the Catholic Church; religious marriage was made equivalent to civil marriage; special honors were given high church dignitaries; ministers of the Church were to be exempted from military service. The Catholic religion was also declared the religion of the state (Art. 1), religious teaching was introduced in the high schools (Art. 36) and religious schools were given a larger amount of independence (Arts. 39 and 40).

The Lateran Agreements considerably strengthened Mussolini's prestige. The majority of Italians enthusiastically welcomed the end of the controversy which had set state and church against each other, and which for nearly sixty years had represented a problem of conscience for many Italian Catholics.

For a few years relations between the Fascist state and the Catholic Church remained good. In 1931 friction developed over the question of the Catholic youth organization (Catholic Action), because it competed, in the field of youth education and organization, with the Fascists and could therefore not be tolerated by them. This, however, was a minor question and could easily be settled. In 1938 and 1939, relations started to deteriorate. Mussolini's close alliance with Hitler could not be accepted easily by the Vatican, which had condemned Hitler's policy of persecution of the Jews. During the war, in view of its international vocation and its universalist doctrine, the Vatican maintained a position of neutrality with regard to aggressive Fascist policies. But as soon as the final outcome of the conflict was no longer in doubt, the Vatican made ready to assume a new political role.

The Church had to anticipate the dangers, both political and religious, which might result for Italy as one of the pillars of Catholicism, in view of the political vacuum that would be left by the defeat and the sudden disappearance

---

[1] The indemnity included the payment of 750 million lire plus a billion lire worth of state securities.

of Fascism. The Vatican feared that at the end of a lost war, Socialism and Communism would gain increasing ground in the country; this was felt to be the main problem that would have to be faced by the Catholic Church in the post-war period. The necessity of establishing a political force through which the Italian Catholics could rally the opposition to Communism was obvious. This fear led to the resurrection of a Catholic party.

In 1942-1943, in fact, a number of leaders of the old *Partito Popolare* and new recruits clandestinely resumed political contacts. In these years they laid the foundations of a new party to be called Christian Democracy. They recognized Alcide De Gasperi[1] as their leader. During the Fascist period De Gasperi had been persecuted and imprisoned; he was liberated from a Fascist jail in 1939 and took refuge in the Vatican, where he worked as a librarian and wrote political articles under a pseudonym for the *Osservatore Romano*.

At the end of 1943 the organizational nucleus of the DC was still quite weak. Almost nothing of the structure of the *Partito Popolare* had remained intact; only the "cadres" still partially existed. Men like Stefano Jacini, Giovanni Gronchi, Achille Grandi and Alcide De Gasperi himself, all leaders of the old party who were to constitute the directorate of the new Christian Democracy, had kept up their contacts throughout the years of Fascism.

However, the DC could always rely on the help of the Church for the reconstitution of its party organization and on the availability of existing semi-political bodies, the most powerful of which, the Catholic Action, had remained almost intact throughout the years of Fascism. The support of the lower clergy, the *parroci*, who exercise considerable influence

---

[1] Alcide De Gasperi began his political career before the First World War as a representative of the city of Trento to the Austrian Congress in Vienna. Before the war the towns of Trento, Trieste, Bolzano and Gorizia and their territories were under the administration of the Austrian Empire. After World War I these territories became Italian and De Gasperi was elected to represent them in the Italian Parliament.

on parish life, was equally important. This support was to result in an important and lasting hold by the Church on the DC, which, in future years, was frequently compelled to play the role of a secular arm.

The political program of the DC followed in the main that of the *Partito Popolare*. The principal points of its platform were the division of church and state, the validity of the Lateran Agreements, the creation of regional governments and the strengthening of communal institutions, complete freedom for the workers to organize trade unions and their right to participate in the management of enterprises, universal social insurance, progressive taxation and land reform. The defense of Christian values and good relations with the Catholic Church were especially emphasized.

The social structure of the party that was to become the largest and most powerful in Italy was extremely diversified. Farmers and industrial workers coexisted with elements of the petty-bourgeosie and representatives of vested interests, corresponding to a number of different and contradictory political positions, from the progressive left to the extreme conservative. This determined the interclass character of the DC.

While the necessity of mediating between these currents assigned a center position to the DC in the Italian political spectrum, historical necessity and the interplay of internal tendencies often compelled the party to switch alternately from the center to the right or the left.

THE MINOR PARTIES

The sixth member of the CLN was the *Partito Democratico del Lavoro* (Labor Democrats): a small party, existing only in southern and central Italy and not represented in the Northern CLNs. Its leaders, Ivanoe Bonomi and Meuccio Ruini, were former Socialists who had left the party in 1912 because their reformist position conflicted with the revolutionary maximalism of the majority. Several groups with heterogenous ideological backgrounds gathered around these leaders, all more or less favorable to a social democratic program.

The *Partito Repubblicano Italiano* (PRI) had a great historical heritage; it came into existence during the struggle for Italian national unity. Its first leaders were Giuseppe Mazzini, the apostle of the Italian political and moral *Risorgimento*, and Carlo Cattaneo. The latter advocated a state based on a federalist structure, which represented the alternative to the centralized monarchical state which was the ultimate outcome of the *Risorgimento*.

From 1943 until the constitutional referendum (1946), from which Italy emerged a Republic, the Republican Party engaged in an uncompromising struggle against the monarchy.

In contrast to the other parties of the CLN, in which it did not participate, the Republican Party never agreed to cooperate with the monarchy. Though relatively small, its strength was based on a few strongholds, scattered all over Italy. It was and still is one of the dominating political forces in the Romagna, Maremma (Tuscany) and in certain Sicilian districts. In 1943 it enjoyed considerable prestige due to its uncompromising opposition to Fascism, which had prompted some of its leaders, foremost among them Randolfo Pacciardi, to fight on the side of the Republicans in the Spanish civil war.

The PRI program resembled the program of the Action Party, with which the PRI has many affinities, as a party of ideas and as an advocate of a spiritual and moral renovation of Italian life. Following Cattaneo's ideas on federalism, the PRI strongly upheld a constitutional system in which the Italian regions would be endowed with a broad autonomy. This federalist principle later found a partial realization in the new Italian Constitution.

The parties, whose history and programs have been outlined here, are the main political forces that appeared after the fall of Fascism; with the exception of the Labor Democrats, they played an historical role in post-war Italy. Some of them have occupied dominant positions and attained great power, such as Christian Democracy. Some, such as the Socialist Party, were to become protagonists in complex and drawn-out political crises; others (the Action Party) disappeared. All of them influenced, sometimes deeply, Italian political life in the post-war years, or laid the basis of political programs which still carry weight and influence. Other groups or movements sprang up locally, profiting from the disorientation and political inexperience of the Italians. They were all shortlived. The only one worth mentioning is the Sicilian Separatist Movement, under the leadership of Finocchiaro Aprile, a lawyer from Palermo.

Separatism developed as a reaction to the neglect in which Sicily had been kept by all Italian governments—the Fascist regime included—from the time of unification. Several generations of Sicilians felt exploited by the industrial and advanced North, and the Separatist Movement was a natural outgrowth of this historical frustration. It went so far as to demand complete independence for the island. The Separatist Party gained considerable following but fell into disrepute when some of its leaders asked for the annexation of Sicily by the United Kingdom. This request was based on historical interests which Great Britain had in the island prior to Italian unification. The Separatist Movement lasted only about three years. Among its many and sometimes absurd requests, the most valid ones were incorporated into the Italian Constitution. In 1949 Sicily was constituted by special statute as an autonomous region.

CHAPTER 4

WAR IN ITALY, 1943-1945

CO-BELLIGERENCY

On the same day that Badoglio's Government declared war against Germany, Italy was declared a "co-belligerent nation" by the Allied powers.

The concept of "co-belligerency" did not alter Italy's legal status, which had resulted from the signing of the armistice. It was, in fact, made clear by the British Government, in an official statement on October 14th in the House of Lords, that, technically, Italy would be considered as an enemy until the signing of the final peace treaty. But the Allies were obliged to give some kind of formal recognition to Italy in exchange for the collaboration they requested; having no precise knowledge as yet of the extent of the collapse of the Italian army, they still counted on Italian military help against Germany, in addition to the full support of the Italian population, particularly in the territories still occupied. Moreover, in recognizing Badoglio, they hoped to strengthen the King's government, which had signed the armistice, as a counter force to Mussolini's newly established Italian Social Republic in the North. They attempted to present the King's government as legitimately backed by the national consensus as contrasted with German attempt to create an Italian satellite state. On the other hand, since they wanted to be left free to dictate the final peace terms to Italy, they rejected the Italian request for an alliance, which had been repeatedly advanced by the King's government. Hence, the idea of co-belligerency, far from having any real worth, was no more than bait cast to the Italian people to enlist their support in the war against Germany.

The declaration of co-belligerency was accompanied by the recognition of the right of the Italian people to choose its own form of government at the end of the war. This principle had already been stipulated in the armistice agreements, and was embodied in the Atlantic Charter. It represented a fundamental political premise at the same time that it met the insistent demands of the majority of the anti-Fascist political parties.

THE MONARCHY AND THE POLITICAL PARTIES

The next step taken by the Allied military authorities, with the same purpose of reinforcing the Italian Government and widening its base among the population, was the request made to Vittorio Emanuele to include representatives of the anti-Fascist parties in his cabinet. At the beginning, the King refused to comply. He did not want men in his cabinet whose attitude toward the monarchy or to his person was, to say the least, unfriendly. Finally, under persistent Allied pressure, he was forced to acquiesce. But even formal collaboration between the monarchy and the anti-Fascist parties at the government level took some time to be achieved. Negotiations went on for several months and revealed how resistant the past political forms were to change.

The attitudes of the various political parties toward the monarchy and the King differed. The Communists, Socialists, Actionists and, of course, the Republicans openly opposed the monarchical form of government; to them the monarchy was the symbol of conservatism and the rallying point of privileged forces and vested interests. The realization of their progressive programs, the changes they planned to bring about in Italian society could not be imagined under a monarchy. These parties, therefore, opposed both the institution and the King. On the other hand the Liberal Party, some Christian Democratic elements and all of the anti-Fascist conservative groups favoured the maintenance of the monarchy, but neither King Vittorio Emanuele, nor his son Prince Umberto, whom they accused of collaboration with Fascism and Mussolini, was acceptable to them. In October 1922 the King had entrusted the premiership to Mussolini and refused to act when he could have done so against Mussolini's totalitarian policies, thus becoming his accomplice. The King again acquiesced in 1938, when he permitted Mussolini to bind the country to an alliance with Germany, despite the anti-German feelings of the people which he fully shared. And in 1940 when, although he knew of the Italian military and economic incapacity, he did not oppose Mussolini's decision to involve Italy in the war. The final, and perhaps the greatest accusation against the King was that he left his capital undefended after the armistice.

The charges against the King's son, Umberto, were more general. The Crown Prince, who had no political powers, could not be held responsible for Italian entry into the war; however, as a military commander, he knew the great risks involved in Mussolini's policies and he never used his position to restrain the dictator, nor his influence in military circles to keep the country out of war. During the twenty years of Fascism he had shown his indifference with regard to political problems. He preferred the more pleasant cares of a glittering social life.

In defense against these accusations the King flatly denied any responsibility. According to the Italian Constitution (the so-called "Albertine Statute"),[1] he replied, the King bore no

---

[1] The Albertine Statute, the first Italian Constitution, dated back to 1848. It had been granted by Carlo Alberto, King of Piedmont and Sardinia, to his subjects to meet the demands of the Italian Liberals and as a token of his intention to free the Italian peninsula from the Austrian yoke. Later, in 1861, when Italy became independent and united, the Statuto Albertino was extended, with little modification, to the whole country.

political responsibility; therefore, he could have done little to block Mussolini's political actions. According to the King, the dictator's accession to power was the inevitable result of the deadlock brought about by the inability of the democratic parties to organize a government majority. To justify his inaction with regard to the Italian entry into the war, the King and his son declared publicly that the Italian people were responsible since they went along with the dictator's aggressive policies. "How could the King have stopped Mussolini's warlike policy when the Italian people were behind him?,"[1] Prince Umberto answered a *Times* correspondent, when asked why the monarch had not intervened in June 1940 against Italian participation in the war.

It became clear that the royal house would act against the interests of the Italian people in order to save the throne. All of the requests made to the Allies for revision of the harsh clauses of the armistice and for more generous conditions in the final peace treaty were based on a clear distinction between the responsibilities borne by Mussolini and his regime and the Italian people; this had also been the line of Allied propaganda directed to Italy before the fall of Fascism. There was evidence that a good part of Allied public opinion, especially in the United States, had accepted this thesis. There was no doubt that the line of defense chosen by the King conflicted with the position adopted by the anti-Fascist parties.

REQUESTS FOR KING EMANUEL'S ABDICATION

When the King, finally yielding to Allied pressure, invited the anti-Fascist parties to enter the Badoglio Cabinet, the parties of all tendencies made as the condition of their participation the abdication of the King and his son. The institutional question, however, that is, the final choice between monarchy and republic, was to be decided by the Italian people at the

---

[1] Interview to the London Times, April 20, 1944.

end of the war, according to the armistice agreements. Meanwhile the crown was to pass to the young Prince of Naples, Umberto's son, then only six years old, under the regency of Prime Minister Badoglio. This was the proposal advanced in early November 1943 by the six parties of the CLN of Naples, the most influential in Southern Italy; it mainly reflected the positions of the two major leaders, the Monarchist Benedetto Croce and the Republican Count Carlo Sforza.

The conflict over the royal succession went on for several months, monopolizing all political activity in the liberated south, especially in Naples and Brindisi. The King refused to abdicate, since he did not recognize any of the charges made against him by the CLN; the political parties, on the other hand, insisted on their demands in an unusual show of unanimity. Among them the Liberals and the conservative monarchic wing of the Christian Democrats also favoured for tactical reasons the abdication of the King and his son. They believed that King Victor Emanuel's personal sacrifice would put them in a better position to defend the monarchic institution as such when, after the war, the issue of monarchy or republic would have to be decided.

Confronted with the impossibility of finding a quick solution of the conflict between King and political parties, the Allied Military Government (AMG) at times took sides with one or the other. The Americans clearly favored the anti-Fascist parties; an economic mission headed by Adlai Stevenson in January 1944 at the end of a fact-finding visit to Southern Italy, presented a famous report to the State Department, in which the monarchy and the Badoglio Government were pictured as discredited institutions, lacking prestige and authority and representing a block on the road to economic and social evolution of a new democratic Italy. The British, on the other hand, following Churchill's instructions, were generally favourable to the monarchy, because they had little faith in the political capabilities of the new democratic parties and a greater awareness of the potential dangers represented by extremist political forces. The difference of opinion between the Allies remained in the background and could not be fully exploited either by the King or by the political parties. The Americans had recognized the priority of the British concerning political decisions with regard to Italy and, although on various occasions they pressed for a more generous and open-minded policy in favour of the Italian people, on the whole they respected the agreement.

SOVIET RECOGNITION OF THE KING'S GOVERNMENT

A new element in the situation was added by the decisions taken at the congress of CLNs held in Bari at the end of January 1944. This was the first important political conference to take place after the fall of Fascism. The participants were delegates from local CLNs and a special mission from Rome, which had crossed the front-line to represent the authoritative voice of the Central Committee of National Liberation. These latter delegates held much more extreme views, demanding the creation of an extraordinary inter-party cabinet which could arrogate to itself all constitutional powers. The proposal was unrealistic, since, apart from other technical difficulties, it did not take into consideration the fact that the AMG would not have withdrawn its support from Badoglio's Cabinet, which was responsible for the execution of the clauses of the armistice. In Central Italy, still under German occupation and, even more so in the north, political positions within the same parties differed considerably. Liberals or Christian Democrats of the south were generally more flexible and ready to compromise on matters of principle. Their political position was hardly comparable to that of the Liberals or Catholics of the north, who were more intransigent and more ready for decisive changes. The underground struggle against Fascism and the Germans, which lasted one year in Central Italy and two years longer in the north, together with other historic factors, accounted for these differences.

After considering several proposals and engaging in long

discussions, the Congress of Bari[1] decided to limit its demands to the abdication of King Victor Emanuel. A few days later an executive junta, created as a standing committee of the Congress, made additional proposals. Following the King's abdication, according to these proposals, his successor, Umberto II, would delegate all his royal powers to a collegiate general Lieutenancy of the Realm, which was to appoint a cabinet made up of representatives of all the parties in the CLN. This plan was finally approved and endorsed by the Allied Control Commission. The pressure put on the King by this agreement was too great to be resisted for long. The monarch could well do without the collaboration of the parties, but he had apparently also lost Allied support. However, at the last minute, two new events occurred to reverse completely the situation and strengthen the position of the monarchy, if only for a short time. The first was a declaration made by Churchill rejecting the junta proposals endorsed by the Allied Control Commission. The British Prime Minister made a new statement in support of the monarchy and once again postponed the solution of the differences between the monarch and the political parties. The second event, much more dramatic, was the Soviet *de jure* recognition of the Badoglio Government and, as a consequence, the decision of the two governments to resume regular diplomatic relations. The announcement came on March 13, 1944, and caught both political parties and the British-American authorities in Italy by surprise. The British and American Governments had not yet granted official recognition to Badoglio. Such a step would have amounted to a return to complete normalcy in diplomatic relations with Italy; and the British and Americans objected to being preceded by the Soviet Union, which, considering its limited

---

[1] On a different plane, one of the most important achievements of the Congress of Bari was the foundation of the Italian General Confederation of Labor (CGIL, *Confederazione Generale Italiana del Lavoro*), which merged into the same labor organization the Communist, Socialist and Christian Democratic workers unions. This act achieved a unity on the labor front similar to that reached among different political forces already existing in the CLN.

66

interest in the area, could easily make a display of formal generosity. The Italian political parties were equally disoriented by the Soviet gesture; how could a socialist power give its support to a government which by unanimous consent was reactionary and deeply compromised with Fascism?

The real reasons for the Soviet move remain obscure; the most plausible explanation is that by acting in this way the USSR was trying to bring about a solution of the political deadlock, a solution, which in the long run, might turn out to be most favourable for the Italian Communist Party. The Soviet Government knew that for the moment there was no possibility of a Communist takeover of power in Italy; considering the difficult economic and political situation of the country, this might not even have been desiderable. The existence of a conservative government in a period when hard decisions had to be taken would eventually benefit greatly the Communists and provide the best atmosphere for their growth and final success.

This interpretation was born out by the position taken by the PCI soon after the Soviet recognition. On March 28th, Palmiro Togliatti, leader of the PCI, arrived from Moscow, where he had spent the years of his exile, to take over the leadership of the Italian Communist Party. His first political statements were most conciliatory: the Italian Communists, in view of the emergency situation, were willing to go along even with the King; they thought that the first and most important goal was to achieve a united front against Mussolini's Social Republic and the Germans. To this end the PCI was ready to subordinate all other political questions and to accept fully the *status quo* until the end of the war, when the Communists could resume their liberty of action.

AGREEMENT BETWEEN THE KING AND THE POLITICAL PARTIES

The PCI's realistic approach was welcomed by both the monarchy and the Allied authorities, and represented an important, almost decisive, contribution to the final agreement between the political parties and the King. The agreement was reached on April 24th, on the basis of a compromise proposed by Enrico De Nicola, a Neapolitan political leader since December 1943. This compromise, which had been first accepted then refused by Victor Emanuel, provided for the transfer of all royal powers from the King to a Lieutenant General: the King would retire from public life without abdicating; Umberto, the Crown Prince, would then be designated as Lieutenant General.

The British-American reaction to the Soviet "de jure" recognition had been strong. The King's government was accused of violating the armistice terms[1] and a protest was lodged with the Soviet Government. The Soviet Government accepted the Anglo-American remonstration and changed its recognition from "de jure" to "de facto"; this involved an exchange of representatives of minor rank rather than ambassadors. This change in the situation considerably reduced the King's advantage. He, therefore, again decided to accept De Nicola's compromise with only one reservation. His powers would be transferred to the Lieutenant General only after the Allied occupation of Rome, which was considered as imminent.

The British-American Allies, who after the gesture of good will made by the Soviet Union, could not afford to wait longer, endorsed De Nicola's compromise and put pressure on the Socialists and Actionists, the only CLN parties still strongly opposed, to accept it. The Communists, too, used their moderating influence to persuade them. Under this double pressure, the Socialists and Actionists dropped their reservations, and, on April 22nd, the new government, still under the premiership of Badoglio but with the participation of all the CLN parties, was finally formed. Its freedom of action and that of the CLN parties was considerably limited by a pledge, requested by the Allies, to accept the present settlement of the institutional question between

---

[1] The Allied thesis was that, under the armistice, Italy could not entertain relations with a foreign state without permission from the Allied occupation authorities.

monarchy and republic until the end of the war, and to postpone until then all projects for social reform. Further limitations concerned propaganda activities of the political parties and their cooperation in recognizing and fully respecting the armistice terms. For the Allies this was tantamount to backing the monarchy and the existing social order.

These conditions were hard, but their acceptance was an absolute necessity. Because of the disastrous economic situation of the country and the condition of the population, which only Allied help could save from starvation, the anti-Fascist political leaders could not take the responsibility for rejecting the Allied impositions in the name of ideological principles, the same principles which until the armistice had constituted the main Allied propaganda line. The conduct of the Allies in this whole matter caused much disillusionment and bitterness among the anti-Fascist. Their efforts aimed at clarifying the new goals of political renovation to the Italian people were considerably hampered and frustrated by the Allied measures. The prestige of democracy itself, a concept whose meaning was still vague and uncertain for many Italians but which stirred their hopes and enthusiasm, suffered considerably.

The operation turned out eventually to be most advantageous for the PCI. Developing the policy that had been initiated by the Soviet Union, Togliatti's strategy assured the PCI of its participation in the government.[1] This position was maintained and strengthened in successive cabinets and gave the party the opportunity to infiltrate gradually on the local level; this infiltration was often favoured by the same Allied authorities who appeared to have accepted, at face value Communist good-will and collaboration. This episode is of fundamental importance for a study of the Italian Communist Party, since it anticipated the line of conduct the party was to adopt in the future. Putting aside the revolutionary "maximalism" of its origins, the PCI's policy was flexible and

---

[1] In the new cabinet the Department of Agriculture was given to the Communists; moreover, Togliatti, became minister without portfolio.

69

accomodating; the party carefully avoided getting involved or committed on questions of principle and ideology, preferring the substantial political advantages to be achieved by viable tactics.

MILITARY OPERATIONS IN ITALY, 1943-1944

During the winter of 1943-1944, the fronts had been stabilized along the Gustav line and the Nettuno bridgehead. The Allied High Command launched a new offensive in the spring. With their massive superiority in air power, which could be brought into full play with the good weather, the Allies swiftly reached Rome, liberating it on June 5th.

The capital had been declared an "open city" in august 1943 and had suffered only few Allied air attacks. The city was almost intact, although the Romans had lived through a difficult period during the German occupation. On the verge of starvation, the city's population had been subjected, especially during the last months, to organized terror by Fascist *Milizia* and the German political police. Young men were frequently rounded up and either forced to enrol in the new Fascist army or, more often, sent to do slave labor in Germany.

Rome was also the center of an intense underground activity, in which old and new political leaders participated at great personal risk. The CLN was the promoter of all political actions; it followed the situation in the liberated south and organized guerrilla and sabotage actions in the countryside, especially in the Alban hills surrounding Rome. German retaliation that followed these actions was fierce and cost many lives. One of the bloodiest episodes of the German occupation in Italy[1] was the massacre of the *Fosse*

---

[1] Several German officers were subsequently tried as war criminals for acts performed in Italy. One of the most murderous, beside the one at Via Rasella, was the so-called Marzabotto's massacre, after the name of a small village in the province of Bologna. There, during the night of September 30th - October 1st, 1944, 1500 civilians and 300 partisans were

Ardeatine at the end of March 1944: 335 Italians from all social classes and particularly lawyers, teachers and intellectuals were shot in a sand quarry outside Rome in retaliation for a surprise attack on a company of German soldiers marching through the Via Rasella, in which 32 were killed.

In the last and most drastic phase of the German occupation, the Vatican authorities gave vital spiritual and material help to the Romans. Abandoned by the civil government and at the mercy of the Germans, the Roman population found protection with the clergy and the Pope. Churches and monasteries became hideouts for political refugees; food and clothing were distributed by the charity organizations of the Vatican to those most in need. Profiting from its authority and its neutral status, the high clergy sometimes intervened to moderate the ruthless decisions of the German command. This action considerably strengthened the prestige and authority of the Church among the Roman population, and helped to erase the memory of the Church's early attitude in favor of the Fascist regime. On the day of liberation the Romans expressed their gratitude to the Pope in a thanksgiving manifestation in St. Peter's square.

After the conquest of Rome, the Allied troops continued northward at a faster pace. In the first days of August the Allied troops entered Florence with the help of the Italian partisan formations, which, during the past several months, had been fighting a guerrilla war on the mountains of the Casentino. Allied soldiers and Italian partisans fought side by side to clean the town from retreating Germans and Fascist snipers.

At the end of September Allied troops were again blocked. They had reached the last line of German resistance, the so-called Gothic-line, running along the Appennines from the Tyrrhenian to the Adriatic sea, between the cities of Bologna and Florence. During the entire winter of 1944-1945 the front-line remained static.

---

shot by a German punitive unit in retaliation for the support given by the people of Marzabotto to partisans active in the area.

The liberation of Rome opened new political perspectives. As had been agreed in April 1944, King Victor Emanuel signed a decree transferring all his constitutional powers to prince Umberto on June 5th; the latter was to exercise them from now on with the title of Lieutenant General of the Realm. On the same day, Prime Minister Badoglio presented his resignation and that of his cabinet to the Lieutenant General who immediately entrusted him with the formation of a new government. This task proved difficult.

The liberation of Rome brought new and more complex political factors into play. Roman political leaders, and the members of the Central CLN, had already shown their intransigence and their radicalism at the Congress of Bari. They had barely accepted the compromise that had led on April 24th to the second Badoglio Cabinet, in which Socialists and Actionists in particular had been uneasy. For these reasons, they advanced a number of conditions for their participation in the new cabinet. The main reservation of the Central CLN concerned Badoglio himself, who, apart from his early connections with Fascism, had shown complete allegiance to the cause of the monarchy; then the Roman anti-Fascist leaders, the Socialists and the Actionists particularly, conceived of the cabinet as the direct expression of the CLN from which it should derive its authority and mandate. The last request was revolutionary, since the Italian Constitution, much modified during the Fascist period but legally still in force, stated that the designation of the Prime Minister and of the other members of the cabinet was a royal prerogative now invested in the Lieutenant. Thus the CLN aimed at substituting itself for the Lieutenant, reducing the latter to a mere figurehead.

The pressure for a solution along the lines advocated by the CLN was so strong that Badoglio, recognizing the impossibility of forming a cabinet, declined his mandate and the Lieutenant was obliged to endorse the choice of Prime Minister made by the CLN. He appointed Ivanoe Bonomi, chairman of the Central CLN and leader of the Labor Democrats, to head the new government.

On June 18th the cabinet was formed, composed exclusively of CLN men, with the exception of one member, the Minister of the Navy, Admiral De Courten, a career officer whose participation in the cabinet had been requested by AMG. During the negotiations for the formation of the cabinet, AMG had also vetoed the appointment of Count Sforza as Minister of Foreign Affairs, because of his republican leanings.[1]

The first act of the new cabinet was a decree (lacking a freely elected representative body, legislative activity was exercised by the government by means of decrees) issued on June 25th, calling for the convocation of a Constituent Assembly at the termination of the hostilities in Italy. It was a solemn pledge to give Italy a new constitution and to solve the institutional problem. This commitment confirmed, at the same time, the anti-monarchic orientation of the majority of the CLN and was a warning to the House of Savoy and its supporters that the problem of a new form of government would be taken up again as soon as the situation permitted it.

Bonomi's Government was not long lived. His range of activity was limited strictly by the state of tutelage in which Italy was kept by the Allied powers and by the armistice terms. Consequently, the policy to be followed by the Bonomi Cabinet was foreordained; the Italian Government, of whatever political orientation, could only work for the lessening of controls, for the improvement of Italy's status and to attempt to overcome the ambiguities of co-belligerency; and for more economic aid and greater Italian participation in the war effort. In all these respects Bonomi's policy could not be different from that of the previous Badoglio Cabinets.

---

[1] This veto, given by the British High Commissioner, gave rise to a violent dispute between Churchill, who still supported Badoglio, and the U.S. State Department, which favoured Sforza and the new democratic forces represented by the CLN. The views of the British prevailed once again, and Allied control over internal Italian affairs was reaffirmed.

1944 was a presidential election year in the United States; therefore, the occasion was favourable for enlisting the support of Americans of Italian origin in Italy's cause. Their response was wholehearted, and as a consequence, while the electoral campaign was on, the American Government granted diplomatic recognition on October 26th. Had it not been for the intransigent opposition of Great Britain, Italy would probably have attained the status of an Allied nation.

Another important result was the allocation of UNRRA aid (see p. 124). However, because of the lack of shipping facilities, UNRRA aid remained largely on paper until the end of the war. Finally the proposals for increased Italian military participation in the war against Germany, constantly requested since the armistice, were partially accepted.

This represented an important step forward. At the beginning, the Allies had been in favor of making full use of the Italian Army, until they realized the extent of the Italian military collapse. In order to be used efficiently the Italian army had to be reorganized and retrained. This was judged too costly and time-consuming to be worth-while; moreover, it would have entailed a price, in terms of political concessions, that the Allies were not ready to grant. The Italian Government, however, well aware that its political future depended on its contribution to the war effort, insisted repeatedly on the rearmament of available Italian manpower. These requests were eventually granted in part, due to a change in the military situation. The Allied effectives in Italy had been weakened by the movement of several important units to the Western front, which opened on June 6, 1944, with the landings in Normandy and had absolute priority. Italian troops were then used to fill the gaps left by these troop transfers. The Italian Army was expanded to a total of about 50,000 men, re-equipped and re-trained under British supervision. In the fall of 1944 these troops entered into action on the easternmost sector of the Gothic Line, successfully participating in the war until its end. In the meantime the Italian Navy and Air Force also made important contributions to the Allied war effort. Italian ships participated as escorts of convoys in the Atlantic as well as in a number of naval actions. The Air Force was particularly active in supplying the Yugoslav partisans and in reconnaissance missions.

FIRST CONFLICTS BETWEEN THE POLITICAL PARTIES OF THE CLN

The results that Bonomi's Cabinet achieved in its dealings with the Allies were positive (although they were attained through favourable circumstances) but its record in the field of internal policy was much less constructive. The cabinet, which lasted about four months, was torn by dissensions and violent debate. There were two major points of friction. The first concerned the function of the CLN itself (both at the central and local level); the other regarded the political purge of former Fascists from all branches of public life. This had been started by a special committee under the direction of the Communist leader, Mauro Scoccimarro. On both points Socialists and Actionists clashed with Christian Democrats and Liberals. The Communists remained somewhat in the background of this clash; although they publicly supported the Socialist and Actionist cause, at the governmental level they were ever ready to turn all situations to their benefit.

The CLN had increased its power so that it was able to impose its authority on the Lieutenant General, influencing the appointment of the Prime Minister. The local CLNs were at least as powerful within their narrower jurisdiction. In central Italy they existed in most of the towns and villages. Since they were the only organized political forces in existence, they had been invested, after the Allied liberation, with administrative powers, previously exercised by Fascist elements. Allied Military Government, not knowing the local situation and lacking personnel trained for specific administrative functions, was inclined to rely more and more on CLN collaboration. As a consequence, the local CLNs became the arbiters of local life. Due to the technical impossibility of holding elections, they selected the mayors and all the most important local officers and often gained complete control of the administrative and political life of the area. In certain cases, following their revolutionary inspiration, they even disposed of the property of former Fascists, or distributed uncultivated lands to the peasant laborers.

CLN power soon began to be questioned by some of its own members. The Liberals, in view of their monarchist orientation and faithful as they were to the values of the old liberal state, were inclined to consider the function of the CLN as temporary. Following the re-establishment of Italian government authority over the liberated areas (by the fall of 1944, AMG had returned southern and most of central Italy to Italian jurisdiction), the Liberals wanted to reinstate normal organs of administration, such as the *prefetti*,[1] police chiefs and other officials of government bureaucracy, to their positions. The local CLNs were to submit to these administrative organs, transferring to them the powers they had taken over. The Liberals and the other conservative forces feared that the progressive tendencies of the CLN might in the long run completely subvert the old social and political structures that, on the whole, they intended to maintain.

The issue of the local CLNs was directly connected with the purge of the administration. All the anti-Fascist parties in the CLN had agreed that Italian life was to be purged of those elements who were compromised with Fascism. This decision was dictated by moral considerations; it seemed justified to prosecute those who had collaborated with Mussolini, especially those who had personally profited from their position, misusing public funds. For the progressive parties the purge had primarily a political purpose: in order to build a new democratic society it was first necessary to eliminate the old political class, which stood for values contrary to democracy and whose political approach was strongly tied to Fascist mental habits and methods.

---

[1] The *prefetto* is a high career official who represents the government in the province. He is the supreme authority in the province and has vast political and administrative powers, among the most important of which is control over the local administrations elected by the people.

Disagreements among the CLN parties arose as to how far the purge should go. During the Fascist regime all government employees automatically had to be members of the Fascist party. Since bureaucracy, under Fascism, became inflated, the purge would touch an important part of the population; moreover, in other sectors of national life, such as private business or the independent professions, Fascist pressure had become so strong that not to hold a Fascist Party membership card might have been dangerous to both career and personal safety. It was, therefore, difficult to establish exact criteria for convinced Fascists as differentiated from fellow travellers.

While the Liberals and Christian Democrats favoured prosecuting members of the Fascist hierarchy and Fascist profiteers, the leftist parties were for a much more extensive application of the purge. They not only wanted to reach the Fascist leaders but to rid wide sections of the bureaucracy, the army and the economy of those elements of the bourgeoisie who had supported Fascism, if not actively at least with open sympathy.

The DC and Liberals were strongly opposed to this interpretation, since a purge to this extent would hit mainly the social classes from which they expected to draw their electoral support. To give a free hand to the extreme left was tantamount, for both the DC and Liberal Party, to undermining their own political power and future possibilities of taking over the government. Both the DC and the Liberals needed the help of the former governing class. But the political future of the Left in the government depended upon the substitution of the former governing class.

The debate on the rôle of the local CLNs and the purge went on for several months and led to a number of conflicts which gradually weakened the cabinet. Bonomi, in addition, despite his CLN origin, leaned more and more toward the monarchy and the conservative parties, thus increasing the dissension between the two competing factions.

In November the crisis reached its final and conclusive stage. The High Committee for Measures against Fascism, the highest organ of the purge, requested that a number of high officials in the Department of the Treasury and in the Navy be dismissed because of their past Fascist sympathies. The Liberal ministers of the two departments threatened to resign. Bonomi backed them fully and solemnly requested the dissolution of the High Committee. The leftist parties, both in the country at large and at the government level, demanded the continuation of the purge.

The cabinet was so split over the issue and the positions of the parties involved were so rigid that the Prime Minister decided to resign. On November 26th, Bonomi who had been designated by the CLN, went to the Lieutenant General and presented his resignation, recognizing by this act the Lieutenant's full constitutional prerogatives—which the CLN had denied in the past. Bonomi's decision, which was supported by the conservative parties, was a heavy blow to the authority of the CLN and at the same time a recognition of the functions and power of the crown.

Political consultations for the new cabinet began almost immediately and lasted for about fifteen days. Again the choice fell on Bonomi, who by now was acceptable to the Lieutenant General and had Liberal and Demo-Christian support. The Socialists and Actionists refused to enter the new cabinet in opposition to Bonomi. The Communists, as always, proved to be more accomodating and, although they maintained their reservations with regard to Bonomi, they agreed to cooperate with him. For tactical reasons they did not want to break with the DC and Liberal party and thought that it would be a mistake to abandon their positions in the government, since these positions were useful in consolidating their influence in the country. As a consequence, three Communist leaders entered the second Bonomi Government—Togliatti as a Deputy Prime Minister, Antonio Pesenti as Minister of Finance and Scoccimarro as Minister for the Occupied Territories.[1] The latter turned out to be a key department, which gave the Communists a considerable advantage in consolidating their position within the resistance movement; in this respect the Socialists lost heavily by their isolation.

The constitution of the new Bonomi Cabinet marked a temporary solution of the dissensions within the CLNs. The authority of the central CLN, although somewhat weakened by the re-evaluation of the Lieutenant's powers and by the non-participation of the Socialists and Actionists in the cabinet, was indirectly recognized and reaffirmed by the way in which the crisis had been resolved. The second Bonomi Cabinet was, in fact, still the expression of the Central CLN, although its center of gravity had moved somewhat toward the right. On the other hand, the powers of the local CLNs were sharply limited, to merely consultative functions. Also, the extent of the political purge was considerably reduced and passed from the hands of a political committee to the jurisdiction of the judicial courts, which pursued it slowly and with more leniency.

The fall of the first Bonomi Cabinet had marked the first clash between the left and the right. However, in view of the still-existing emergency situation, the tight Allied control and other tactical reasons, neither side had pushed it to the extreme. The differences, however, remained latent and left most of the issues still pending. An open clash, for which both sides were preparing, was only postponed by one year, until the end of the war.

THE RESISTANCE MOVEMENT

A paramount factor in the history of this period, which was to influence deeply Italian society and political life for a long

---

[1] The Ministry for Occupied Territories, in addition to some administrative duties in preparation for the liberation of the country, was also competent to keep in contact with the resistance movement, active in northern Italy.

time after the conclusion of the war, was the resistance movement, which first appeared in the fall of 1943 and matured in the two subsequent years.

The value of the Resistance cannot be understood, if its military contribution alone is taken into account. Although important, its military action represented only one aspect of a spontaneous popular movement, whose real significance was moral and political.

The forces that participated in the resistance came from different backgrounds. The most immediate contribution came from partisan formations. At maximum capacity they could immobilize and engage eight full German divisions. Although a precise estimate is difficult to make, it has been calculated that the number of partisans active at the beginning of the summer of 1944 was over 100,000. At the end of the war an official estimate of the number of persons who had at any time engaged in partisan activities was 232,841 and of those who had regularly participated in the resistance movement, 125,714. The composition of the partisan brigades—as a force of about 8-9,000 partisans were called—was most heterogeneous; some were soldiers and officers of the army units dissolved after the armistice; others joined the resistance movement to escape the military draft of the neo-Fascist Republic. But most of the partisans were patriots who went into hiding to fight resurgent Fascism and the Germans. At first their action was unorganized and limited to *coups de main* against neo-Fascist and German units and sabotage of communication lines. When they had accomplished their missions, the partisan bands returned to the mountains where they could more easily resist German counter-attacks. Later, reinforced with Allied help, they were able to control large areas with a number of important centers.

Active underground groups like the GAP (Patriotic Action Group) and SAP (Patriotic Action Squads) were part of the partisan movement. The area of their activity was primarily the large industrial towns of the north where they organized strikes, sabotage of war production, spread anti-Fascist propaganda and carried out important missions in

80

concert with the Italian Government in Rome or with Allied headquarters.

The partisans paid dearly in sacrifice and lives. Partisan bands underwent severe difficulties, especially during the winters when, pressed by Germans and neo-Fascists, they were obliged to hide in the mountains without food or contact with other partisan units. Sometimes, for short periods, resistance units were compelled to disband. When their members returned to civilian life they were often caught by the police, tortured and executed. Frequently the Fascists were more cruel than the Germans. The toll of lives in the resistance movement was high. Well over 70,000 Italians who had some connection with resistance activity died in the two years 1943-1945, and about 40,000 were severely injured.

All social classes took part in the resistance, although the majority were industrial workers. Their greater political awareness and the strong influence of working-class political parties would account for this. The partisan army was in fact closely tied to political parties. The "Garibaldi" brigades, which were the best organized and comprised from 50 to 55 per cent of the entire partisan force, were under Communist control. Most of the members of the "Rosselli" and *Giustizia e Libertà* brigades, the second strongest units after the Communist ones, were affiliated with the Action Party. Later, the DC and the Liberal Party organized partisans. These two parties, however, regarded the resistance movement as primarily of military importance, insofar as it could help bring the war in Italy to a speedier end. At the same time, politically it implemented the Italian contribution to the war against Germany on the Allied side. For the leftist parties the Resistance was not only a national and patriotic force organized to oust the Germans from the country, but also represented the armed force of a revolutionary movement which was to reshape the political and social structure of the country at the end of the war. The conception of the Actionists, with regard to the nature of these changes, differed considerably from the ideas of the Communists, but their interpretation as to the ultimate ends of the resistance movement was similar. It was a preparation for the revolutionary political process which was to follow the conclusion of hostilities.

An episode in the partisan war is characteristic with regard to these varying aims. At the end of the summer of 1944, two thousand partisans, belonging mainly to the "Garibaldi" and *Giustizia e Libertà* brigades, ousted the German garrison from Domodossola, a town on the Swiss border, about 100 kilometers from Milan; they occupied the whole Ossola valley, proclaimed a Democratic Republic and started introducing radical reforms in the territory under their control. These prefigurated their ideas of what a future Italian society should be.

Both the conservative elements of the Italian Government in Rome and the Allied Military Command watched closely the political trends of the resistance movement. During the winter 1943-1944 Allied material help to the partisans had been scanty. Apart from the technical difficulties of supplying armed groups scattered over large and sometimes inaccessible areas, the Allied Command did not seem particularly willing to make full use of the partisan forces, fearing that these units, originally scattered and disorganized, might eventually form a partisan army like Tito's in Yugoslavia. Considering Communist preponderance in the Resistance, they thought that this might cause a critical political situation at the end of the war. However, after the second front in Normandy was opened and several Allied divisions were removed from Italy to France, the contribution of the partisans behind the German lines was judged necessary to speed up military operations in Italy and possibly to reduce the losses of the Allied armies.

In the summer of 1944 more weapons and supplies were parachuted to the partisans, and this aid enabled them to organize their offensive operations on a bigger scale. As a consequence of increased activities, partisan losses also increased, and at the end of the summer 1944 it was necessary to reorganize the partisan forces. As a result of lenghty dealings between the emissaries of CLNAI[1] which directed these forces, the Allied command and the Italian Government of Rome, the partisan brigades were transformed into Volunteers for Freedom Corps, under the command of General Cadorna, a regular army general sent across the front line in northern Italy. Luigi Longo, a Communist leader, and Ferruccio Parri, of the Action Party, were appointed deputy commanders. On December 8th another agreement with the same objective, to give the movement official recognition, was reached between the CLNAI and the Allied Command.

The Allied Command, with the assent of the Italian Government, recognized the importance of the CLNAI in the occupied territories, agreed to endorse all appointments to administrative posts made by CLNAI, and committed itself to provide the partisan forces with financial and military support. The partisans, on their part, recognized the authority of AMG and, as soon as the north was liberated, agreed to turn over their arms to them. As a result of these two agreements, the partisans were assured of more support and more assistance from both the government in Rome and the Allied Command; while the Allies and the Italian Government hoped that through these arrangements they could exercise more control over future political developments.

END OF THE WAR IN ITALY

In the spring of 1945 the Allied Command launched its final attack on the Gothic Line. On April 21st, Bologna fell, opening up the Po valley for the Allied armoured forces. The fall of Bologna gave the partisan forces the signal for an insurrection. All major northern towns were attacked by partisans and by April 25th, the CLNAI was in control of all major centers, a few days before the arrival of the Allied

---

[1] The CLNAI (*Comitato di Liberazione Nazionale Alta Italia,* Committee of National Liberation for Northern Italy) was the clandestine political organ of the resistance movement.

troops. Mussolini and his retinue, who had left their head-quarters in Milan in an attempt to escape to Switzerland, were intercepted by a partisan formation sent by the CLNAI. They were tried and executed on the spot and their bodies were hanged head down in a gasoline station in the square of a working class district in Milan.

In the days immediately following the occupation of the northern towns by partisans, before the arrival of the Allied forces, several thousand Fascists were executed, on the personal initiatives of individuals or partisan commanders. The CLNAI could be held responsible only to a limited degree for these spontaneous acts of vengeance.

After five years of a disastrous war, the last two years fought on home territory, the country was exhausted; the long work of reconstruction lay ahead. It was to be not only a physical reconstruction of houses and factories but a political one as well, with new political structures. The greatest task of all was to re-educate the Italian people, who had been morally corrupted by twenty years of Fascism and the exigencies of war. The resistance movement, and the political and moral redemption gained through it, was an inspiring example of the moral courage that was necessary for the job of rebuilding the country.

PART TWO

The post-war period

CHAPTER 1

THE CRUCIAL YEARS, 1945-1948

The end of the war in Italy ushered in a new phase in the history of the country, a phase characterized by the struggle of the political parties for power. This struggle was to dominate political events in the two years from 1945 to 1947. The military situation and the controls imposed by the Allied Military Government during the war forced political life in the gradually liberated territories into rather restricted channels. The parties were hampered in their organization and their propaganda efforts aimed at encouraging the Italians to participate in political activity and at clarifying the objectives of the moral and civil reconstruction. The limitations imposed by the Allies deepened the gulf which for historical and social reasons had separated the southern and northern regions of the Italian peninsula.

In the North the higher social level but primarily the impact of the partisan resistance against Nazi-Fascism brought about a deeper awareness, especially among the masses, of the political objectives that were taking shape in the postwar period. Whereas in the South the absence of a tradition of armed struggle against Nazi-Fascism and the state of ineffectuality in which the political parties had been kept by the Allied Military Government during the years from 1943 to 1945 only accentuated those conditions of political backwardness which had characterized the southern provinces. This disequilibrium weighed negatively on Italian politics for a considerable period after the liberation, causing antagonism and lack of understanding.

The end of the war and of the military regime imposed by the Allies witnessed the natural explosion of all the energies that had been repressed for a long time both in the South and the North. After the period of emergency was over and the unification of the country realized, a series of pressing problems requiring rapid if not immediate solutions posed themselves: economic reconstruction, the institutional choice between monarchy and republic, and finally the new constitution which was to define the structure of society and of the state. For the parties these problems merged substantially into one objective—the conquest of power. According to what solutions were adopted, the political class that up to now had held the reins of power would either be maintained, partially replaced or totally liquidated. The political battle of the years 1945 to 1948 evolved around this fundamental question.

The Communists and the Socialists interpreted the struggle against Fascism primarily as a struggle against the capitalist bourgeoisie. According to this concept, the anti-Fascist struggle continued even after Mussolini's death and the collapse of his regime. Fascism had been defeated as a political movement but the capitalist and bourgeois class which had embraced the movement in 1922 in self-defense against the pressure of popular forces, and which sooner or later could have repeated history, still remained to be defeated. The three problems—the reconstruction, the institutional form and the constitution—were for the Communists and Socialists essentially instrumental problems; through their solution the old political class was to be replaced by a new one.

For the Liberals and the other conservative forces the solution of these problems was an end in itself. Their objective was to reconstruct the state and the economy; but this was to be accomplished according to traditional patterns and structures, making use of the same political forces if substituting some individual personalities. The Liberals considered

88

that Fascism had been an historical parenthesis, "a boil," in the words of Croce, which had appeared on a fundamentally healthy body and had rendered it gravely ill. The problem was therefore to cut the boil out and inject new life and energy into an old but still healthy organism. In conclusion the Liberals, notwithstanding the modifications desired by the most progressive wing of their party, aimed at the reconstruction of the state and through it at a society which politically and spiritually would be the heir of pre-Fascist society.

The position of the Actionists and the Christian Democrats lay midway between those of the Social-Communists and Liberals. Both, though in a different way, desired the renovation of Italian society, but renovation for them was not a question of the substitution of classes. The Actionists considered that the reconstruction of a democratic and progressive society was conditioned by a fundamental moral regeneration of all people of all classes. The Resistance, which had redeemed them from the guilt of Fascism, represented the starting point for such a national rebirth. The Christian Democrats for their part favored a gradual modification of the economic and institutional structure of Italian society. Improved social justice and a more equal distribution of wealth was their objective in a society founded on Christian values. The populist traditions of the old *Partito Popolare* and evangelical principles were the inspirational motives of this essentially reformist program.

In the aftermath of liberation the renovation of Italian society was a common objective of all anti-Fascist parties. Over the limits of this renovation and its ideological and tactical premises sprang the differences which made up the vast spectrum of political positions from the extreme left, revolutionary in its objectives if not in its methods, to the right, progressive in its program but conservative in spirit.

The picture of Italian political life then was rich and differentiated, due also to the very high level of political participation. It was naturally reflected in the quality of the discussion; exceptionally lively if sometimes limited by abstractions, it reached a level of idealism and enthusiasm never to be equalled in the years that followed.

Such a variety of solutions was, however, destined to remain temporary. The dramatic problems of the postwar situation demanded immediate attention. On the one hand, the impatience of the proletarian masses who expected almost messianic, rapid and radical solutions, and on the other hand, the desire of the high and middle classes for a rapid return to normalcy, quickly reduced the number of possible solutions to two sole alternatives: the revolutionary and the moderately conservative. A whole series of internal political events, which shall be discussed in the following pages, eliminated the possibility of intermediate solutions and aggravated the political struggle. A further factor, although external to the Italian situation, was added later: the advent of the cold war which presented the country with the choice between the positions of the Communists and the Western world.

By the end of 1945 the period of anti-Fascist solidarity between the member parties of the CNL had already clearly outlived itself. The struggle for power was restricted, however, to the Social-Communists on one side and on the other the Christian Democrats and Liberals, who converged under the pressure of the extreme left-wing parties gradually toward identical positions of defense.

The Social-Communists had the support of great masses of the people as well as a paramilitary organization at their disposal which had been formed and strengthened during the resistance. In the aftermath of the liberation the Allied command ordered the demobilization and disarming of the partisan units, but this was only partially carried out. Great quantities of weapons were hidden and the partisan units controlled by the PCI, that is, practically sixty-five per cent of them, remained in touch with each other and were secretly reorganized. In addition, the Social-Communists maintained almost complete control over the trade union organizations, which made it possible for them to carry the political struggle into the factories through various workers' organizations: from the cell to the "Internal Commissions" to the "Manage-

90

ment Councils,"[1] but primarily through the powerful weapon of political strife. April 17th, a few days before the partisan insurrection and the Allied occupation, the CLNAI affirmed the right of the workers to participate in the management of industries. "Management Councils" were created in the factories right after the liberation primarily due to the initiative of the Communists. They disappeared fairly rapidly with the gradual return of enterprises to their former managements which had temporarily been dispossessed.

THE "GREAT FEAR"

Thanks to these advantages the Social-Communists could subject the country to strong pressure which was at the same time political and psychological. In the countryside, in the absence of a police force, the more extremist elements of the left-wing parties brought pressure to bear on the middle and great landowners who had been considerably compromised with the Fascist regime. In certain areas in Emilia, where the Fascist movement got its start in 1920, for a few months after the liberation squads of Communist ex-partisans organized real punitive expeditions that resulted in destruction and killings. Property was also menaced in the industrial cities: workers' organizations instituted all sorts of controls over the management and the proprietors, some of whom were evicted from their enterprises.

The upper and middle classes lived for many months under the *grande paura*, in the fear of general insurrection and a coup d'etat. It can now be reliably stated, however, that the fears of this period were only partly justified: an armed insurrection as a means for the conquest of power appears to have remained outside of the plans of the PCI. There is no doubt that some of the leaders of the most

---

[1] They were both factory committees. The "Internal Commissions" had mainly trade-union tasks safeguarding workers conditions in the enterprise and respect for union contracts. For "Management Councils," see p. 3.

extremist currents in the party had contemplated this solution, but it was discarded by Togliatti.

In order not to jeopardize the already precarious balance of existing forces in Europe, the Western powers could not have permitted the establishment of a Communist or para-Communist government in a country which, according to the wartime inter-Allied agreements, was slated to be within the Western sphere of influence. An armed insurrection directed by the Communists would therefore have immediately brought about an Anglo-American intervention. The results of such an intervention could not have been in doubt. One of its first consequences, over which the Communists were particularly apprehensive, would have been the outlawing of the party and its exclusion from any public political activity. In the case of a possible violent action the Communists could not have counted on the support of the Soviet Union, which was then too occupied in Eastern Europe to realize the advantages of its wartime victory. For this reason the pressure on the country that was applied by the PCI through action in the streets had a purely tactical function and served to support the policies of the party at the governmental level.

Within the government, in which the Communists participated until the end of May 1947, the party engaged in a long-term action, designed on the one hand to undermine the governmental initiatives taken under the responsibility of the other parties, and on the other hand to modify the structure of the state and the economy. By rendering the tasks of reconstruction and reorganization of the state difficult, the Communists intended to discredit their adversaries in the opinion of the small and middle bourgeoisie. They expected that these classes would eventually be forced to appeal to the Communist Party as the only possible alternative.

Parallel to this erosive action, the Communists attempted to prepare the institutional machinery in a way that would facilitate, at the moment of their takeover, the tasks of their government. The action taken by the Communists in the Constituent Assembly should be interpreted in this sense. Several provisions of the Italian constitution, which was elaborated in 1946-1947, bear the indelible stamp of the work of Communist representatives. Their aim was to fashion an instrument that would permit the PCI, once it had taken power, to modify profoundly the structure of Italian society within the framework of constitutional legality.

Since insurrectional action had been discarded by the Communists as too risky, the political and psychological pressure that was exercised through the mobilization of the masses and served to weaken and render difficult the functioning of the government in charge, was aimed rather at the conquest of power from within. The Communists sent their own representatives into the postwar governments in order to insert themselves into key positions in the administration and above all in order to engage in a critical and corrosive action. During the two years, 1945 to 1947, the Communist ministers in office systematically assumed an openly critical attitude, using the press and all other propaganda means at their disposal, with regard to the governments in which they themselves were members without, however, ever having the responsibility of its direction. But the Communists, although supported by the Socialists, did not succeed in utilizing conclusively the initial advantages they enjoyed as a result of their control of the masses. Defeated in the course of the years on the governmental level, their efforts to gain power were definitively blocked.

The reasons for this failure are tied to the political events of the years 1945-1947. They may be broken down briefly into three main factors: the systematic refusal of the middle classes to respond to the Communist appeal, the rapidity of the process of reconstruction, the political ability of Alcide de Gasperi who succeeded, in April 1947, after a long and difficult cohabitation, in evicting the Social-Communists from the government, thus canceling one of the basic conditions for their success.

The liberation of Northern Italy had as its immediate consequence the injection of new and powerful elements—the partisan forces and the political tendencies represented in the CLNAI—into the political life of the country. Although these elements adhered to the same parties that were already active in central and southern Italy and were represented in the government in Rome, they were considerably more extremist.

The anti-Fascist experience lived in 1944 and 1945 in the northern provinces was quite different from that in the center or even in southern Italy. Two years of partisan warfare, the organization of the underground struggle, the cruel and merciless fight against the Nazi-Fascists, left a deep mark on those who lived through the experience. The North had its heroic period of resistance; the memories of the recent struggle, the lost comrades and the sacrifices were still very much alive. These experiences transposed to a political level manifested themselves in an insistent demand for renovation and in intransigence to compromise. This spirit was aptly called the "wind from the north" (*vento del nord*). Interpreted by the representatives of the CLNAI, the *vento del nord* was to clear the Roman political atmosphere, liberating it from inertia and fear, and also clarifying the objectives for a renovation of the base of Italian society. Now that the entire country had been liberated and the war was over, the moment had arrived to face the problems that were shelved in order to maintain the unity of the parties in the CNL—so necessary during the two years of war and emergency when the country was divided by the line of the front.

The essential factors for a renovation were closely tied to the difficult problems of reconstruction, whose nature was interpreted differently by all parties of the left and the right. The moral and material ruins left by the war were so vast as to appear insuperable. But from the point of view of those who advocated the most extreme solutions, they offered the opportunity of starting from nothing or at least of making deep inroads on the political and social organization inherited from the past regime. For the parties of the left—the Communists, the Socialists and the Action Party—the problem of modifying the political and social structure of the nation had priority. It had to be resolved in order to profit from the immediate, favorable situation. Later, after reconstruction had followed the old patterns and the existing institutions had returned, favoring old-established interests, any renovation would have been more difficult and would have met with major obstacles. For the moderate and conservative parties, on the other hand, who considered reform possible rather as the fruit of a slow and gradual evolution, the problems of reconstruction of the economy and of the administrative structure of the state had absolute priority.

In the face of differences of such degree, differences that had already begun to emerge before the end of the war but that became more immediate when the problems were posed concretely, it was natural that the political forces that hitherto had coexisted within the CNL should tend to reassume their liberty of action and to define their respective positions.

THE PARRI GOVERNMENT

The first natural consequence of the *vento del nord* was the end of the Bonomi Government. Under the pressure of the demands[1] of the representatives of the CLNAI and in particular of the Socialists and Actionists, Ivanoe Bonomi

---

[1] The demands of the CLNAI agreed upon with the central CNL in a series of meetings held in Milan and Rome can be summarized in the following points: 1) The struggle against monopolistic and capitalistic concentrations which dominated the state; 2) gradual accession of the

was compelled to hand in his resignation. On June 12th he gave his mandate of government back into the hands of the Lieutenant of the Realm who immediately started consultations for a new government. They were long and arduous. Within the CNL the relationship of forces between the major parties, the Communists and the Socialists on the one hand and the Christian Democrats on the other, was such that neither of the two parties would have permitted the other to modify the ratio of strength to the advantage of one party. For that reason the DC rejected the candidacy of Nenni under the pretext that a government headed by the Socialist leader would not have been well received by the Allies at a moment when the negotiations for the peace treaty were being initiated. The candidacy of De Gasperi was rejected by the Socialists for similar competitive reasons.

Finally, after long discussions, the nomination on the part of the CLNAI of Ferruccio Parri, the leader of the Action Party in Milan and former supreme chief of the partisan forces, appeared to all parties as the solution that would best assure the political equilibrium.

The choice of Parri was received with enthusiasm by all those who had directly or indirectly participated in the movement of the Resistance, especially in the North, and who confidently expected the enactment of the programs of renewal and democratization heralded by the parties. Parri enjoyed great prestige as a partisan organizer and for his integrity and firmness of principle. The fact that this was his first experience in government did not appear to be a disadvantage; on the contrary, many people approved that a new man, inexpert in the subtleties and duplicities of politics, should assume the highest executive responsibility. A period that hopefully would usher in a political regeneration started under apparently favorable auspices.

From the point of view of party politics, too, the choice

---

workers to the management of enterprises; 3) the resumption of the purge; 4) the recognition of the consultative functions of the local CNL.

of Parri appeared positive: the Action Party, which was an *avant garde* and elite party, was not preoccupied with political tactics; it voluntarily shirked them. It was most apt to guide the new government in a transition period which seemed a prelude to a final resolution. If his attempt had proved to be positive, he could have counted on the great sympathy of the public and have consolidated the position of a new party barely known in Central and Southern Italy. Outside of this it seemed that the Action Party could represent an intermediate solution between the programs of the extreme left and the cautious reformism of the moderate parties. Because of its ideological character it could have formed a bridge between the values of freedom and democracy in the best political-cultural tradition of the pre-Fascist era and the ideals of social regeneration which had surged up from the Resistance. For this reason also the most lively and the most politically conscious strata of the public greeted the designation of Parri with enthusiasm.

After Parri's acceptance consultations for the formation of the cabinet were initiated. The representatives of the six parties in the CNL took part. Among them Pietro Nenni was appointed Vice Premier, De Gasperi became Minister of Foreign Affairs—a key position considering that the country was on the eve of the conclusion of the peace treaty—and Togliatti received the portfolio of Justice. The new Prime Minister addressed the Italian people on the 23rd of June in a speech which, modeled on a famous example, was called a "fireside chat" because of its informality and lack of rhetoric. The public, which had been subjected in the preceding two months to an intense oratorical debate filled with slogans and formulas, sometimes threatening, sometimes messianic, responded with sympathy and confident expectation to this simple and cordial style.

Perhaps it was precisely because of the hopes that were engendered that Parri's fall, which occurred five months later, was accompanied by disillusionment and a deep bitterness, especially among those who had understood the importance and unique character of the Actionist experiment. The causes of this failure have too often been attributed to Parri's lack of political experience and ability as a tactician. Although these factors may have contributed to it, there is no doubt that the main causes for the fall of Parri's Cabinet are to be looked for in the difficult situation within the country and the conflicts among the major parties. Caught in the middle Parri found himself with scant possibility of defense.

DIFFICULTIES OF THE PARRI GOVERNMENT

The liberation of northern Italy and the end of the war suddenly released masses of partisans, war veterans and ex-inmates of German concentration and prison camps who flowed back into civilian life. The situation in which these hundreds of thousands of individuals found themselves was desperate: in the midst of destruction, ruins and poverty, with their families dispersed by war and without assistance from the state. The problem of an orderly transfer of these masses back into society and active life was for the time being impossible to solve. Considering the extent of the physical destruction and the financial bankruptcy of the state, it was unreasonable to expect that the country's economy, traditionally afflicted by unemployment, could rapidly absorb these masses and transform them into a labor force.

The partisans, war veterans and ex-deportees therefore enlarged the number of unemployed which inevitably represented a serious element of disturbance in the life of the country. Too many weapons left over from the war and partisan resistance were still circulating in the country, thus adding a menacing character to the pressure exercised by these masses who demanded work and a place in society. The discontent was exploited by the extreme leftwing parties. Many political manifestations ended in violence and in many cases the police and the *Carabinieri*, who were forced to intervene to reestablish order, encountered the resistance of the demonstrators.

A threatening atmosphere of tension was very rapidly

created. The propertied classes and those who had privileged positions to defend lived in fear of violence, riots and a general uprising directed by the Communist Party, whose following in this situation appeared to be constantly increasing. The absence of adequate public powers was deplored and soon the "strong state" was regretted and the use of energetic means of repression to bring about order advocated.

After a period of disorientation the forces that traditionally had controlled the economic power began to react to what appeared to them as an emergency situation, attempting to retake the initiative lost to the popular classes. In this case the industrial haute bourgeoisie, who desired a rapid reconstruction of industry in order to defend its privileged position, allied its interests with those of the petit and middle bourgeoisie, whose traditional control of the administration was strongly endangered by the political purges and the powers assumed by the CLN. Such a state of affairs bred a reactionary spirit with its traditional class hatred.

The growing attitude of hostility was directed not only against the popular classes and the parties which defended their demands but inevitably also against the Resistance movement, considering the great part the popular classes and left-wing parties had played in it. Its values were discounted with the result that the Resistance came finally to be denounced as a great Communist conspiracy for the conquest of power; conversely, the old regime and its defense of the "traditional values" was remembered with nostalgia.

Symptomatically, it was precisely in Rome and above all in the South where this spirit was most widespread that a new political movement, calling itself *Uomo Qualunque* (average man) appeared in the summer of 1945. The name was adopted from the name of a newspaper which had inspired the movement. The paper appealed to the "good sense" of the middle classes and in a satiric way bitterly criticized "the new bosses" and political professionalism with its empty ideologies. It defamed the Resistance, paid nostalgic homage to the past regime, and disseminated a slogan which was widely quoted, "One was better off when one was worse off."

Considering the period in which it came into existence and the aims that it espoused, the Parri Government was not a government of a class but a government of the whole people. It assumed a conciliatory and optimistic attitude with regard to popular agitation and demands. For that reason it was accused of weakness and partiality by the Liberals and Christian Democrats. As the head of a democratic and anti-Fascist government Parri could not react with police repression to the demands of those who had fought against Fascism and who had suffered most under its rule. He was committed to realize in the political life of the country the values that had been established by the resistance movement. He could therefore not order the police to fire at former members of the Resistance with whom he had fought for the same ideals.

Parri's inaction can also be explained by the absolute inadequacy of the police means at his disposal. Badly armed and equipped, the small number of the forces of order were frequently overcome during manifestations that they attempted to control. The scarcity of police forces prevented the government and Parri, who in addition to being Prime Minister was also Minister of the Interior and thus directly responsible for public order, from intervening resolutely against common delinquency, which had assumed alarming proportions, profiting from the general disorder.

This situation, which was openly criticized within the cabinet by the Christian Democrats and Liberals but, more important, publicly through the information media under their control, soon created an atmosphere of hostility that rendered the work of the Parri Government difficult.

There were other reasons in addition to this fundamental one for the opposition felt profoundly by the middle classes. Parri, in answer to the requests of the Socialists, Communists and members of his own party, had reopened the problem of the purges, which had been shelved by the second Bonomi Government. Parri intended to broaden the purge, which up to then had been limited, to members of the state administration and private industry who had openly favored the victory of the Fascist movement and to further their economic interests had supported the bellicose policies of Mussolini.

One of Parri's major objectives was also to curb the power of monopolistic heavy industry, as became evident from the economic plan that he elaborated for the purpose of getting industrial production under way again. The plan established an important income tax which would have hit the major industrial combines accused of having accumulated large profits during the Fascist regime. It also established a system of distribution of raw materials, very scarce at the time due to lack of foreign currency, which would have been to the advantage of small and medium-sized business enterprises. The aim of the Parri plan was the reconstruction of industry on the basis of a better equilibrium and better opportunities for small and medium enterprises. The plan met with the open opposition of the Liberals supported by large sectors of the public, which, though not directly affected, saw in the Parri plan an attack on private property. It was supported for political motives naturally by the parties of the extreme left. For that reason Parri, who aimed at establishing greater economic equilibrium, was accused of complicity with the Communists and of favoring their plans for gaining control of the economic life of the country.

The great institutional question lay in the background of these conflicts. Hoping to exploit the predominantly republican orientation of the time, Parri wanted to hasten the decision on the form of government; conversely, the Liberals and the monarchists favored a postponement, hoping that the cause of the monarchy would be served with the return to economic and political normalcy.

The first reunion of the *Consulta*, the consultative assembly which had been established in the preceding March by the Bonomi Government, was held on September 25th. The Assembly was composed of 440 members designated by the parties from among veterans of the anti-Fascist struggle; the new organism fulfilled the function of a provisional parliament until such time when a new representative organ

101

would come into being as a result of the first elections. The institutional question having been posed to the *Consulta*, it was decided that the election of the Constituent Assembly, whose purpose was to prepare the new constitution, would be coupled with an institutional referendum to decide in favor either of a republican or a monarchist system. The government was to fix the date for the double polling.

Another question, which was directly tied to the preceding one and which also divided the parties of the government coalition, was the date of the administrative elections that were to elect local and provincial councils, that is, representative organs of local government. These had been suppressed during the Fascist period. Consistent with their aim of postponing as long as possible the date of the institutional referendum, the Liberals and Christian Democrats favored holding the administrative elections first, to be followed by elections for the Constituent Assembly. Parri, supported by the Social-Communists and Republicans, decided the reverse.

THE FALL OF THE PARRI GOVERNMENT

This succession of disagreements on methods and specific questions, added to a definite intention to terminate the Parri experiment, which moderate and conservative opinion followed with ever greater resentment and hostility, induced the Liberals to precipitate the crisis.

In a letter sent by the executive council of the Liberal Party to all other parties of the coalition, the government was accused of a number of shortcomings: "lack of unity, vacillation, incompetence, bureaucratization and bad administrative principles and disordered and uncontrolled legislation." Finally, on November 21, 1945, Leone Cattani, the leader of the PLI, called on Parri and formally notified him of the Liberals' decision to withdraw from his government. This decision brought on the danger of a government crisis but did not make it inevitable. Considering the small number of

Liberals in the cabinet, the resigning ministers could have been replaced. But a few days later the Christian Democrats decided to follow the Liberals' example and retired their own representatives from the cabinet, thus putting an end to the Parri Government (November 24, 1945).

The crisis of the Parri Government represents a crucial moment in post-war Italian politics: politically, it ended the influence of the Action Party and of the ideals of the Resistance by which it was inspired more than any other party. The program of the Parri Government was established around two essential objectives. The first was to fight Fascism not only as an historical reality but also as a moral and attitudinal problem. The second was embodied in the demands for social and economic progress based on a structural reform of Italian society. The fall of Parri and the gradual disappearance of the influence of the Actionists eliminated the first goal. There was a progressive return to the old mental habits which were not openly Fascist any longer but paternalistic and authoritarian. Democracy was realized in the structures and the institutions, but not in spirit; the fundamental freedoms were formally guaranteed but their meaning was partially negated by the favoring of vested interests. The second objective —structural reforms—were partially carried out only after 1948 by the parties in power. Their benefits, however, were largely lost because vested interests succeded either in watering them down or making them for the most part ineffectual.

With respect to government policies, the fall of Parri ushered in a long period of Christian Democratic predominance. The left-wing parties for some time still maintained the initiative and due to the continued active support of the masses remained a major political force in the country. But the counter-offensive of the moderates was beginning to take shape. In the course of two years they were to succeed in reversing the situation which originally had been to their disadvantage.

The crisis of the Action Party also resulted in a sharpening of the political struggle. Between the forces of the extreme left on the one hand and the moderates and conservatives

103

on the other a bridge was now lacking which formerly had been an important means of mediation. The Socialists in particular no longer had a political force on their right on which they could lean. Hence they were compelled to re-weld their ties with the Communist Party, thus opening the way to the Popular Front.

The day of his resignation Parri called a press conference of the representatives of foreign newspapers in Rome and publicly denounced "the fifth column inside his government (read Christian Democrats and Liberals), which, after having systematically undermined his position, was now preparing to restore to power those political and social forces that had formed the basis of the Fascist regime." Parri's denunciation, which was perhaps expressed in an excessively dramatic way, requires an explanation. It reflects primarily the moral intransigence of a man and his party, an intransigence which could not compromise with the possibilism and flexibility of the other political forces in the government. The Christian Democracy and the Liberal Party, because of their electoral bases, were especially sensitive to the discontent and protest which the activities of the Parri Government had aroused among the conservative upper and middle classes. There is no doubt that this was a most important factor in the decision of the Christian Democrats to withdraw their support from the government. For that reason Parri's condemnation of the return to power of the classes that had supported the Fascist regime would seem justified in the sense that the fall of his government signified the return of the initiative to the parties that represented moderate and conservative forces which opposed all efforts aimed at renewing Italian society.

In any event Parri's denunciation was only partial. His fall was also the work of the Communist Party, which though it supported him in appearance, mobilizing the masses in demonstrations because of his fall, it maneuvered behind the scenes in such a way as to weaken him. The Communists feared that if Parri had consolidated his power and if his experiment in government had succeeded, he and his party could have won the favor of the masses whose sole guardian the Communist Party intended to appear. The Action Party represented a potentially dangerous competitor of the PCI for the favor of the democratic, politically aware proletariat because of the prestige Parri had gained during the period of the partisan struggle and because of his intransigence to all compromise.

CHAPTER 2

ELECTIONS AND POPULAR REFERENDUM

THE FIRST DE GASPERI CABINET

In view of the important political events which were taking place, the power vacuum left by the Parri crisis was rapidly filled. During the evolution of the crisis of the Parri Cabinet the Christian Democrats played a decisive role; the decision to withdraw from the government was taken by the party leadership with the conviction that the political situation was ripe for a government directed by the DC.

Profiting from the disorientation that followed an abortive attempt to constitute a new government headed by a personality above the parties[1] and unexpected aid from the Socialists whose leader, Nenni, officially proposed his candidature, De Gasperi accepted the charge to form a new government from the Lieutenant of the Realm. On December 10th he presented his new cabinet. It was to be the last cabinet formed with the participation of all six parties of the CLN.

The Socialist proposal, intended to embarrass the Christian

---

[1] The names of some elderly politicians with great prestige were advanced as candidates to form a new government, such as Vittorio Emanuele Orlando and Francesco Nitti, formerly prime ministers in the pre-Fascist period. The parties opposed these designations, which were made by the Lieutenant of the Realm in an effort to lessen the tension in the country due to the antagonisms that had developed around the program of the Parri Government.

Democrats by forcing them to assume the responsibility of government at a politically difficult moment, resulted in a considerable advantage for the moderates and the conservatives. Despite the fact that the De Gasperi Cabinet was based on the support of all six parties of the coalition, his center of gravity veered to the right, as the events of the following months were to demonstrate.

The advent of De Gasperi inaugurated a period of considerable government activity in every field—from internal to foreign policy where with tenacity and ability he made efforts designed to improve Italian prospects at the peace table.

De Gasperi soon won the full confidence and cooperation of the Allied authorities, who had not hidden their distrust of Parri.[1] By Dec. 31, 1945, Allied Military Government ceased to operate and the jurisdiction in the northern provinces, which up to then had remained under Allied control, was transferred to the Italian Government. In addition American economic aid within the framework of the UNRRA[2] program was stepped up.

In internal policy one of De Gasperi's first acts was to replace the CLN appointees in local administrative functions, which they had taken over in the northern provinces right after the Liberation, by officials from the very bureaucracy that the Social-Communists wanted to eliminate. A definite termination of the purge trials followed, and on Jan. 3, 1946, after long discussion in the Consultative Assembly, the new law for administrative elections was enacted. It combined the proportional with the majority system and stipulated the application of the latter to communities with less than 30,000 inhabitants. The passage of this law terminated the debate over the priority of political or administrative elections. The

---

[1] An American banker of Italian origin, Amedeo Giannini, president of the powerful Bank of America, declared in the course of a press interview while in Italy in Sept. 1945 that the U.S. would not have sent economic aid to Italy if the government had continued to function in the manner of the Parri Government.

[2] See page 124.

latter were fixed for the first polling to take place in the spring while the political elections were postponed, though only for a few months.

ELECTIONS

Preparations for the administrative elections were immediately started. The first balloting took place on five consecutive Sundays, starting on March 10th. These were the first elections in twenty years; for that reason the electoral campaign and its results were followed with great interest at home as well as abroad. Despite the political pressures and the fears they engendered, incidents were rare and freedom of expression was fully guaranteed.

The results of this first balloting, which to some extent represented a general rehearsal for the coming, much more important, elections for the Constituent Assembly, confirmed the expectations and prognostications. The three parties—the Christian Democratic, the Socialist and the Communist—emerged as the parties with the greatest popular following. Of the 5,596 (out of 7,572) administrative districts (*comuni*) included in the first electoral balloting, 1,955 went to the Christian Democrats and 2,256 to the Social-Communists who had presented joint lists nearly everywhere. Four hundred local administrations went to independent lists while the Liberals, the Labour Democrats, the Republicans and the Action Party divided the remaining 985 *comuni* between them.

A new political formation also emerged from these elections, the *Uomo Qualunque*,[1] which had been transformed from a movement into a political party in February. It won control of 23 of the local administrations. Its success, which was destined to increase during the elections to come, testified to the discontent and incomprehension among certain sectors of the public who were attached to the memory of the past

---

[1] See page 99.

regime and who opposed democratic political procedures. However, it represented a transitory phenomenon which reached its zenith in the course of the next two years after which it ceased to exist. In any case, it should be noted that the first neo-Fascist groups infiltrated into the *Uomo Qualunque* and as soon as the general political situation permitted, they gave life to the *Movimento Sociale Italiano* (Italian Social Movement), the official heir of the old Fascist party.

The results of the administrative elections clearly indicated the probable results of the elections to the Constituent Assembly to be held on June 2nd. Judging by the number of votes that were cast for parties having a republican orientation as well as the results of an internal polling within the Christian Democratic Party, which showed that 73 per cent of its members favored the republic, the prognostication was unfavorable for the monarchy. Spurred to greater activity by these indications the monarchist leaders intensified their propaganda, to which the republican parties responded with equal vigor. During the two months of April and May a close campaign was waged for the Constituent Assembly and the institutional referendum.

PRELIMINARIES TO THE ELECTIONS

The debate over the law that was to regulate the elections for the Constituent Assembly and the referendum was concluded by the *Consulta* on February 23rd. In view of the fact that the conclusions reached by the provisional parliament were consultative and not compulsory, the government was obliged to make the final, executive decisions. The essential questions may be outlined as follows:

1) Either to entrust the decision as to the form of the government to the elected members of the Constituent Assembly or to put a decision up to the Italian people by means of a referendum.

2) The delimitation of the tasks of the Constituent Assembly, which was to be elected.

3) Characteristics of the electoral law: the system of a uninominal college or the system of the purely proportional; a compulsory vote with fiscal sanctions or an optional vote.

With respect to the first question, a decree law (number 151) had been enacted by the first Bonomi Cabinet, providing that the members of the future Constituent Assembly make the choice between the monarchic and republican forms of government. In the course of the debates in the *Consulta* (from October to February) the pressure exerted by the monarchists seconded by De Gasperi again put this delicate problem in question.

The groups favoring the monarchy insisted that the decision should be made directly by the people by means of a national referendum. In support of this solution they relied on the traditional attachment of a large part of the population, both working classes and the bourgeoisie, to the royal family, while they feared that this purely emotional factor would not influence the members of the Constituent Assembly, who would probably be content to pronounce historic political judgment on the institution of monarchy.

The monarchists' insistence on a popular referendum provoked violent protests from the left-wing parties. De Gasperi endeavored to solve the problem quite shrewdly by seeking the opinion of the Anglo-Americans. Although the latter refused to give an official opinion, both governments unofficially declared themselves in favor of the referendum. Strengthened by their support, De Gasperi succeeded in having his thesis on the referendum adopted by the cabinet which had the final decision in the matter.

The question of the competences to be attributed to the Constituent Assembly was also resolved to the disadvantage of the left. The latter demanded that the Assembly be delegated the same powers and jurisdiction of a regular parliament over all political and legislative questions which might arise in the course of its deliberations. They conceived the Constituent Assembly as a truly representative organ which, in addition to its specific function of formulating the text of the new constitution, would be endowed with the legislative powers of control over the operation of the government that are normally invested in the Chamber under a democratic system. On the contrary the DC, supported by the right-wing parties, wished to limit the competence of the Constituent Assembly to the formulation and approval of the new constitutional chart of the state. According to their views the Constituent Assembly should not exercise normal legislative functions which should be within the competence of the government, with the exception of some extraordinary matters such as the ratification of treaties and the approval of electoral laws.

This question was also resolved with the aid of the weight carried by the Allied governments' opinion. The Department of State in particular voiced approval in the matter of limiting the competence of the Constituent Assembly solely to the formulation of the articles of the constitution. For that reason the governmental decree which defined the matter finally confirmed the thesis supported by the right, that is, "that during the period of the Constituent Assembly until the convocation of the parliament, legislative power shall remain a competence of the government with the exception of electoral laws and international treaties whose approval will pertain to the assembly to which the government is responsible."

The last point, the question of the compulsory vote, was resolved with a compromise. The left was opposed to the principle of compulsion because it saw in it an attempt by the right to mobilize "the indifferents," whose vote was presumed to favor conservatism. So much importance was attached to this decision that the Communists even threatened to withdraw from the government if optional voting was not adopted. The thesis of compulsion won but with such limitations that it was practically ineffective. Instead of fiscal sanctions, which were to be imposed on abstentionists, it was decided to publish the names of the abstentionists in public lists, thus merely exposing them to a moral reproof.

The electoral law which established the number of deputies to be elected at 573 was passed by decree law (number 74) of March 10, 1946, making the choice definite in the question of the electoral system. Instead of a system based on the uninominal college, supported particularly strongly by the Liberals and the representatives of the pre-Fascist political class, upon which they had founded their own political fortunes, it was decided to adopt a proportional system with balloting by list and picking up residual votes in a unique national college.

A few weeks before the elections the distinctive symbols to be used on the lists for the institutional referendum were selected: a crown for the monarchy and the head of a woman framed by an oak branch to symbolize the republic.

JUNE 2nd, 1946

The campaign preceding the voting on the Constituent Assembly and the constitutional referendum was heated and was filled with dramatic moments, one of which was the abdication of King Victor Emmanuel III.

The compromise reached between the political parties and the crown in April 1944 had relegated King Victor Emmanuel III to an inactive role outside of political life. It deprived him of his constitutional powers which were delegated to his son, Umberto, in his capacity as Lieutenant General. On the eve of the referendum, following the urgent advice of the monarchist leaders, King Victor Emmanuel finally decided to do what he had up to then refused to do: abdicate. It was a last moment gesture clearly designed to influence psychologically the electorate. The crown was transferred to his son, Umberto, whose Fascist past was less compromising and who during his lieutenancy demonstrated a certain progressive orientation. This gesture was calculated to introduce the concept of a democratic monarchy willing to recognize the necessity of great social transformation. As the monarchy had been liberal—the most flexible monarchist propagandists affirmed—it could conceivably also have become socialist without recognizing or claiming not to recognize the obvious contradiction, in a country still bearing the weight of its feudal past, of the institution of monarchy with the principles, ideals and practices of a truly progressive democracy.

Immediately after the act of abdication King Victor Emmanuel left Italy and moved to the neighborhood of Alexandria in Egypt, going into voluntary exile "according to the practice" as the press office of the royal house hastened to underscore; he thus attempted to establish a parallel with the example of his by far more illustrious predecessor from the *Risorgimento.*[1]

The abdication of the King was fully exploited by the monarchists, who, however, soon realized that the decision had been taken too close to the date of the elections to bear the anticipated fruit. At this last moment the monarchist parties and committees began to press the Allied Control Commission, the last Allied organism remaining in Italy after the end of AMG, with requests for intervention in favor of a postponement of the referendum. Admiral Ellery Stone, the head of the Commission, rejected every overture and declared himself incompetent to intervene.

Meantime the dual electoral campaign continued at a closer and faster pace. The republican parties concentrated their efforts on demonstrating the monarchy's guilt and connivance with Fascism, affirming that the retention of the King would consolidate privilege and block social reforms. The supporters of the King presented the monarchy as the best assurance against subversive tendencies and Communism, thus reiterating a familiar theme of Italian politics: they affirmed the necessity of conserving the old institutions to

---

[1] Carlo Alberto of Savoia, in 1848, defeated by Austria in the first of the three wars waged for the unity of Italy, abdicated and retired to voluntary exile in Oporto, Portugal.

avoid the present danger of change. The middle-class voter, already made fearful by the atmosphere of intimidation engendered by the parties of the extreme left right after the liberation, and by the results of the administrative elections, anticipated apocalyptic consequences to result from a republican choice. It would have been, according to a then current, very popular slogan, "a leap into the dark."

The church too did not fail to intervene on behalf of the monarchy through the intercession of cardinals, bishops and the local clergy. On the eve of the vote, the Pope clearly defined what according to the church was the essence of the question. "What is the problem?" asked Pious XII. "The problem is whether one or the other of those nations, of those two Latin sisters (the Pope's speech referred also to the political elections taking place in France the same day) with several thousands of years of civilization will continue to lean against the solid rock of Christianity,...or on the contrary do they want to hand over the fate of their future to the impossible omnipotence of a material state without extraterrestrial ideals, without religion and without God. One of these two alternatives shall occur according to whether the names of the champions or the destroyers of Christian civilization emerge victorious from the urns."

The campaign for the referendum was joined with the campaign for the election of the Constituent Assembly. Christian Democracy was especially active in it. Although the party had declared itself in favor of the republic, it left its own members and sympathizers free to vote either for the republic or for the monarchy. This was a wise decision considering the inter-class character of the party and the results of the internal referendum previously taken, which showed that within the party a republican majority coexisted with a strong monarchist minority. The DC, by-passing the question monarchy or republic, preferred to call the attention of the voters to the major importance of the elections for the Constituent Assembly, on whose composition the fundamental choice between a democratic or a totalitarian state would depend. Christian Democratic propaganda, which was

114

actively supported by the Church and particularly by the minor clergy, addressed itself especially to the female electorate, who for the first time had been granted the right to vote.

THE ELECTORAL RESULTS AND THE SECOND DE GASPERI CABINET

The results of the institutional referendum, following the prognostications on the eve of the elections, were favorable to the republic, with a margin of about 2,000,000 votes. The monarchists made accusations of fraud and procedural irregularities. They claimed for the monarchy in particular the void votes, altogether 1,148,136, although the final result would not have been affected; and they accused the competent authorities of having proclaimed the results before all the ballots had been counted. But none of these objections could have placed the ultimate result in doubt, which was 12,717,923 votes for the republic against 10,719,284 for the monarchy.

King Umberto had no other choice but to accept the will of the people. On June 13th he left the country and retired to Cascais in Portugal, not without, however, making a proclamation reiterating the accusations of procedural irregularities. Thus his reign, which had lasted little more than a month, came to an end and all his powers were temporarily assumed by the Prime Minister, De Gasperi.

The results of the elections for the Constituent Assembly confirmed the trends shown in the local partial elections held in the spring. The main positions remained nearly the same although in different alignments. The Socialists and Communists had presented separate lists not only for tactical reasons but also because, at the congress of the PSIUP in April, a strong autonomous tendency affirmed itself, one that was opposed to the fusion with the Communists projected by the majority.

Liberals and the Democratic Labor Party established the National Democratic Union in an attempt to increase the strength of the right whose electoral weakness had appeared clearly in the administrative elections. The Union tried to attract the middle-class electorate by including in the lists of its candidates Croce, Bonomi, Orlando and Nitti, names widely known in the country and commanding considerable personal prestige.

The definitive figures of the election results, announced four days after the vote, confirmed the primacy of Christian Democracy and the strength of the extreme left-wing parties. Together the Socialists and Communists would have surpassed the DC by about 400,000 votes.

Results of the Elections to the Constituent Assembly

	Votes	%	Seats Gained
Christian Democracy	8,080,644	35.1	207
Italian Socialist Party of Proletarian Unity	4,758,129	20.7	115
Communist Party	4,356,686	18.9	104
National Democratic Union	1,560,638	6.8	41
Uomo Qualunque (Average Man)	1,211,956	5.3	30
Italian Republican Party	1,003,007	4.4	23
Freedom Bloc	637,328	2.8	16
Action Party	334,748	1.5	7
Other Lists	1,025,130	2.7	12

The Qualunquists made notable and unexpected inroads at the expense of the Liberals; the latter, after having dominated political life in pre-Fascist Italy, were reduced to a mere 40 deputies. The Action Party with its 335,000 votes suffered a major defeat which renewed internal antagonisms,[1] actuating a grave crisis within the party.

The great mass parties, strongly organized, emerged as the victors in these first elections. The industrial proletariat,

---

[1] A first split in the Action Party had taken place on Feb. of the same year when the La Malfa - Parri group left the party.

particularly in the large cities of the North, and the agricultural proletariat of the Center-North and Central Italy (Emilia, Tuscany, Umbria) voted for the Social-Communists. The middle classes, the peasants of the North eastern areas (Veneto) to a large extent voted DC. The conservative opinion, especially in the South, divided its votes between the *Uomo Qualunque* and the National Democratic Union (Liberals).

The majority of the Italian people voted in these first elections for moderate and conservative parties which were opposed to great political and social changes. However, the margin which separated these parties from those which advocated revolutionary changes could still be overcome. The Social-Communists in particular viewed the backward South, where vast masses of the underprivileged remained under the influence of political bosses or of the Church, as a huge reserve of votes which potentially could be exploited by them. The struggle for power was therefore far from over. After the 1946 elections, in which the political parties had their first accounting and experienced their first test of strength, this struggle entered into its most important phase.

The limitations of the victory of the moderate forces appeared almost immediately within the Constituent Assembly. Notwithstanding its 8,000,000 votes and 207 mandates, the DC's position inside the Assembly was from the beginning very tenous. A few months later, on Oct. 25, the PSIUP reconfirmed its pact of "Unity of Action" with the Communist Party,[1] thus constituting a bloc of 219 seats out of the total of 556. This alliance forced Christian Democracy, a center party, to make a delicate search for allies among the right-wing parties. This necessary maneuvering for alliances, which was not always successful, put the Social-Communist bloc, whose influence on the work of the Constituent Assembly was notable if not predominant, into an advantageous position.

---

[1] The first pact had been signed in Paris in 1934.

9.

The first meeting of the Constituent Assembly took place on June 25, 1946. Giuseppe Saragat, Socialist leader and head of the autonomous tendency within the party, was elected president. Two days later, Enrico de Nicola, a politically independent lawyer from Naples, who enjoyed great prestige among all the parties for his forthrightness and democratic loyalty, was chosen temporary head of state.

While the Assembly began its work, which was destined to take a year and a half, consultations for the formation of a new government were taking place. It was again Alcide De Gasperi, as leader of the party which had received the highest number of votes, who became head of the new cabinet. The coalition of the parties of the CLN, which up to then had provided the basis for all the governments that had succeeded each other since the fall of Rome, had become outdated. The differences between the Liberals and the extreme left, but even more so the electoral results which had profoundly redistributed the ratios between the CLN member parties, put an end to a fictitious equilibrium and prompted a search for a different political combination. The new formula was to be realized with the participation in the government of the three mass parties: Christian Democracy, which occupied the key ministries, the PSIUP and the PCI, with the addition of the Republican Party. The Republican Party had experienced a slight, if only temporary, strengthening, during the elections; before the referendum it had steadfastly refused to participate in the government because it resolutely rejected the monarchy. The Actionists and the Liberals, however, remained outside of the government, the former because they were weakened by an internal crisis between the left and right-wing tendencies, which in a few months was to bring about the party's dissolution. The Liberals stayed outside in protest against the methods with which the referendum had been carried out.

CHAPTER 3

THE PROBLEMS OF ECONOMIC RECONSTRUCTION

THE ECONOMIC SITUATION AT THE END OF THE WAR

The problems of political and institutional renewal, which each party attempted to solve according to its own principles, could not take precedence over the much more dramatic and pressing problems of economic reconstruction.

For the majority of the Italians, who had withstood during the war years physical and moral suffering difficult to imagine for anyone who had not lived through them, the end of the conflict raised the hope for a quick return to better conditions of life. This was the reason for the impatience and the protests of certain sectors of the population over the differences among the parties, which seemed to impede uselessly the search for solutions to the many economic and administrative problems and to stall progress on their requests for immediate and energetic action.

In the course of the years 1945, 1946 and 1947 the governments tried to repair the most pressing damage and to attain a standard of living which would guarantee a minimum livelihood to everyone. These efforts were not always well conceived; frequently old errors were repeated in the work of reconstruction, or the limited means at the government's disposal were badly distributed. But nonetheless in less than three years the first phase of reconstruction could be considered finished. Its limitations and the methods by which it was undertaken will emerge with greater clarity through an examination of the political events of the years 1946, 1947 and 1948. Before a more comprehensive evaluation is made of what was accomplished, it is helpful to have a clear picture of the situation of the Italian economy in 1945 and the damages that had been inflicted on it by the events of war.[1]

The most serious and widespread destruction was caused by the movement of the front and the exactions imposed by the retreating German Army, much more than from the bombardment which the major cities and industrial centers had been subjected to from the end of 1941. In order to get an idea of the situation found by the Allied troops as they advanced slowly up the peninsula during the years from 1943 to 1945, it is enough to take as an example the condition of the food supply. The hunger rations of the large towns, such as Rome and Naples, were so precarious that the problem had to be resolved from day to day frequently with the help of the Allied commands themselves. During the winter of 1944-1945 the country lived through its hardest days. Large strata of the population were dangerously undernourished and almost completely destitute. The average daily caloric intake went down from 2,795 calories a day per inhabitant (the average in the years 1936-1940) to 1,733 calories in 1945. The natural ingenuity of the people manifested itself in thousands of ways in the tiresome search for the essential means of subsistence, but frequently ingenuity alone did not suffice, and it was necessary to have recourse to humiliating means. Morality sank to an extremely low level, and prostitution and the black market flourished, feeding on the presence of Allied forces who were well provided for.

The end of the war and the rapid demobilization of the Allied armies freed huge quantities of food supplies which had been accumulated for military purposes. They were used

---

[1] The national patrimony valued at 700 billion lire in 1938 was estimated to have been reduced by one fourth at the end of the war.

120

in the aid programs of the American Government and were sufficient to overcome certain emergencies, but the general situation of the country's economy after the first and somewhat cursory survey appeared disastrous. All sectors of the economy had been hard hit but some—housing and communications—showed the most serious damage. The standstill in construction which had been imposed by military necessity and the destruction caused by bombardments and military operations made the housing problem especially hard. More than 2,000,000 rooms of civilian habitations were destroyed and 1,800,000 were seriously damaged, corresponding approximately to ten per cent of the housing space before the war.

The damage to public works was even more serious: bridges, roads, aqueducts, public buildings that were used by the occupying armies and had therefore become military targets were the most directly affected by the war. Sixty per cent of the state roads had been put out of commission and over 8,000 bridges were destroyed. Seventy per cent of the harbor installations had been rendered unusable as well as 40 per cent of the schools, hospitals and railroad stations. The damage to the railroads was assessed at 900 billion lire, representing approximately 40 per cent of all railroad installations. Sixty per cent of all locomotives and freight cars were destroyed or damaged beyond repair, as well as 90 per cent of all passenger cars, and 80 per cent of all the electrified lines. Still in the sector of transport the Italian merchant fleet, which before the war had been the fourth largest in Europe by tonnage, was severely decimated, having been reduced from 3,500,000 tons in 1938 to approximately 450,000 tons.

The statistics for the losses suffered in agriculture and industry were briefly as follows:

Agriculture: Production in 1945 compared to that of 1938 showed a decrease of 60 per cent; livestock was reduced by 75 per cent. The total damage was estimated at approximately 550 billion lire, but in addition to the losses that could be directly assessed, there was also incalculable damage resulting from the diminishing productivity of the soil caused by the lack of fertilizer and manpower during the entire course of the war. The yield per hectare[1] of cultivated grain which in 1938 was 56 bushels on the average had in 1945 been reduced to 45 bushels.

Industry: The total losses sustained by industry were assessed at 450 billion lire, corresponding to approximately 20 per cent of all the installations existing in 1939. At the end of 1945 the level of industrial production was reduced to 25 per cent of the pre-war output. Some sectors were particularly hard hit: the production of electric energy, for the most part of hydraulic origin, had diminished to 35 per cent of its highest output (in 1941).

Nevertheless it should be stressed that the losses suffered by industry were less than the losses of all other productive sectors. This was due to the fact that the greater part of the industrial enterprises were situated in northern Italy and were spared the destruction of a war fought yard for yard; furthermore the partisans and civil authorities had guarded and successfully defended these factories against destruction and dismantling, which the retreating Germans had carried out in other areas. The most devastated areas were those where the war had dragged on the longest and where the dismantling operations of the Germans had been the most systematic, that is, in the central and south central regions. On the other hand, the productive capacity of industry and the possibility for its rapid recovery depended on other factors which explain the discrepancy between the losses due to war damage (approximately 20 per cent) and those due to the slowdown in production which were much higher (55-60 per cent). The wear and tear on installations as a result of using the machines to maximum capacity, either due to the Fascist policy of autarchy or war production, the conflicts between workers and management which broke out in violence immediately after the liberation, the difficulties in communications which caused the scarcity

---

[1] One hectare is 2.471 acres.

in the supply of raw materials and hindered the distribution of the finished product, all were circumstances that contributed to keeping production at the lowest level.

In addition to these technical reasons, more basic causes conditioned production in a much greater degree, that is, the shortage of raw materials and foreign currency reserves necessary for their acquisition and the state of public finance. Italy, a country already traditionally poor in raw materials, whose reserves were exhausted by the necessities of war, expected with the normalization of international trade to be able to increase its own exports and thus acquire the hard currency necessary to buy raw materials. But obviously in order to start this process, a basis for departure was indispensable. This was entirely lacking. It was a vicious circle that could be broken only by foreign help in the form of loans and aid.

FOREIGN AID

The political uncertainty caused by social unrest discouraged private investments, national or foreign, and the financial resources of the state were in such a condition as to exclude any decisive action.

The Minister of the Treasury, in an interview with the press on November 28, 1945, revealed the state of the public finances. The public debt, which in 1939 had amounted to 145 billion lire, amounted to approximately 906 billion, while the budget deficit for the fiscal year 1945-1946 was expected to reach 230 billion.[1] The masses of paper money in circulation, inflated during the period 1943-1945 by the German and the Allied issues, increased even more, since the printing of new paper money was the only means for the Treasury to face the enormous commitments imposed by the first phases of the reconstruction. Consequently prices, which in 1945 were 20 times

---

[1] The budget deficit for 1945-46 reached instead 380 billion lire.

the pre-war prices, continued to rise at an ever increasing rate, aided too by the accelerating rate of the circulation of money.

Finally, a further weight on the national economy was the unemployment and underemployment. As a result of demobilization, the return of the prisoners and reduced economic activity, unemployment was increasing alarmingly; according to the first statistics available in 1946, over 2 million unemployed were registered, but those who were not on the lists and the high number of underemployed, either in the state bureaucracy or in private industry, should be added to this figure. The excessive manpower in industry alone in 1946 was put at approximately one million units.

In a picture as negative as the one described the most encouraging prospect was the promise of American aid. It was to permit the acquisition of those raw materials that were indispensable to reactivate the industrial enterprises of the North, without whose contribution the whole complex mechanism of the national economy could not have been put in motion.

After a preliminary series of aid projects administered by the Allied Military Government (in the summer of 1945) and the granting of credit of $ 130 million as a countervalue for am-lire[1] put in circulation by American troops, a more important long-term program was elaborated. While the initial aid was spent mainly to cover the needs of the population for essential food supplies, the aid that followed was meant to finance the acquisition of machines and raw materials.

A greater part of the funds for the financing of this second program was furnished through UNRRA (United Nations Relief and Rehabilitation Administration).[2] UNRRA

---

[1] Currency which was put in circulation by the Allied Military Government for the needs and pay of the occupation troops.

[2] The international organization for aid to countries damaged by the war was constituted in November 1943 by 44 countries. At the end of its activities (June 1947) UNRRA had distributed over $3,658,400,000. The contribution of the United States to the UNRRA program was by far the

signed an agreement with the Italian Government in January 1946 after having already distributed the preceding year $ 50 million in aid expenditures. The organization agreed to furnish food supplies, raw materials and machinery to Italy with the dual aim of improving the dietary level of the Italian population and of aiding industry to reach a normal level of production. UNRRA aid to Italy between January 1946 and June 1947 amounted to over $435 million.[1] The deliveries totaled over 10 million tons. The main components were coal, carburants, grain, food supplies, raw materials and machines.

ECONOMIC POLICIES OF THE RECONSTRUCTION

The availability of American aid raised the question of how it should be used. Should it be distributed through the government according to particular criteria and specific conditions and its utilization controlled, or should full freedom be left to private initiative? It was easy to see how this question was directly tied to the more general problem of economic reconstruction: should reconstruction be directed by the state or left to the initiative of free enterprise? The problem was a fundamental choice whose political implications were of basic importance.

The position of the extreme left-wing parties on this

---

most important, comprising over 73 per cent of all expenditures. Between the termination of the UNRRA aid program and the beginning of the Marshall Plan Italy continued to receive industrial supplies directly from the United States Government in accordance with the AUSA program (Interim Aid from the United States of America).

[1] In addition to Italy major recipients of UNRRA aid were (in millions of dollars): China: 520, Poland: 481, Yugoslavia: 420, Greece: 350, Cechoslovakia: 264, Ukraine: 188, Austria: 136.

With the proceeds of the sales of the UNRRA—supplied products to private individuals (only a part was used for direct assistance programs)— a fund in lire was constituted, administered jointly by the Italian Government and by the UNRRA Mission in Italy. This fund was spent in a series of rehabilitation programs: the fight against malaria, tuberculosis, building reconstruction programs, etc.

question has already been described. They believed reconstruction should be oriented with a precise political objective in view: a gradual dismantling of the monopolies in order to eliminate their great political influence in the country. Thus formulated, the program of the extreme left could have met with the agreement of all democratic forces that were sincerely progressive. In reality the hidden intention was to gradually bring a greater part of the heavy industry under the control of the state.

The major industrial enterprises in Italy for many years acted as monopolies or semi-monopolies. This system originated at the end of the last century when the Italian Government adopted a policy of government protection. Industry of national importance developed late in Italy by comparison with the major European countries (England, France, Germany). The government at that time favored industry from the beginning for political and military reasons, and made possible its development with a system of customs barriers, although this hurt the consumers and other sectors of the economy, especially agriculture in the South.

During the Fascist period, as a result of Mussolini's debt of gratitude to the great industrialists who had favored his takeover of power and later due to his bellicose policies, Italian industry was given favorable conditions for further development, especially in those sectors that were tied to the military effort. When many enterprises[1] suffered a crisis, for the first time in 1921-1925 because of the necessity to reconvert to peacetime production and again in the 1930's at the time of the great depression, the state intervened. To save them from bankruptcy it acquired considerably devaluated shares with public funds. As a result of these policies, in 1933 the IRI (Institute for Industrial Reconstruction) was constituted and entrusted with the adminis-

---

[1] A good part of these industries such as the mechanical industry, the shipyards and iron and steel based their production on war material supplies.

tration of all the state shareholdings in industries, banks and financial societies acquired with government recovery subsidies. It should be pointed out, however, that the state, instead of directly taking over the management of the industries it controlled, limited itself to having its official representatives on the boards of directors. The representatives of private investors easily exerted their influence on the government officials with the consequence that private interests finally prevailed over the interests of the state. Such a system of state intervention was clearly to the benefit of the great industrialists for whom it represented a wholly gratuitous form of insurance. If the industry was making money, the shareholders received their profits; if, however, the industry was in the red, the state intervened with its recovery program to plug the deficit with public funds.

At the end of the war the least efficient branches of industry, which were particularly tied to war production (metallurgy, shipyards, naval transport), were owned jointly by the state and by private groups, whereas the healthier industries (automobile, chemical and textile) were in the hands of private monopolies which with their own corporative organism, the *Confindustria* (Italian Confederation of Industry), constituted a very powerful pressure group. Through this group and with the support of the Liberal Party and the most conservative wing of the DC, private monopoly intended to reacquire the economic and political predominance that it had always enjoyed in pre-Fascist Italy and under the Fascist regime.

The parties of the extreme left and the democratic reformist parties, though with different objectives in view, found themselves in accord in recognizing the necessity to put order into the complex and disorganized sector of state participation in industry, as well as to undertake a struggle against the monopolies in order to limit their economic and political power. The democratic reformists intended to eliminate the monopolies by means of legislation modeled on the type of the anti-trust acts common in the United States, in order to reestablish a system of free enterprise and a situation in which there would be major opportunities for all businesses.[1] For the Communists, on the other hand, anti-monopoly legislation was merely one of the instruments designed to hit the great capitalist industry in such a way as to modify basically the economic organization of the country. In the political situation in the years immediately following the war, at a time when the structure of the new democratic state was still weak and uncertain, a substantial reduction of the political power of great industry would have removed one of the major obstacles to the conquest of power by the extreme left.

In the months after the liberation, exploiting the momentum of the working masses, the Social-Communists exercised their greatest pressure within industrial enterprises in view of this aim. The partly well-founded accusations of complicity with Fascism that were launched against the great industrialists in the ardent anti-Fascist climate of those months and the demand for an ever greater participation by the workers in the management of the factories through the "Management Councils"[2] were within the framework

---

[1] The following data concerning Italian stock companies show the degree of capital accumulation in 1938:

Class of Capital in lire	Enterprises	Total nominal capital
Up to 50 million	83.94 %	8.14 %
From 50 to 500 million	13.23 %	17.41 %
From 50 million to 5 billion	2.49 %	29.22 %
From 5 to 50 billion	0.33 %	39.40 %
Above 50 billion	0.01 %	5.83 %

[2] The "Management Councils" had been instituted by the CLNAI by a decree dated April 25, 1945, as "the affirmation of the new economic democracy which had been born out of the war of liberation." The "Management Council" was conceived as an organ composed of the representatives of capital and those of the workers who were elected from among the workers of the enterprise in a free and democratic way. It was the aim of the "Management Council" to discuss all questions regarding technical problems of production and the better use of manpower within the enterprise.

In reality, according to the intentions of the Communist Party, the "Councils" were to have a primarily political function: to weaken the authority of management and to carry out the class struggle within the framework of the establishment. Despite the fact that two projects had been presented for legal recognition of the "Councils," their de facto existence was never formally legalized. During the summer of 1946 there were about

of this initial offensive. But it was very soon blocked. The management of enterprises gradually recaptured the initiative, resisting all attempts on the part of the workers to exercise pressure. The latter were soon compelled to withdraw a good part of their requests in exchange for increases in salary made necessary by the rising cost of living.[1]

Hourly wages in the industrial triangle (Turin-Milan-Genoa) increased considerably in the last months of 1945: 9.30 lire in August to 12.78 (September) and then from 13.50 (October) to 20.12 (November). In December 1945 a general agreement between the CGIL (the single existing trade union which though predominantly under Communist influence organized until 1949 all Communist, Socialist and Demo-Christian workers) and the *Confindustria* established the minimum pay for all industrial workers in the North, conceded a special allowance (called contingency indemnity, which was justified by the high cost of living), introduced a sliding scale for the contingency indemnity (that is, the indemnity or allowance would automatically increase with the increase of the cost of living), and, finally, established the right to equal salary for men and women.

The agreement was celebrated by the trade unions as a great achievement. But in reality it was a political victory for management. In exchange for wage increases and the improvement of contractual conditions, the workers lost the possibility of insisting on their requests for participation in the management of industries. Furthermore, by conceding to the workers of the North better conditions in comparison

---

500 "Management Councils," which had been united into a National Committee of Coordination. According to the Social-Communists, this was, in collaboration with government organs, designed to have the function of implementing the planning of the country's economy. Soon, the attitude of private management hardened with regard to the "Management Councils," whose number and influence diminished rapidly.

[1] The indices (1938 is equal to 100) of listed goods went from 862 (August 1945) to 981 (September 1945) and successively to 1,107 (October 1945) and 1,118 (November 1945), while goods sold on the black market had the following increases for the months cited above: 3,190, 4,647, 4,609 and 4,591.

with those in other areas of Italy, and particularly compared with the conditions of the agricultural workers, the industrial bosses demonstrated their intention to continue the traditional policy of dividing the working class by creating within it privileged elites.

After the first inevitable retreats of the working class, the Social-Communists were forced to transfer their action to the government level, trying to bring their influence to bear on the economic and financial policies of reconstruction.

FINANCIAL PROBLEMS OF RECONSTRUCTION.
THE CURRENCY REFORM

The immense program of investments which was required for reconstruction posed the problem of how to acquire the financial means, which it would have been impossible to raise through normal channels. Inasmuch as American economic aid could only cover a part of the requirements, the costs of reconstruction had to be financed for the major part by local capital. For that reason it was necessary to tax the savings and assets of the Italians. Two basic measures were proposed: the floating of a reconstruction loan and the imposition of an extraordinary and progressive tax on property.

The reconstruction loan was decided upon easily since its necessity was unanimously recognized. The loan was floated in the autumn of 1946 and closed in January 1947. It furnished 231 billion (112 of which were in cash and the rest in Treasury bonds), a considerable but insufficient amount in view of the vast needs of the state.

The extraordinary tax on property, which took the form of a compulsory levy, on the other hand, encountered resistance and was the subject of long polemics tied in with the intentions of its proponents with regard to another important operation: the change of currency. This measure would not only have blocked considerable quantities

130

of money, which were being sent abroad by those who had little faith in the future of the country, but it was an essential condition for the levy of an extraordinary tax, since it would have permitted an exact census of liquid assets. Furthermore the circulation of money could have been partly blocked through a change of currency and thus have an anti-inflationary effect.

The conservative forces soon manifested their opposition to the change of currency as well as to the extraordinary tax. They wanted reconstruction to be financed exclusively through public loans, thus leaving complete freedom of investment to private initiative. The absence of public controls on credit and of any extraordinary tax would have facilitated most efficiently such investments. Such a policy, corresponding fully to classical principles of economic liberalism, denied to the state the function of guide and manager in the process of reconstruction, and limited its tasks to public utility works and the infrastructures. Considering the insufficiency of the means that could be collected through loans, to finance these the state could only print new paper money which would have caused a worsening of inflation as its logical consequence.

The change of money and the tax on property were supported mainly by the Social-Communists but were also approved of by the Republicans, the Actionists and a part of the DC.

According to their sponsors, both measures would have stopped the inflationary process, which was well under way, blocked speculation and furnished a large receipt to the Treasury out of which reconstruction could have been financed.

The logical consequence of the extraordinary tax on property would have been the elaboration of an economic plan for the employment of the capital thus collected. The left counted on this to weaken the private economy and to transfer major powers to the government.

The battle for and against the change of currency and the tax on property continued for almost a year, interrupted by constant postponements and pretexts of technical difficulties that were in part real. The government pronounced itself several times in a sense favorable to the change of currency, but major opposition to it came from the Minister of Finance, Corbino (in office from December 1945 to September 1946), a *laissez-faire* economist and the proponent of a policy based on classic principles of market economy. The continuous postponement of the measure, which should have been carried out immediately in order to produce results, and the gradual reinforcement of conservative influence on the government during the second De Gasperi Cabinet resulted finally in the shelving of the project. The tax on property, on the other hand, was approved and applied, although with remarkable slowness; instead of a progressive tax as intended in the original proposal, it was changed into a proportional tax and thus affected small properties more than large ones.

During the summer 1946, when it became increasingly clear that the change of currency would not take place, basic production indices, also as a consequence of the liberalization of the governments foreign trade policy, rose considerably.[1] There was as well a notable pickup in stock exchange values and an exceptional recovery in exports which went up between April and September 1946 from an index of 2.8 to 13.1.

The decision to forego the change of currency signified a fundamental turn in the economic situation of the country and had most important effects on the political situation. With it the management of economic reconstruction definitely passed into the hands of private initiative and developed according to a traditional policy of the state collaborating with rather than controlling private business.

The immediate effects of this turn, however, were to aggravate the financial situation of the country. The recovery

---

[1] The basic production figures were: *electric power* from 1,235,000 kwh. (May) to 1,421,000 kwh. (September); *steel* from 67,113 tons (April) to 108,038 tons (September). The index of chemical products went up from (1938 equals 100) 49.1 in May to 72.4 in September.

of industrial production and of private investment which was to continue in the first half of 1947 put an inflationary spiral into motion which up to then had been contained within reasonable limits.

Until then the government met the urgent expenses required for reconstruction, in addition to Allied loans, by floating treasury bonds. The recovery of production and the subsequent increase in investments, however, deprived the government of important capital which could have been used for public financing. Private capital was no longer invested in state bonds; it reverted to more profitable investments in industrial stocks. In order to face its payment commitments the state was therefore forced to print emissions of paper money in ever growing quantity. The increased money circulation as a result of the recovery of the exchanges and production, together with the constant increase of currency in circulation, caused a full-fledged inflationary situation. From June 1946 to June 1947 the money in circulation increased from 394.7 billion lire to 577.6 billion lire. This was a new serious hurdle on the road to economic reconstruction and the attainment of a level of normalcy, and it provided a new political opportunity for the left.

10.

CHAPTER 4

THE TRIPARTITE EXPERIMENT

THE SECOND DE GASPERI GOVERNMENT

The second De Gasperi Government, constituted in July 1946 following the institutional referendum and the elections for the Constituent Assembly, established the so-called "tripartite coalition" which was to last for about one year. In reality the parties represented in the cabinet were four: in addition to the Christian Democrats, the Socialists, and the Communists, the small Republican Party also was given two portfolios. The Republicans, who were participating in the Government for the first time, remained politically isolated from the very beginning. They did not carry sufficient political weight either to assume an independent position toward the three large parties of the coalition or to develop the role of mediator between the Communists and the Demo-Christians. For that reason the differences between the Social-Communists on the one hand and the Christian Democrats on the other were manifest in an even more direct fashion than in the past; in less than a year they were bound to reach the point of rupture.

The program of the new government had two main objectives: the defense of public order and the continuation of the work of economic reconstruction. It has already been pointed out how the policies of the Communists and the Christian Democrats differed. These differences inevitably

134

were reflected also over the means to be used for the restoration of public order. The Demo-Christians, who under the influence of the conservative forces had by then chosen to impose an economic policy favoring private initiative to the utmost, considered the defense of public order a clearly political objective. The party intended not only to combat the petty crime and general immorality that are the inevitable heritage of every post-war period, such as delinquency, the black market, smuggling and in general the violence of those who had put themselves outside the law due to the exceptional situation. Unquestionably the reestablishment of normal conditions of public morality was of first importance, but one of the most important aspects of public order was the restoration of social peace and the reaffirmation of the authority of the state. In the framework of these objectives the restoration of public order meant the limitation of strikes, especially those that were political in nature; the reestablishment of discipline in industry; the elimination of the atmosphere of psychological threat which the masses, organized politically by the extremist parties, exercised on the country; the reinforcement of the authority of the state to enable it to control and quell any action in the streets. In substance, the aim of De Gasperi and the DC was to deprive the left-wing parties of their most effective weapon, that of political pressure exercised through their control of the masses. The right maintained that it was only by reestablishing an atmosphere of security that conditions favorable to the development of private initiative and the reconstruction could be created. With this goal in view, De Gasperi, who in addition to the tasks of Prime Minister also held the portfolio of the Minister of the Interior and as such was responsible for public order, undertook to reinforce the police organs in order to reconstitute the weapon traditionally at the service of the state and the political forces in power.

In the aftermath of liberation in the North many demobilized ex-partisans, who were under the influence of the extreme left-wing parties, had joined the police force. These elements were partly replaced by ex-Fascists liberated from concentration camps following a recent political amnesty. This measure had been taken purportedly in order to achieve the "pacification of the spirits." Continuing the same trend started in his first cabinet, De Gasperi took new measures to clear the administrative organs. The prefects, who had been appointed by the CNL, were dismissed or forced to resign and substituted by career functionaries of conservative, anti-Communist sentiment. At the same time, in Emilia, the bastion of Communism, there was a major clean-up of hidden arms caches. These search operations, which were extended to other regions and continued for many years, resulted in the gathering of enormous quantities of war material. The arms were frequently in the possession of Communist Party members and this circumstance provided the DC and the right-wing press the opportunity to affirm the existence of a paramilitary organization supported by the Communist Party and to denounce the menace that it represented to the democratic life of the country.

The Communists, on the other hand, fought to maintain their positions in the police and administration. They strongly opposed these measures, employing all means at their disposal to obstruct De Gasperi's policies. They carried on resistance within the government by accusing De Gasperi of wanting to restore power to Fascist elements, and more intensely in the country at large by encouraging resistance and opposition to all of his directives.

Riots and popular manifestations took place in answer to newly named prefects, and resistance actions, which in many cases assumed the character of full-fledged rebellions, were undertaken within the police corps. During the month of July a series of strikes was organized in the large industrial cities. Initially protests of an economic nature

136

against the rapid rise in the cost of living, they became confounded with the political struggle against De Gasperi's policies. On September 11th there were grave disorders in Mestre in the course of which a local police station was attacked and sacked. In addition to the uncovery of arms caches, the denunciations and condemnations that followed in which extreme left elements were involved also increased the tension between the Communists and their sympathizers and the state authorities; a situation which reproduced itself in the council of ministers.

Such resistance inevitably inhibited and hampered government action. De Gasperi and the Christian Democratic ministers, who had the major government responsibilities, were forced continually to reach compromises with their Communist and Socialist colleagues in the cabinet over a part of their program. Progress in one direction was paid for by concessions in another, which the Prime Minister was compelled to make so that the tension inside the cabinet should not reach the point of rupture. It was a game of *do ut des* (give and take) and frequently put the DC in a difficult position with respect to public opinion and its own voters.

For instance, one of the first acts of the second De Gasperi Government was to grant a special indemnity (called "indemnity of the republic" to honor the results of the institutional referendum) to wage earners in industry and agriculture. The indemnity was agreed upon with the Communist Party which needed to achieve concrete advantages for the working classes in order to conserve their loyalty and maintain their fighting spirit. The "indemnity of the republic," whose cost amounted to about 30 billion lire, resulted in an increase of prices and therefore serious loss to other categories of wage earners with fixed salaries, such as white collar workers.

These compromises, which were denounced by the right-wing press as evidence of real collusion between the DC and the PCI, increased the discontent of the middle classes. They regarded with suspicion the coexistence within the

137

government of parties that were ideologically so opposed, and accused De Gasperi and the DC of immobilism and inefficiency, especially in combating the inflation which was wiping out their profits and savings.

The second balloting of the administrative elections held in October and November (the first balloting took place on the eve of the referendum[1]) demonstrated to what extent the discontent was general. As was to be foreseen, Christian Democracy paid the price. In the great cities, in Rome, Naples, Turin, Florence and Genoa, the DC suffered a serious defeat by comparison with the results of the elections of June 2, 1946.[2] The party lost 100,000 votes in Rome and 40,000 in Naples; most of these votes went to the *Uomo Qualunque*, a party best suited to represent the protest and discontent of the middle classes.

THE SPLIT IN THE SOCIALIST PARTY

One of the most important aspects of the administrative elections was the evidence that the PCI was gaining considerable ground over the Socialist Party. In Rome and Naples where the PCI and PSIUP had presented joint lists of candidates under the name of "Bloc of the People" it was more difficult to determine how the votes were distributed between the two parties. But from the calculation of the preferential votes and from the results obtained in cities where the PCI and the PSIUP presented separate lists, the regression of the PSIUP became clearly apparent. In the opinion of well-qualified commentators, this phenomenon was not only the consequence of superior Communist organization but was also due to the fact that important sectors of the Socialist electorate were opposed to the policy of direct

---

[1] The second balloting of the administrative elections involved 1,976 communes.

[2] In Milan, Florence and Genoa the majority of the local governments was won by the Socialists and Communists.

collaboration with the PCI. One of the consequences of the electoral losses of the PSIUP was the reopening of the differences that had always existed inside the Socialist Party between the fusionists and the autonomists (which corresponded to two traditional currents, the maximalists and the reformists).

The fusionist-maximalists supported a policy of direct collaboration with the PCI which would eventually have brought about a fusion of these two parties. The way to fusion had been opened by the recent renewal of the Unity of Action Pact. The autonomist-reformists, on the other hand, demanded a clear differentiation from the Communists, whose political methods and direct ties with the Soviet Union they condemned. The differences were due not only to the traditional division and the two opposed solutions, the dictatorship of the proletariat and parliamentary democracy, but for some time the basic problems of foreign policy had also become another highly controversial issue. Since the start of the political and diplomatic conflict between the Soviet Union and the Western powers, which began in 1946 and was to bring about the cold war and the creation of political blocs, the PSIUP had consistently espoused a position of neutrality toward both great powers.

Pietro Nenni had repeatedly affirmed, especially on the question of neutrality, the fundamental differences between the PSIUP and the PCI. Nevertheless, perhaps because of its policy of firm friendship with the PCI or its strong historical and ideological sympathies for the USSR, neutrality was in reality expressed in open hostility toward the Western capitalist countries and therefore indirect support of Soviet theses. In view of this ambiguity, which appeared ever more clearly with the deepening of international conflicts, shifting more every day from the diplomatic to the ideological level, the autonomist tendency took a clear position of dissent from the official policies of the party. The need for a choice between Stalinism and Western democracy and between the different ideological and cultural values which both systems implied became more and more clearly apparent. Considering the impossibility of achieving a compromise between these two opposed positions within the party itself, which by now was decidedly committed to a policy of collaboration with the PCI, a split within a short period appeared inevitable.

On January 9, 1947, on the occasion of the national congress of the Socialist Party held in Rome, the dissident Socialists, organized into two currents, the "Socialists Initiative" and "Socialist Critique" headed respectively by Giuseppe Saragat and Matteo Matteotti, left the hall in which the proceedings of the congress were taking place and moved to the Palazzo Barberini. There they founded a new democratic socialist party which took the name of Socialist Party of the Italian Workers (PSLI). Approximately 50 of the 115 Socialist deputies elected to the Constituent Assembly adhered to the new party.

A split of such importance renewed the process of reapportioning and reconstruction within the organizational structures of PSIUP and the newly-born party, necessarily compelling their leaders to suspend government and administration activities. As a result of the new situation and his new tasks, Pietro Nenni announced his own resignation as Minister of Foreign Affairs, as well as the resignation of the other Socialist ministers, in a letter which reached De Gasperi in the United States where he was on a good will mission. When the Prime Minister returned to Rome on January 20th he took cognizance of the Socialist decisions and presented the resignation of the whole cabinet to the temporary head of state, De Nicola, thus opening the fourth government crisis in less than two years after the end of the war.

THE THIRD DE GASPERI CABINET

De Gasperi's trip to the United States had been particularly successful. The Prime Minister was the object of manifestations of sympathy and solidarity with Italy on the part of both the responsible statesmen and the public at large. In the international climate of that moment these demonstrations acquired a special significance. After more than a year and a half of difficult negotiations between the four victorious powers, the peace treaty with Italy was ready for signature and ratification. The conditions were hard and produced bitterness and antagonism among large sections of the public. During the negotiations for the formulation of the treaty, the American Government maintained an attitude favorable to Italy. But it ran counter to the intransigent attitude of the other victorious powers or was negated by the need to reach compromises necessary to arrive at a final agreement. De Gasperi had become convinced after his conversations in the United States that the American Government would be disposed to support an action by the Italian Government, to be undertaken immediately after the signature of the treaty, with the aim of revising some of its hardest provisions.

The trip was also a sign of the end of the political and diplomatic isolation in which Italy had found itself since the end of the war, and it anticipated a fundamental political choice in the history of the country. The conflict between East and West was rapidly reaching its most acute phase. For that reason De Gasperi's trip and his requests for economic aid, which were in part satisfied, and the promises he received presupposed Italy's future alignment in favour of the West.

The economic aid which had been granted, in addition to that from the UNRRA program, was substantial: it included a loan of $100 million from the Export-Import Bank, concrete prospects for financing Italian industry and the unfreezing of Italian property in the U.S.A. The Americans specified, however, that the eventual administration of more economic aid was tied to "the stability and consolidation of the Italian democratic regime." The exhortation to drop the Communists and Socialists from the government was plain.

141

The political crisis that had been provoked by the Socialist split seemed to offer a good occasion to put an end to the unnatural collaboration between Christian Democrats and Communists, as the right-wing of the DC and large sectors of the public had been demanding. It is quite certain that De Gasperi himself had thought for a long time about how to achieve this disengagement, but at the moment of its realization he encountered serious difficulties. In order to constitute a government that would exclude the Communists, the DC needed the support of the other parties, but the consultations initiated by De Gasperi right after he received the nomination from the President of the Republic remained unsuccessful. In order to avoid exposing his left flank too much to Communist attacks, inevitable if they were to be excluded from the new government, De Gasperi looked for allies among the small parties of the democratic left, among those forces that would have permitted him to constitute a government without the extreme left and without at the same time opening himself to the criticism of being influenced by the right. None of these parties (Action Party, Republican Party, Socialist Party of the Italian Workers) accepted De Gasperi's proposal. There were many reasons for their refusal: some considered the maintenance of the Communist Party in the government as essential to represent the working classes; others thought that the operation presented the most serious unknown risks and feared that the Communists would react to their eviction by mobilizing the masses in manifestations of protest and resistance that would lead to chaos or outright civil war. In addition, the November elections had demonstrated that it was to the advantage of the smaller parties to remain in the opposition at a time of economic difficulties when participation in the government would have made them unpopular with large sectors of the public.

The situation was summed up in an editorial of *Il Popolo*, the organ of the DC, in its issue of January 29th: "the man in the street asks himself why you have agreed that the Communists sit with you in the government? The main reason for this

142

evolution which has justly been called 'forced cohabitation' is the general reluctance of all the so-called democratic forces to try to form a government without the extreme wings. The real weight, and effectives, of the Communists in the chamber and in the country, however, should not be overlooked. A minority government formed by the DC would give rise to bitter polemics and the continuation of tensions that could compromise the constructive atmosphere necessary to the last phase of the work of the Constituent Assembly."

It must be added that the new government would have had the delicate and unpleasant task of signing the peace treaty (which took place on February 10th), and it would have been too dangerous for the DC to assume exclusive responsibility for an act destined to revive protests from many quarters. The final reason for the postponement of the operation of disengagement was most likely the approaching vote in the Constituent Assembly on Article Seven of the draft of the Constitution, which provided for the inclusion of the Lateran Pacts in its final text, guaranteeing the Catholic Church an especially privileged position. Considering the direct ties the Demo-Christians had with the Church and the Vatican, Article Seven had a special importance for them. They feared that in excluding the Communists from the government, the latter would promote a concentration of forces of the lay left which could have voted down the article under discussion and modified the juridical relations between the state and the Catholic Church in an unfavorable way for the latter. De Gasperi was therefore forced another time to fall back on a coalition government (the third one) in accordance with the tripartite formula, notwithstanding the opposition of a large section of his own party. The new cabinet was formed on February 2nd. In addition to the Demo-Christians, it included PCI the Socialists which after the January split had readopted their old name of PSI (Italian Socialist Party) and two independents.

143

The third De Gasperi Cabinet, the shortest of the eight governments headed by the DC leader, appeared quickly to be what it was in reality—a solution based on a temporary compromise and an attempt to gain time in order to prepare a government of democratic concentration without the Communists. On March 24th, Article Seven was approved by 350 votes in the Constituent Assembly, including the votes of the Communists, while the Socialist parties, the Republicans and the Actionists voted against it. Public opinion was extremely surprised by the Communist decision, which fully supported a privileged position for the Church, one that all other parties with a lay tradition (except the Liberals) decidedly rejected. The event was unheard of and incomprehensible, and the small but fighting groups of the lay left, defenders to the utmost of the rights of religious minorities, reacted violently, accusing the Christian Democrats and Communists of complicity. The Communist daily *L'Unità*, in justifying the Communist vote, defined it as "the highest example of national responsibility for religious peace and the unity of the workers." The Communist leaders knew that a good part of their own electorate was still profoundly influenced by religious tradition and intended to avert the danger of an open declaration of war against the Catholic Church.

Whatever the motives and the tactical reasons that caused the Communists to take this position on Article Seven, it merely represented a parenthesis in the open political conflict between Communists and Christian-Democrats which had by now reached the breaking point. It continued to manifest itself within the government, thus condemning it to almost total immobility, while the internal situation became ever more critical because of the threatening progress of inflation. The only measures that could stop inflation were demanded from many quarters. These were to freeze salaries and reduce public expenditures. Both measures naturally encountered resolute opposition from the Communists, who insisted on a policy of state intervention in the economy to be realized with a vast program of public expenditures.

The increase of tension on the international level, especially following the proclamation of the Truman Doctrine to aid «those freedom-loving peoples...against the aggressive movements which seek to impose their own totalitarian regimes,"[1] contributed to the final break between the parties in the government. The Communists, in line with Moscow policy, condemned the Truman Doctrine and compared its aims to "ideological political motivations analogical to those habitual to German imperialism." The Christian Democrats and the entire moderate and conservative opinion extolled Truman's decision, seeing in it as well a guarantee for the security of Italy.

All these factors imposed a solution on De Gasperi which could not be put off any longer. In a speech on the radio on April 28th the Prime Minister again denounced the disloyalty of the two other parties of the government, the Socialists and the Communists, accusing them of refusing him "solidarity within the state administration and in the legislation on public matters," and he renewed the appeal to all those who could offer him a "concrete collaboration." The denunciation of the Social-Communists, as well as the exhortation to "concrete collaboration," obviously addressed to the minor democratic parties in favor of a coalition government, precipitated the crisis. It occurred on May 12th, three months after the formation of the government. Taking as a pretext new attacks against him that had appeared in the Social-Communist press, the leader of the DC turned in his resignation and the resignation of his government to the President of the Republic.

---

[1] The Truman Doctrine was proclaimed to provide military and economic aid to Greece and Turkey, both threatened by Soviet political moves.

Thus began one of the longest and most important government crises in the post-war history of the country. To resolve it a new approach was sought. The mandate to form a new government was first given to Nitti, then to Orlando so that they might try to form a cabinet of "democratic concentration." But as it had happened in the past both of these independent statesmen failed; although they enjoyed great prestige, they lacked the unconditional support of a major party. Only a leader who would be backed up by an important political force could have attempted with likely success the most delicate maneuver of disengagement from the Communist Party. For that reason the mandate was again given to De Gasperi who for many days tried to work out new solutions and new combinations.

He first tried to form a government of "general concentration," with all the parties participating, in which the influence of the extreme left would have been limited by the numerical preponderance of the other political groups. But the attempt failed, due to the refusal of the Liberals to join a government which also included the Communists. He then renewed the invitation to the parties of the democratic left (Social Democrats, Actionists and Republicans) for a center-left government which although leaving the Social-Communists out could not be characterized as too conservative. But the attempt failed again as it had three months earlier. There was only one solution left: to form a minority cabinet[1] composed of Christian Democrats alone with the participation of some independent "technicians"

---

[1] That is, a government that did not have a preconstituted majority within the Constituent Assembly, which functioned as a temporary parliament and would vote the confidence to the new government after having evaluated its program. Although he presented his cabinet without a pre-established majority, De Gasperi hoped that he would be able to gather, as in reality happened, the outward support and favorable vote of other political forces.

On May 31st the formation of a one-party cabinet was announced. It was defined as "the government of rebirth and salvation of the country." With this cabinet the DC produced its greatest effort. All of the best-known Christian Democratic leaders participated in it; two important positions in the cabinet were also given to two independents: Luigi Einaudi, an economist of world renown, was given the Vice-Presidency and the Ministry of Finance and Treasury and Cesare Merzagora, a well-known financier, the Ministry of Foreign Trade. They were both very close to business and financial circles, and Einaudi was even one of the most authoritative leaders of the Liberal Party. His qualification as independent should therefore be interpreted in the sense that his position in the cabinet was only personal and did not imply the official participation of his party.

The formation of the new government took on an historic significance in that it marked the end of one period of Italian political life and the beginning of another. The collaboration between the anti-Fascist parties, which started in 1943 in the CNL and was continued after the elections in 1946 with the tripartite formula, was definitely ended. In general it had rendered good services to the country during the period of the war against Nazi-Fascism. But after the failure of the Actionist experiment, which had been the sole intermediary solution between Social-Communist extremism and moderate and conservative clericalism, it had exhausted its reason for being. The wartime period of common political action, although necessarily limited by the political and ideological heterogeneity of the parties but nonetheless operative, was gradually replaced by a political battle conducted with no holds barred. This antagonism, which monopolized the energies and attentions of the various governments and paralyzed their action, would have ended by plunging the country into political and economic chaos. This was what the extreme left anticipated. Such a situation would have provided the most favorable conditions for great success at the polls which could have eventually brought it to power.

The value of De Gasperi's decision was precisely in having outwitted these tactics and in having taken away from the Communists their most effective weapon, perhaps the only one still at their disposal.

It should be stressed, however, that the victory of Christian Democracy and the forces it represented in the country was directly dependent on the success of the new government. The responsibility which the Demo-Christian leader assumed was therefore extremely grave. If the experiment of his government had failed, if it had been incapable of improving definitely the serious political and economic situation of the country, the political initiative would have almost inevitably been returned to the Social-Communists.

A test of strength was underway in which Christian Democracy had to commit all its resources and energies. The left, which continued to be in control of the masses, was to do everything to throw obstacles in De Gasperi's way, but by now it had lost the possibility of influencing government decisions. While this gave the government back its freedom of action, any failure of the government's program could not have been imputed to Social-Communist obstructionism but would have been attributed directly to the DC.

The new De Gasperi government brought the political clarity and precise assumption of responsibilities that large segments of the public had insistently demanded; but at the same time it was destined to produce inevitably sharper division between the forces for and against the restoration of traditional structures and economic forces. "The rebirth and the salvation of the country" was now destined to be realized in accordance with a conservative program. The position of a center party open to all social classes, which the DC had always sought to maintain, was compromised, at least for the moment, because of the urgency of the situation and by the parliamentary alliances, which the

De Gasperi Government as a minority government was forced to make. On June 21st the new cabinet received a vote of confidence in the Constituent Assembly by 274 votes for to 231 against. The Liberals, Qualunquists and Monarchists voted in favor of the government, that is, all the forces of the right and the extreme right which had demanded vociferously the end of the government with Communist participation.

This vote made the De Gasperi Government a center-right government and for that reason presupposed essential concessions to the right: the renunciation, at least for the time being, of those reforms that had been an essential part of the Demo-Christian political program.

For a large section of the population, which though anti-Communist favored renovation and progress, the solution of the political crisis of May 1947 was a victory dearly paid for.

11.

CHAPTER 5

TOWARD THE FOUR-PARTY COALITION

STRUGGLE AGAINST INFLATION

De Gasperi's courageous decision did not have the apocalyptic repercussions anticipated by many. There was no huge mobilization of popular forces as had been feared, nor were there any violent manifestations in reaction against the new government. The leftist parties appeared to have been disarmed by De Gasperi's move and perplexed over the stand they should adopt in opposition, or they were so convinced that the "one-party" experiment (*monocolore*) would fail in a short time that they judged it useful to assume a position of wait-and-see.

Shortly, however, the hopes of the Social-Communists for an immediate new crisis were disappointed and their prediction that Christian Democracy could not govern alone and control a situation that particularly in the financial sector appeared most difficult, proved a fundamental error in calculation. The most important objective of De Gasperi's policies was to combat inflation and save the buying power of the *lira*. By stopping inflation and saving the state from bankruptcy, De Gasperi knew that he would be rendering the most important service to the country and he could win the support of large numbers of small and medium-range employees and of all those with fixed earnings whose salaries and savings were menaced most by inflation.

Two months after the formation of the new government anti-inflationary measures were enacted. Bank credit was restricted to industries and a series of measures were taken for a strict control of the supply of goods. As invariably happens in an inflationary period, when people prefer goods to paper money, the former were accumulated in the storehouses of industrial and commercial firms. Both measures were closely tied together. Since the financial means that would have permitted accumulation of goods were lacking, the supplies were injected into the market with the effect of lowering the prices. The mounting spiral of the cost of living was also stopped in the sector of foodstuffs by the injection into the market of great quantities of low-priced goods that had been acquired by the government abroad or by the distribution of food parcels that were a part of American aid. Other important measures were taken to improve the situation of the State Treasury which was headed for bankruptcy. In order to increase its funds the government increased indirect taxes, especially those imposed on food supplies and attempted further to regain for the Treasury some of the funds which had gone to industry through the Stock Exchange, requesting the banks, especially those controlled by the state through the IRI, to invest parts of their deposits in state bonds.

The first consequences of these policies were not long to manifest themselves. Even before they operated to reverse the trend in the economic sphere, they caused almost immediately an important psychological change. Businessmen realized that inflation was being seriously curbed and in return they expressed their confidence in government policies by changing their practices. Speculation was reduced and industrial production, after a period of arrest in conjunction with the deflationary measures, continued to develop on a sounder basis. At the end of the month of November the central office of statistics already noted a decrease of 5 per cent in the price index of wholesale goods, while between the end of September and November the decrease in wholesale foodstuffs was between 21 and 23 per cent.

With the decrease in prices the speed of money circulation was reduced and savings increased, as was evident from the total number of bank deposits, which grew rapidly in the last month of 1947 and the first month of 1948. The benefits of this policy extended in the long run to the state budget, whose deficit[1] in the fiscal year 1948-1949 was reduced with respect to the preceding year's budget by 27 per cent.

THE TEST OF THE "MONOCOLORE" GOVERNMENT

The Socialists and Communists could not fail to realize the political implications of the financial policies of the De Gasperi Government. Certain at first that the De Gasperi experiment would fail, they became aware of having committed a serious political mistake by not having taken any action against it.

On September 8th the Social-Communist opposition attempted a counter action. The PSI leader Nenni presented a motion of non-confidence in the Constituent Assembly in order to precipitate the fall of the government and thus end the *monocolore* experiment. The motion was rejected with a large margin in favor of the government, 271 against and 178 for. Along with the Demo-Christians the representatives of the *Uomo Qualunque* Party and the Liberals voted against, with the result that the majority shifted further to the right. This new shift to the right provoked reaction from the Social Democrats and Republicans, who a few days after the first motion introduced a second motion of non-confidence in the government. The PSDI and the PRI presented their motion in the name of the "constitutional opposition" in order to differentiate their initiative from that of the Social-Communists, whom they accused of anti-constitutional practice. The government also won this second test,

---

[1] The deficit of fiscal year 1948-1949 amounted to 503 billion.

although with a reduced majority (270 votes against and 236 for). Admittedly, however, the Social Democratic and Republican motion had a purely tactical aim; it served as an admonition to the government in the name of those democratic and progressive forces which though anti-Communist did not approve of the conservative evolution of the DC and the government.

This double parliamentary victory considerably strengthened the government, increasing its support both among the political parties and in the country at large. The greater confidence of the country in the government program and particularly in its economic policies became an important psychological factor in the struggle against inflation. But the most significant proof of the change in public opinion could be noted in the results of the new administrative elections, which took place on October 12th in Rome.

Despite the involvement of the left in the electoral campaign, the results were clearly favorable to the DC, which practically doubled its votes, as compared with the preceding elections (November 10, 1946), while the Social-Communists, who again presented a joint list, decreased in percentage from 37 to 33 per cent. The trend was evident: the vote of confidence given the government by the Constituent Assembly was confirmed by the public.

Since its battle had been lost on the parliamentary level, the left resorted to a tactic of mobilizing the masses, organizing a series of manifestations, strikes and political agitations. Their purpose was to create such a state of tension in the country that the government would be compelled to resign. The campaign reached its peak during the month of November when a continual series of incidents took place between demonstrators and the police. Due to De Gasperi's efforts, the police had in the meantime been reinforced and issued more up-to-date equipment. The work he began was continued energetically by the new Minister of the Interior, Mario Scelba.

The police succeeded in controlling the popular demonstrations, but the drastic means they employed, from tear gas bombs to riot stick charges, sometimes resulted in deaths and tended to increase further the tension in the country and to exasperate the demonstrators. The deep cleavage between the popular masses and the government, which had previously existed, was thus enlarged. In political life it was expressed by an intensification of class hatreds. Since the Christians Democrats by this time had reassumed complete liberty of action, they responded with equal violence to the Social-Communist propaganda, which was engaged in an all-out effort to discredit the government and provoke a new crisis. The anti-Communist campaign was also intensified during this period, partly due to the evolution of the East-West relations. It was to reach its peak in the months during the campaign for the political elections of April 1948. The inferiority complex which in the period immediately after the war had put the middle classes on the defensive with regard to the working classes was slowly disappearing, although it was to take many years before it vanished altogether. The energetic policies of the government and the initial perplexity and lack of preparedness of the Communists had demonstrated the vulnerability of the left.

The resumption of anti-Communist action was linked with the resurrection of Fascist movements. The *Uomo Qualunque* Party was at the same time in the process of disintegration. It had come into existence as a protest against the inaction and the spirit of compromise of the DC. It was therefore natural that the Qualunquist movement would have lost its *raison d'être* after the ejection of the Social-Communists from the government and the determination demonstrated by De Gasperi. Elements of the *Uomo Qualunque*, encouraged by the final break between the anti-Fascist parties, regrouped into a number of semi-clandestine neo-Fascist movements, which shortly united to form the M.S.I. (Italian Social Movement) which soon was to appear in Italian political life as the official heir of the old Fascist Party.

A further consequence of the success of De Gasperi's Government, as well as the increase in the anti-Communist climate which was spreading in the country, was to compel the other political parties to take a stand. Up to then the Republicans and Social Democrats had maintained an independent position between the two opponents, being sceptical as to the life expectancy of the De Gasperi Government. They were now forced to make a hurried choice. Considering the democratic traditions of the Republicans, and the reasons that had led to the break between the Social Democrats and the Socialists, their choice was foreordained. Both parties decided not only to support the government, but indicated as well their desire to participate in it. Their decision was influenced by two aims: one was to stop the evolution of the government toward the right and reorient its position more to the center; the other was their desire not to remain isolated during the further phase of the struggle between the forces of communism and democracy, a struggle that would obviously be drawn out, both in the national and the international spheres.

Profiting shrewdly from this possibility to enlarge and consolidate the basis of his own majority, De Gasperi entered into negotiations with the leadership of both parties. The negotiations were concluded on December 11th and resulted in a reshaping of the government. The two leaders, Saragat (PSDI) and Pacciardi (PRI) entered the government as Vice-Premiers. Thus in the course of six months a combination of heterogeneous political forces, profoundly divided on political and ideological issues, was replaced by another, totally different one. This combination resulted in a four-party government, made up of the PSDI, the PRI, the DC and the Liberals, who had been participating in the government in the person of Einaudi. It was to last almost five years.

In the same month, on December 22nd, the Constituent Assembly concluded its work, which had been in process for a year and a half, approving the Constitution of the Republic by a great majority (453 in favor to 62 opposed). The Constitution entered into law on January 1, 1948. New elections were then scheduled to take place on April 18th of the same year in order to elect the new representative bodies—the Chamber of Deputies and the Senate.

ECONOMIC AND POLITICAL SITUATION AT THE END OF 1947

The year 1947, a neuralgic year for democracy in Italy, ended with the political situation considerably changed by comparison with that of the preceding year. Thanks to the policies advanced by Einaudi, who played a prominent role in postwar Italian history, inflation had been brought under control. The overall economic situation was improving, and the prospects for the reestablishment of a normal rythm of production was by then assured. The confidence of the business community had been considerably reinforced by the government policies of the last six months, and the process of reconversion to peacetime production had been initiated. Even more encouraging results were being obtained in the various sectors of production. Electric power output, the reconstruction of the merchant marine and of the oil refineries were proceeding at an accelerated pace, while important progress was being made in the textile, chemical and metallurgical industries. The rehabilitation of the agricultural economy was slower, because of the especially complex historical and structural factors involved.[1] Nevertheless important progress had also been made in the field of agriculture, thanks to massive imports of fertilizers, seeds and insecticides, which also made it possible to eliminate the malaria epidemic. The import of livestock permitted the increase of stocks which had been impoverished by German raids and indiscriminate slaughter.

---

[1] At the end of 1947 the industrial production was 88% of the 1938 level, while agricultural production had only reached 82%.

With the increase of production it was possible to gradually eliminate wartime rationing, although wheatpools were retained for a much longer period in order to assure the availability of essential products.

At the end of 1947, the first phase of economic reconstruction could be considered as accomplished. The reconstruction process was nevertheless still incomplete, and financial stability was achieved only by 1949-1950. The standard of living was as yet far below normal levels. The road to economic normalcy still appeared long, and aid from friendly nations was indispensable to further its way. However, the worst damage had been repaired, the ghost of bankruptcy was fading, and a minimum standard of living had been assured to the majority of Italians.[1]

As has been pointed out, the political makeup of the government had also changed radically within a few months. The tripartite system, in which the Christian Democrats, Communists and Socialists had faced each other without any possibility of collaboration, had been replaced by a coalition of more homogeneous parties, thus opening the way to a clearer and more constructive government policy. The new political formula of "quadripartism" was endorsed by the elections of April 1948. It ushered in a long period of political stability, which made the completion of the reconstruction process possible.

By the end of 1947 the struggle between the extreme left and the moderate forces, which had begun on the morrow of the liberation had decidedly turned to the advantage of the latter. Although the left had won important gains in the drafting of the Constitution in the Constituent Assembly—so much so that it was said that the Constitution would have required no modification to permit the functioning of a Communist popular democracy—the Social-Communists had by now failed to reach their main objective: the modification of the political and economic

---

[1] Per capita income in 1947 was 119,506 lire, which was almost double that of 1946 (61,057).

structure of the country in a revolutionaiy sense. The failure of the extreme left was followed by the failure of the democratic and progressive left as well. The reformist program, which aimed at inserting structural reforms into the process of reconstruction that would have destroyed the great concentrations of economic power and instituted social democracy as well as political democracy, could not be carried out. The ideals of the Resistance, which in 1945 had been so alive, had been lost in the daily struggle for power to which the parties were committed. The anti-Fascist solidarity among the parties of the CNL was definitely dissipated, thus opening the way to the resurrection of neo-Fascist movements.

In the next five years the political situation was to crystallize around the two power blocs, the Social-Communist opposition on the one hand and the government parties on the other; the cleavage which separated them was to become so deep that any dialogue was out of the question. The pressure of international events which obliged the Western powers to commit themselves to a major effort in order to contain Soviet expansionism became the determining factor. In Italy it absorbed the entire attention of the public, as it did in other European countries. The internal political struggle ceased to be a conflict between political programs and became a struggle between two opposed ways of life.

CHAPTER 6

THE PEACE TREATY

At the end of the war Italy found itself almost totally isolated in the sphere of international relations. The end of the occupation regime led to the abolishment of Allied Military Government and the restoration to the Italian Government of administrative jurisdiction over the entire nation. Since December 1945 the Italian Government had exercised full sovereignty in matters of internal affairs. Foreign affairs, however, still remained under Allied supervision in accordance with the armistice terms. The Allies constituted a "Control Commission" headed by U.S. Admiral Ellery Stone, whose function was to see that the armistice clauses were fully executed.

Until such time as the peace treaty should be signed, Italy was relegated to a kind of limbo, awaiting a judgment which, as could be foreseen, would be hard and which the Italian Government had the scantest possibility of influencing.

The drafting of the treaty took long and the differences between the victorious powers made negotiations difficult. The questions to be resolved were numerous and of the most varied kind: territorial questions with regard to the Italian borders with Yugoslavia, Austria and France; the colonies; military problems which concerned the final fate of the fleet, and financial questions with respect to reparations for damage caused by the military actions of the Italian Army.

Following the decisions taken at the Potsdam Conference by the three great powers, the first conference to discuss the peace treaty with Italy was convened in London in September 1945 on the level of the foreign ministers of the four victorious powers: France, Great Britain, the United States and the Soviet Union. Subsequent meetings took place in Paris in the spring and summer of 1946. The foreign ministers drew up the draft of a treaty, which was presented for approval to the representatives of the twenty-one nations participating at the actual peace conference, which took place in Paris between July 30 and October 15, 1946. The suggestions made at the conference were taken up again in the autumn by the council of the four foreign ministers, and the treaty in its final form was signed by the Italian representatives on February 10, 1947. After a long and stormy debate the Constituent Assembly authorized its ratification on July 31, 1947.

The most important clauses of the peace treaty, and the obligations and losses imposed by it on Italy, are dealt with briefly in the following pages.

MILITARY AND FINANCIAL CLAUSES

According to the military clauses of the peace treaty, the strength of the Italian Army was restricted to 185,000 men, in addition to 65,000 *Carabinieri* who as militarized police could be considered an integral part of the army. The Air Force was limited to a maximum of 25,000 men and 350 planes. The Navy was likewise reduced to 25,000 men and a considerably limited tonnage, comprising two warships too old to be used in combat, four cruisers which were also outdated, four destroyers, twenty torpedo boats and other smaller vessels. The units in excess of this, among which were two modern battleships and various cruisers, were divided between the United States, Great Britain, France, the Soviet Union, Greece and Yugoslavia.

After the ratification of the treaty, Great Britain and

the United States restored their share of the vessels to Italy in a gesture that was particularly appreciated by the Italian people, for whom the dismemberment of the fleet was a painful blow.

Other clauses of minor importance stipulated the demilitarization of the borders and the dismantling of their fortifications in order to prevent the possibility of a serious and prolonged defense of the country's borders.

The financial clauses were concerned primarily with the reparations demanded by those countries with whom Italy had been at war. The Italian Government accepted the principle of reparations, because it, too, reserved the right to present its own claims for reparations from Germany for combat operations carried out on its national territory. But it protested vigorously against certain clearly exaggerated claims that were requested, particularly by the USSR, which had demanded an indemnity of a total of $600 million. Thanks to the good offices of Great Britain and the United States, who viewed with apprehension the consequences of a further economic weakening of Italy, an agreement was reached whereby the USSR received $100 million, Albania $5 million, Greece $105 million and Yugoslavia $125 million. Part of these amounts were paid by the expropriation of goods belonging to Italian citizens in the territories of the creditor nations, and part in currency and industrial deliveries. France, Great Britain and the United States renounced their claim to Italian property within their respective territories and received in exchange a limited indemnity from the Italian Government.[1] This partial renunciation appeared more reasonable than generous, considering the enormous costs of the occupation by the Allied Armies which Italy had to sustain in the years 1943 to 1945 and which had contributed notably to the devaluation of the lira and the increase of inflation.

---

[1] The United States received $5 million and $15 million was paid to France. To Great Britain the Italian government paid all the pre-war debts due from Italians to British nationals.

The question of the Italo-Yugoslav borders was tied
to the territorial settlements which resulted from World War
I and which had since that time continually been a source
of conflict between the two nations. The primary reason for
the antagonism was the conflict between the two ethnic
elements, Italian and Slav, living together in the same area.
They were distributed so unequally that in many cases,
particularly in the rural areas, claims as to the numerical
prevalence of one over the other led to continual disputes.
In addition, the policy of suppression of ethnic minority
groups pursued by the Fascist Government during the twenty
years of its rule transformed the ethnic character of the area,
and rendered a just decision even more difficult.

The center of the area under discussion was the city of
Trieste, predominantly Italian with a very fine natural harbor,
which from the end of the 18th century had been one of
the most important outlets of the Austrian Empire and, after
its dismemberment, for the Central European states. The
economic value of Trieste remained very great, justifying
the demands of the young Yugoslav state which wanted to
turn it into a base for its commercial operations with Central
and Eastern Europe.

For Italy Trieste was of sentimental and historical as
well as economic interest. The annexation of Trieste after
the end of World War I had in fact concluded the
movement for Italian national unity. The claims on Trento
and Trieste and the surrounding areas with their partially
Italian populations had represented since 1870 the leit motif
of the Italian irredentist movement and the main formal
justification for Italy's entrance into World War I on the
side of the Allied nations. The secret Treaty of London of
1915 established the territorial compensation that Italy was
to receive at the end of a victorious war, which among other
areas included Venezia-Giulia with Trento, Trieste, Gorizia
and the whole Istrian Peninsula, with the exception of the
city of Fiume and the Dalmatian Coast. These were later

claimed by the Italian Government. At the end of the war, notwithstanding the opposition of President Wilson who, disregarding the London agreements, favored regulating the problem of the Italo-Yugoslav borders on an ethnic basis in accordance with one of the principles expressed in his Fourteen Points, Italy received partial satisfaction. The Treaty of St. Germain (September 10, 1919) ceded to Italy almost all the territories promised in the Treaty of London, while the decision on the problem of Fiume and Dalmatia was left to future negotiations.

In September 1919 Fiume was occupied in a local uprising led by the poet Gabriele D'Annunzio and nationalist elements from the army. Although the action was disapproved by the Rome Government, the latter waited complacently for fifteen months before deciding to put an end to the rebellion. The Treaty of Rapallo, in November 1920, settled the question of Dalmatia. By it the Italian Government renounced its claim to that region in exchange for the cession of Zara and several coastal islands. In 1924, with the Treaty of Rome, the question of Fiume was finally resolved by its cession to Italy.

At the end of World War II Yugoslavia, on the strength of its rights as a nation that had been invaded and occupied by Italo-German troops and had then emerged victorious, claimed from Italy, Zara, the Istrian peninsula, Fiume and Trieste with the entire Venezia-Giulia region. If these demands had been fully satisfied, Italy would have returned in practice to its 1915 borders in this region.

The position of Yugoslavia was especially strong, not only because of its war effort, which had been sustained for over three years by Tito's partisan army, but also because at the time of the surrender of the German troops, the Yugoslavs had succeeded in occupying all of Istria, reaching Trieste which they held for forty-five days. Later on, following an agreement for the delimitation of the occupation zone made with the command of the Anglo-American troops who had reached Trieste from the West, the Yugoslav troops were forced to retreat, leaving the city under the control of an Allied military government. All of Istria, with the exception of the city of Pola and a good part of Venezia-Giulia, were assigned to Yugoslavia as its occupation zone. The solution was temporary, awaiting a decision by the peace treaty, but it clearly constituted an advantageous position for Yugoslavia.

If one compares this with the Italian position, it is easy to see how wide the differences were between the two parties. The Italian thesis was set forth by De Gasperi in a letter dated August 22nd to James Byrnes, American Secretary of State. In it he also presented the Italian position with regard to all other problems dealt with in the peace treaty. The letter proposed as a basis for the delimitation of the Italo-Yugoslav border that the line drawn by Wilson should be applied, that is, the proposal which the American President had made in 1919 as an alternative to the borders attributed to Italy by the Treaty of London. This line took into particular consideration the ethnic factor, although it would have left 80,000 Italians in Yugoslavia. De Gasperi asked for ample guarantees for linguistic and cultural safeguards. From a territorial point of view the line was advantageous to Italy. Italy would have kept a major part of Istria, including the rich bauxite mines. In Venezia-Giulia minor rectifications would have been granted in favor of Yugoslavia. The same letter affirmed the necessity for an autonomous statute for the cities of Fiume and Zara, considering their predominantly Italian character.

The negotiations to find a solution to this controversy, deeply felt by both peoples, were long and difficult. Because of its status as a country *sub judice*, Italy did not participate directly, but the Italian Government tried every means of influencing the final decisions, starting with direct negotiations with Yugoslavia, which brought no results whatsoever, and leading to energetic requests to the Allied governments, especially the United States which more than the others favored the Italian position. In September 1946 the Rome Government finally advanced a proposal to hold a plebiscite; this, however, was rejected.

An important step toward the resolution of the controversy was made in March 1946 with the dispatch of a quadripartite commission into the territories that were concerned. Its task was to trace a frontier line which would take into account the opposing demands and would be acceptable to the four major powers. As was to be foreseen, the commission did not succeed in formulating a common proposal; each of the representatives of the four powers came up with a different border line.

The Soviet line penetrated more deeply into the Giulian territory of Venezia-Giulia, in almost exact agreement with the Yugoslav request. The English and American lines differed little, but the latter was more advantageous to Italy. The fourth proposal, presented by France, was a compromise which took special cognizance of the ethnic factor. It was on this basis in fact that the final accord was reached later on, after repeated wrangles between the Russians, who for political and ideological motives took up the defense of Slav interests, and the Anglo-Americans who were closer to the Italian point of view. The fate of Trieste remained to be solved, a question which for practical reasons it was decided to set apart from the border question.

The proposal to turn the city and its surrounding area into a free territory under UN administration encountered the hostility of both the Italian and the Yugoslav Governments, but at the time it seemed the only possible solution. In expectation of the choice of a governor and considering the difficulties of drafting the final statute, in view of the reserves of the four powers to the agreement, a temporary statute was adopted. The entire territory of Trieste was subdivided into two zones: Zone A and Zone B. The former included the city of Trieste and remained under an Anglo-American military government; the latter included all of Istria and was turned over to Yugoslav military administration. This temporary solution was destined to remain in effect for seven years, until October 1954. Consequently, the peace treaty only partly solved the problem of the borders between Italy and Yugoslavia, leaving the fate of

12.

the Free Territory of Trieste undecided. The future of the controversy, which was directly tied to the evolution of the international situation and internal developments in Italy, poisoned the relations between the two bordering nations which in the fall of 1953 reached a point of explosive tension.

All the clauses of the peace treaty concerning the eastern borders appeared to the Italian people, and especially to the generations that during World War I had fought bitterly for these territories, as the hardest part of the treaty. They now saw their efforts nullified and their sacrifices rendered vain. The hope for the restitution of Trieste remained and was in the years to come exploited by groups and parties in a demagogic way, especially in electoral campaigns, thus constituting for the country, whose development toward democracy was beset with difficulties and incertitudes, an experience which was in direct opposition to the development of a genuine democratic consciousness.

SOUTH TYROL (ALTO ADIGE)

Among the requests for territorial revisions with regard to the Italian borders, one was made by Austria concerning the province of Bolzano. This zone, which in Italy is known as the Alto Adige and in Austria as the South Tyrol, came to Italy at the end of World War I, although more than two-thirds of its population was of German language and culture. A large-scale immigration of Italians into the area and massive investments for the exploitation of electric power resources between the two wars transformed the Alto Adige into a region in which Italian economic interests became more and more important.

The problem of the German community had been partly solved by the Hitler-Mussolini agreement of 1939, which established a nationality option for the German-speaking element. As a result of this agreement 185,365 inhabitants (out of 266,885) chose German citizenship, and a good part of them (about 70,000) moved within the borders of the Third Reich. After September 8, 1943, Germany incorporated this zone militarily and politically, but the necessities of war slowed down the implementation of a policy of outright annexation to the German Reich. In 1945, when its independence was reestablished, Austria asked for the annexation of the South Tyrol and justified the request because of the German-speaking ethnic group, which after the end of the war had grown again with the return from Germany of most of those who had chosen to leave after the option in 1939. The Austrian request received backing by France and by conservative political circles in Great Britain who favored reinforcing the small and weak Austrian state in line with a policy of restoring the power equilibrium in Central Europe.

Italy rejected the request, giving its reasons in the letter already cited from De Gasperi to Secretary Byrnes. The Italian position was that it was a manifest injustice to favor a country which after the *Anschluss*[1] had accepted the objectives and methods of Nazi policies and had fought the war against the democracies to the end, while Italy had redeemed itself by its contribution to the anti-Fascist struggle with its military and partisan action after September 8th. The injustice appeared even more brazen if one considered the openly pro-German and pro-Nazi attitude that had always been manifest among the German element in the Alto Adige. De Gasperi pointed to the investments made by Italy that had benefited the region, in particular the construction of power plants (which furnished 13 per cent of the national production of electricity) and the mechanical industries in the Bolzano area. The Rome Government's vigorous defense of its position in the area and the better bargaining position of Italy *vis-à-vis* Austria, which had been part of the German Reich and as such had participated in the war against the Allied powers until 1945, eventually won out.

---

[1] That is, the integration with Nazi Germany which occurred following the occupation of Austria by German troops in March 1938.

In March 1946 the council of the four ministers of foreign affairs decided in favour of the Italian thesis, although it recognized Austria's right to minor border rectifications and greater protection of the linguistic, cultural, economic and administrative autonomy of the German community. A few months later, in September 1946, before the peace treaty was finally settled, De Gasperi resolved the problem of the autonomy of the German community in direct negotiations with the Austrian Foreign Minister Karl Gruber. This meeting and later meetings led to the De Gasperi-Gruber agreements. According to them, Austria recognized the Italian border of the Brenner, while Italy guaranteed large administrative autonomy to the Alto Adige and to the nearby area of Trentino. The agreements further established absolute equality of rights to the German-speaking elements, to have access to public office where bilingualism was officially introduced and to German-language schools. Other concessions in the field of economic exchanges between the Italian and Austrian border zones were also granted by Italy.

Shortly after its signature the text of the De Gasperi-Gruber agreements was transmitted to the major powers who, following the desire of the signatories, incorporated it in the peace treaty (Amendment Four). The favorable solution of the Alto Adige problem was Italy's sole compensation for the clearly unfavorable treatment it received in almost all other questions settled by the peace treaty.

Unfortunately the Alto Adige question has sprung up again many times in the post-war history of Italo-Austrian relations with a violence that would have been difficult to imagine in the atmosphere of collaboration which led to and followed the Italo-Austrian agreements of 1946.

The commitments made by Italy in the De Gasperi-Gruber agreements have been carried out in the letter if not in spirit. In January 1948, the Constituent Assembly approved the Special Statute for the region of Trentino-Alto Adige, which was to give full constitutional recognition of the autonomy of the German-speaking population.

The creation of the Trentino-Alto Adige resulted in re-opening the Austro-Italian dispute over the South Tyrol. Instead of limiting the special statute region to the province of Bolzano, where the German population was the majority (61.97% against 33.13, according to the census of Dec. 1953) and therefore the problem of assuring autonomy rights was most acute, the Italian legislators also included the province of Trento, where the German-speaking elements represented a small and almost negligible minority. The inclusion of the province of Trento in the newly constituted region resulted in an Italian majority in the regional Assembly. This solution left the German population of Alto Adige highly dissatisfied. An organized movement led by the *Südtiroler Volkspartei*, the party representing German elements, soon developed, asking for a more fair application of the 1946 agreements. This movement, which from 1953 on was to be strongly backed by the Austrian Government for reasons of internal policy, fell into the hands of extremist elements. From the original requests for autonomy they began to demand outright annexation of the Alto-Adige to Austria; and their protest action degenerated into open terrorism, with real commando raids on hydro-electric installations and military frontier posts. As a result of these developments the relations between Italy and Austria became increasingly tense. Recourse to the mediation of international organizations (International Court of Justice and United Nations General Assembly in 1960) and direct dealings between the two governments have thus far (Fall 1965) failed to solve the problem, as terroristic activities, inspired and carried out by former Nazi elements, have grown with menacing violence. The local economy has been seriously affected by the long and violent conflict. It is therefore not only in the common interest of the Italian Government and of the Alto Adige German population, but also in the interest of the peace in Europe that an agreement between the two parties be reached.

Italy was obliged to accept other territorial losses on its borders with France. This was the price democratic Italy had to pay for Mussolini's ignominious intervention against France when, in June 1940, it was about to collapse under the impact of the German army. As territorial compensations, France demanded the two Alpine villages of Briga and Tenda, the zone of Montcenis and other minor border rectifications. The French request and its acceptance by the Allies had a purely punitive character; notwithstanding the presence of linguistic minorities, these territories had belonged to the Kingdom of Sardinia prior to the unification of Italy, and their acquisition by France could therefore not be readily justified on historical grounds.

The Italian Government, which had renounced the statute establishing special protection for Italian settlers in French Tunisia in a gesture of reconciliation, tried to counter French demands by stressing the economic and strategic importance of Briga, Tenda and the Mont Cenis area for Italy. The hydroelectric power plants built there with Italian money and labor supplied a good part of the Ligurian and Piedmontese industries and furnished about 60 per cent of the electric power for the city of Turin. Furthermore the cession of Montcenis 25 miles from Turin, to France would have rendered the access to the rich Po Valley undefendable.

Italian objections were for the most part rejected and the contested territories were granted to France, with the stipulation that Italy would have the right to utilize the hydroelectric resources. Later, when the old resentments had subsided and both nations found themselves in collaboration for the creation of a United Europe, the French Government in a gesture of friendship offered to restore some of the most important annexed zones. Unfortunately, a negative vote in the French National Assembly blocked the government's initiative.

Another region on the border with France, the Aosta

Valley, where French-speaking populations had enjoyed economic and cultural autonomy until they were suppressed by Fascism, was given a Special Statute in January 1948. This Statute which implemented article 116[1] of the Republican Constitution recognized the official use of the French language and provided for the special organs of local administration.

The question of the disposition of the Italian colonies required long and arduous negotiation stretching out over many years.

Italy decided to renonuce spontaneously some of its colonial territories, knowing that it could not hold them in the light of unequivocal statements made several times during the war by Allied leaders and certain British commitments toward Greece and the former emperor of Ethiopia. Italy ceded the twelve Aegean islands (the Dodecanese), which had been in its possession since the end of the Italo-Turkish war (1911-1912), to Greece, and to Ethiopia it ceded all the African territories that had been acquired during the Fascist regime.

In De Gasperi's letter to Secretary Byrnes the Italian Government asked that it maintain sovereignty over the pre-Fascist colonies of Eritrea, Somalia (for the latter the alternative solution of a mandate was proposed) and Libya, at the same time declaring its readiness to furnish military bases to Great Britain.

The Italian demands were based on the necessity for an outlet for excess manpower, and the government supported its argument by pointing out the extent of Italy's financial investment in its overseas territories for the past fifty years in expectation of adequate returns. Both arguments, however, were weak. It was easy to demonstrate in the first place that regardless of incentives and encouragements, the Italian

---

[1] Art. 116 reads: "Particular forms and conditions of autonomy in accordance with special statutes adopted by constitutional law are attributed to Sicily, Sardinia, Trentino-Alto Adige, Friuli-Venezia Giulia and the Valle d'Aosta.

colonies, because of their poverty and lack of resources, had never attracted settlers in such numbers that they could have relieved the worrisome problems of overpopulation and unemployment in Italy. Furthermore, the huge amounts spent by the Italian Government prior to and under Fascism had been decided upon more in support of a badly conceived policy of boosting Italian prestige than any precise and justified economic calculations, so that the colonies had always been a heavy burden.

The US proposed entrusting Italian colonial territories to UN administration. In the absence, however, of any agreement between the Allied powers, each of whom had special interests, in particular with regard to Libya which was disputed between Great Britain and the USSR, it was decided to put the question off until after the signature of the peace treaty. By the terms of the treaty Italy was committed to renounce all of its overseas territories. This renunciation was hard for those, who, raised on nationalistic and Fascist rhetoric, found it difficult to abandon their dream of power tied to a different period with different values.

Efforts to settle the problem were pursued without results in 1948 and in 1949 when the question was turned over to the UN General Assembly. Finally, at the end of 1949, it was decided that Libya would be given its independence in 1952 and that until then it would be administered by the United Nations with the help of a consultative committee composed of representatives of Great Britain, Italy, Pakistan and Egypt.

So far as the former Italian possessions in East Africa were concerned it was decided that Eritrea should form a federation with Ethiopia, while keeping a broad administrative autonomy. Somalia, the poorest of all the contested territories, was given to Italy as a trusteeship administration for ten years: which represented some recognition for Italian efforts and investments in the area.

The peace conditions aroused disappointment and bitterness all over the country. The immediate reaction to the decisions of the four powers was one of protest. Particularly to some sections of the public opinion still imbued with nationalistic spirit the treaty appeared as a patent injustice. Later, when a more objective consideration of the facts could be made, judgment of the treaty became more moderate, although a deep sense of disillusionment remained. The conviction was widespread that the promises made by the Allied governments before and after the signature of the armistice, the generous contribution in blood and sacrifice of the Italian people in the war of liberation against Nazism, the sincere enthusiasm and the willingness to contribute to the moral and material reconstruction of the international community (Italy had repeatedly requested to become a member of the UN), would have justified more favorable conditions and above all more dignified consideration during the drafting of the treaty. The Italian Government had several times requested to be allowed to participate in the conferences formulating the peace treaty in order to advance its own ideas. With the exception of two passionate speeches delivered by De Gasperi at the London Conference and at the Peace Conference in Paris —which were barely taken into account by the Allies— Italy remained totally unrepresented in the treaty negotiations. Consequently, those who claimed in demagogic fashion that a *Diktat* had been imposed on Italy by the victorious powers and not a just peace, reached on the basis of an objective consideration of the responsibility of the Italian people, found easy game.

The repercussions of the peace treaty, due mainly to the long, drawn-out debate over the Trieste and colonial questions, although they only affected a minority, lasted several years and were exploited by various left-wing extremist parties and even more by the right-wing parties which the peace treaty had to a certain extent helped to resurrect. If their attempts did not produce more serious consequences. it was due mostly to the good sense of the population. The majority of the Italians had abandoned the nationalistic and imperialistic ambitions of the past regime.

Political judgment of the peace treaty with Italy should take into account the climate of open antagonism between the Anglo-Americans and the Soviet Union.

The political and diplomatic conflict between East and West which was to reach its most violent manifestations in the years from 1947 to 1951 came into the open for the first time after the war during the negotiations for the Italian peace treaty. On the one hand Italy benefited from the early settlement of its peace conditions before the East-West conflict had yet reached its peak. (Germany and Japan were obliged to wait long years during the cold-war period before regaining their full sovereign status). On the other hand, the Italian peace treaty suffered from incipient East-West conflict and the continuous compromises that were necessary to reach agreement weighed against Italy in many of the most important decisions. Furthermore, because of the long period it took to prepare, the treaty came to regulate a situation which by then had been surpassed by events. The Western governments were conscious of this fact, particularly the United States, which more than any other power involved had defended Italian interests and which realized the necessity of compensating Italy in other ways, such as economic aid to further its rebirth.

The signature of the peace treaty by the Italian Government and its ratification by the Constituent Assembly encountered initial opposition in right-wing political circles, but to reject the treaty, as some proposed, would have seriously endangered the independence of the country, since it would have reduced its own sovereignty and prevented its joining the community of nations as a full-fledged member, an objective which all Italian governments after the war pursued as an essential goal. Considering the political and economic condition of Italy, in need of aid and

174

friendship, its isolation could not be further prolonged. For that reason the treaty was signed, in February, and in July 1947, after heated debate, the Constituent Assembly authorized its ratification.

CHAPTER 7

THE REPUBLICAN CONSTITUTION[1]

Following the elections and the institutional referendum of June 2, 1946, the 556 elected representatives of the Constituent Assembly began the work of drawing up a new constitution for the country. The first draft was entrusted to a committee of 75 members; after the first draft had been prepared, it was submitted to a more selective committee of eighteen, predominantly eminent jurists, who gave it its final form. The draft constitution was then presented to the Assembly, which began its deliberations in January 1947, taking it up article by article. It was modified and approved in the course of 173 sessions.

The Constitution of the Republic comprises 139 articles and eighteen "Temporary and Final Dispositions," which in fact represent additional provisions that are an integral part of the body of the charter. Its excessive length was almost unanimously criticized; among other drawbacks it prevented its wider dissemination. Actually, some articles could have been omitted and incorporated into separate laws, with the

---

[1] The Republican Constitution succeeded the so-called Albertine Statute, the constitution that had been granted by Carlo Alberto, King of Sardinia and Piedmont, to his subjects in 1848 and later extended to united Italy. The original document was deeply modified during the Fascist period to such an extent that it was entirely changed both in letter and spirit. In practice the Albertine Statute had been a flexible constitution which could be changed by an external law without a constitutional amendment.

result that the document would have gained in clarity and precision.

Articles 1-12 are entitled Basic Principles and constitute a preamble; they are followed by Part I (Arts. 13-54) and Part II (Arts. 55-134). The first part defines the rights and duties of the citizen in their various aspects: civic, social, political and economic (each of these aspects is dealt with in a separate chapter). Part II, the longest part, is entirely devoted to a description of the structure of the government and establishes the competencies of the various organs of the republic. The final part comprises the "temporary and final dispositions," mentioned earlier. As does every modern constitution, the Italian Constitution follows the principle of separation of powers, though it is modified by a series of reciprocal controls.

THE PARLIAMENT

At the center of the institutional system is the legislative power, which is embodied in a two-chamber parliament,[1] composed of the Chamber of Deputies and the Senate. The chief importance of parliament lies not only in its functions but equally in the fact that it is the only body elected directly by the people, who delegate to it its sovereignty. The functions of debating and approving laws (the initiative of proposing laws can come from the government, the parliament and also from the people)[2] are exercised jointly by the two chambers (Art. 70). Any proposed legislation, of whatever nature, must in fact be examined and approved by both the Chamber of Deputies and by the Senate; a simple modification of the text under discussion by one of the two chambers automatically requires that it be sent back to the other chamber

---

[1] Hence the "parliamentary" character of the Italian Republic.

[2] This is one of the innovations with regard to the preceding constitution, the Albertine Statute. Art. 71 stipulates that 50,000 voters may present the proposal of a law to parliament, on the condition that it be formally drafted as a law and be subdivided into articles.

for approval. A law can be definitely approved and enacted by parliament only if both chambers reach complete agreement on an identical text.

The Chamber of Deputies and the Senate have for that reason the same attributes, the same rights and equal standing. They differ, however, in numerical composition, and in the method of election.[1]

Outside of its legislative function, parliament also exercises political control over the executive branch, by means of its vote of confidence or non-confidence.

THE GOVERNMENT AND THE PRESIDENT OF THE REPUBLIC

The government, or cabinet, is the organ in which the executive power is vested. It includes the prime minister, and other ministers as heads of the twenty-six existing departments (*ministeri*)[2] and is invested after its formation by a vote of confidence of both chambers. Confidence is voted only after the government program is outlined by the prime minister and approved by a simple majority of the parliament. If no majority can be constituted in support of the government, the prime minister is compelled to hand in his resignation. A confidence or non-confidence vote, according to whether it is proposed by the government, which wants to verify its majority, or by the opposition, might come about any time during the government's tenure of office.

---

[1] A deputy represents 80,000 inhabitants or a fraction of 40,000; he is elected by all those who have the right to vote in accordance with the plurinominal system on the basis of proportionality. The minimum age for a deputy is twenty-five years. A senator is elected by 200,000 inhabitants or by a fraction of more than 100,000. Only those citizens who have completed their twenty-fifth year can vote in the senatorial election. Senators are elected on a regional basis, according to a law which is a compromise between the uninominal and the proportional system. The minimum age requirement for a senator is that he must have completed his fortieth year.

[2] The number of departments varies according to technical and sometimes political exigencies.

178

The other branch of the Italian constitutional system is the Presidency of the Republic. Unlike the United States President, who assumes the double function of head of the executive department and head of state, the Italian President has limited powers. He is elected[1] by a vote of both chambers of parliament, who meet in a joint session in which three delegates for each of the nineteen regions with the right to a vote participate. As head of state he performs a number of symbolic and representative functions. He promulgates laws that have been approved by parliament; he appoints high state officials, when the law requires it; he accredits and receives diplomatic representatives; he dispenses state honors; etc.[2]

His primary political functions, through which he participates in the government of the country, are the designation of the prime minister and the dissolution of parliament, which has to be followed by new elections within 70 days. Another presidential prerogative is the right to veto laws passed by parliament.

Although these prerogatives appear formally most important, the extent of the president's political power is very much limited. The designation of the prime minister must be approved by a vote of confidence of parliament, and it is therefore conditioned by the existence of a majority. The dissolution of the chambers is equally contingent on precise conditions: notably if it is demonstrably impossible to constitute a majority; this is an act of such gravity that so far it has never been used by any president in office. Finally the suspensive veto of a law approved by parliament is equally restricted: if parliament chooses to pass the law again, the president is compelled to withdraw his veto.

The president's intervention is essential in putting the

---

[1] The election of the president is conducted by secret ballot. In the first three ballotings his election requires a two-thirds majority; if this cannot be constituted, an absolute majority is sufficient for the next balloting. The president remains in office for seven years.

[2] See: Art. 87, other functions of the president.

constitutional machinery into motion, but when this has been accomplished, his functions become mainly representative as head of the state. It must be added, however, that the exact interpretation of presidential prerogatives is a subject of controversy, both in doctrine and in practice. The two presidents, Luigi Einaudi and Giovanni Gronchi, who have completed their seven-year terms since 1948, have given a different interpretation of the constitution. While the first adhered strictly to its letter, the second constantly endeavored, and frequently quite successfully, to exercise the role of mentor and guide in governmental policies. The interpretation which the current President Antonio Segni makes of the presidential function may be of great importance in the establishment of its definitive scope.

THE OTHER CONSTITUTIONAL ORGANS

In these main aspects the Republican Constitution follows the general lines of the old Albertine Statute, with the role of the president corresponding to that of the King, as it was exercised until the fall of Fascism. It differs notably with the establishment of four new organs:[1] 1) the Constitutional Court, 2) the regional administration, 3) the Supreme Council of Magistrature and 4) the popular referendum.

1) The Constitutional Court, is, together with the parliament, the government and the presidency one of the most important constitutional organs. It is composed of fifteen judges, who remain in office for twelve years; one third are chosen by the highest judicial officials,[2] one third by parliament and the remaining third by the president of the republic.

---

[1] Another difference from the Albertine Statute which should be stressed is that Senate members were appointed by the King.

[2] The judges of the three highest tribunals, the Court of Cassation, the Court of Accounts and the Council of State.

The essential functions of the Constitutional Court (which is modeled on the American Supreme Court) are to pass on the constitutionality of national and regional laws and to decide in conflicts of competency between the highest constitutional organs. Minor functions are the power to impeach the president and the members of the government and to decide on the admissibility of a referendum.

Considering its prerogatives, the Constitutional Court emerges as the highest guardian of constitutional legality and the liberties guaranteed by the constitution. The drafters of the constitution were prompted to establish it by the necessity of guaranteeing the free institutions against all threats. The way in which Fascism had come to power was uppermost in their minds, and the manner in which it had transformed the spirit of the former constitution, the Albertine Statute, to suit its purposes, precisely because of the absence of an authority that could have defended its integrity.

One of the most important activities of the Constitutional Court, from the time of its creation (1956) until today, has been to abolish gradually the Fascist legislation that had remained in force each time that it conflicted with the liberties and rights guaranteed by the new constitution. Police laws, the limitations of personal freedom, which were quite evidently inspired by Fascist totalitarian practice have been declared invalid by the court. This work of bringing laws up-to-date will go on for a long time and must proceed with wisdom and perseverance until the old Italian legislation is brought into harmony with the democratic principles of the Republican Constitution.

2) Another institution which was incorporated into the Republican Constitution in order to increase local administrative autonomy and to combat centralization, is the regional administration. The regions represent a further addition to the traditional administrative subdivisions of communes (*comuni*) and provinces (*province*).[1] As in the communes and

---

[1] Italy is divided into 19 regions, 99 provinces and about 8000 communes.

provinces, the region has organs of government, such as the regional council (equivalent to a small local parliament) and the *giunta* (a regional executive) and its president.

The regions enjoy considerable legislative and administrative autonomy, in accordance with the functions enumerated by Art. 117 of the constitution. The most important of them are: urbanism, tourism, agriculture and forestry, professional instruction, roads, public works, etc. Art. 119 establishes regional financial autonomy in order to permit the regions to carry out their functions. The regions may levy their own taxes and receive their quota of the national taxes.

An even larger degree of autonomy has been given to Sicily and Sardinia and to three frontier regions: the Trentino-Alto Adige, the Friuli-Venezia Giulia and the Aosta Valley, which have been classed as "regions with special statutes." This special type of autonomy has been granted in order to take into account the specific conditions of the populations of certain areas. So far as Sicily and Sardinia are concerned, their requests corresponded to ancient demands which were justified by the fact that the local administrations were directly involved in solving the grave economic and social problems of these two particularly depressed areas. The other regions, being frontier areas, included large linguistic minorities (French in the Aosta Valley, German in the Trentino-Alto Adige and Slav in Friuli-Venezia Giulia). Consequently it was deemed advisable that they should be granted broader autonomy, in order to garantee the rights of these minorities.

3) The Superior Council of Magistrature was conceived to assure the independence of judges of all categories, removing them from the jurisdiction of the executive In fact, one of the major preoccupations of the lawmakers was to guarantee the complete independence of the magistrature, whose powers had been sharply curtailed under Fascism, leaving the citizen defenseless before the state. While in the past the judge—a judgeship is not an elective office in Italy—had been directly dependent on the executive (the careers, sala-

ries, transfers of magistrates and everything that concerned the organization of justice was within the competence of the Ministry of Justice), the establishment of the Superior Council of Magistrature has modified this relationship in assuring the freedom of the judge.

The council is composed of twenty-four members, fourteen of whom are elected by judges of all categories and grades, seven by parliament, while the three remaining are the President of the Republic, who presides over the council, the Chief Justice and the Chief Prosecutor. Art. 106 relegates to the Superior Council the right to make "appointments and transfers, promotions and disciplinary procedures concerning magistrates."

4) Finally the democratic institution of a referendum has been introduced (Art. 75) in order to enable the people to participate directly in the elaboration of laws.

Conversely, the constitution also establishes the right to propose a popular referendum for the total or partial abolition of a law. Such a referendum, which represents another way in which the sovereignty of the people can be expressed may be called if it is requested by 500,000 citizens or by five regional councils.

GOVERNMENT BY THE PARTIES

The Republican Constitution was deeply influenced by the ideas and trends current in the immediate post-war period. It represents an attempt to reconcile the general aspirations for progress and renewal with the conflicting solutions put forward by the different political parties. For that reason the work of the Constituent Assembly was a compromise between sharply differing positions. all the more so since it was carried out at a time when these divergencies were deepening and becoming increasingly evident. The results of this compromise were not always positive. Behind the formal facade of unity were concealed equivocations and

183

contradictions that were destined to cause contrasting interpretations of the constitution.

An analysis of the impact on the constitution of this precarious though even political balance would require a more systematic description and commentary on the Italian Constitution than is possible here. However, it should be pointed out to what extent this phenomenon became established during these years, and how deeply it altered the original spirit of the constitution.

The development of a *partitocrazia* ("rule of the parties") had begun in Italy before the constitution was in the process of being drafted. The phenomenon was common in other democracies of Continental Europe but became especially developed in Italy. The term *partitocrazia* connotes a political regime in which the power of decision in matters of government has been transferred from the constitutional organs to the political parties, and especially to those parties that are members of the government majority. This has occurred in Italy between 1945 and the present, with the result that the parties have arrogated to themselves the right to control every important aspect of political life. The control of power by the parties has established itself in particular with regard to the constitutional organs, thus evading the principle of division of powers and nullifying the checks and balances which had been precisely defined between the major constitutional organs.

In general this evolution may be attributed to three causes: 1) the plurinominal system, in which candidates for parliamentary election are chosen by the directing organs of the parties; 2) highly organized parties and the strong discipline that binds the members to abide by the decisions taken by their leaderships (secretariats, directorates, councils of direction), and finally 3) the trend among the Italian electorate which by an overwhelming majority casts its votes for programs and ideas represented by the various parties rather than for the candidates themselves. In reality, rather than three separate causes, these are all aspects of the same phenomenon, since party discipline and voting for party

184

programs are both, from the historical point of view as well, a direct consequence of the introduction of the plurinominal system of balloting.

The most direct consequence of the *partitocrazia* has been a considerable weakening of the independence of judgement and authority of both chambers, which the Republican Constitution places at the core of the entire constitutional system. The parties in fact exercise complete control over the deputies and senators, who owe their own election to the parties and therefore have to follow their instruction if they intend to be reelected. For that reason parliament looses its most important political function, that of control of the activities of the government.

Parliamentary majorities are composed by agreements between the party secretariats, and government crises occur when these agreements are broken. In view of this situation, the confidence and non-confidence votes, as well as the debates which precede them, have a strictly formal character and merely confirm the divergencies or the agreements which have developed outside of parliament. Through parliament, the basic constitutional organ, party control easily extends equally to other constitutional institutions.

Along with those critics who condemn the evolution of the system, there are some who point out its positive aspects. They consist mainly in the fact that the system prevents a dictatorship of the assembly of the type common in the French Fourth Republic, which was responsible to a considerable extent for the paralysis of government action and the subsequent takeover by the Gaullist regime. The defenders of the *partitocrazia* reply to those who object to this fundamental violation of the guarantees of democracy to the effect that the democratic principle remains untouched, inasmuch as the will of the parties expresses the will of its members. Those who do not participate in party life always have the possibility of approving or disapproving party policies at the polls.

In reality the party system has assured in the post-war period major political stability, more than that which would

185

have conceivably resulted if the parliament had been free of external pressures; but the results obtained in these years cannot be generalized as good or bad. Though it should be admissible that this practice is formally not in opposition to codified law, it nevertheless collides with the intent of the legislator. The establishment of some form of control over the life, the methods, the activities and financing of the parties is, in fact, a matter of first necessity.

It is impossible to conclude a discussion of the Italian Constitution without mentioning the serious problem of the failure to implement some of its provisions. Fifteen years after the charter was enacted some of the new institutions that were established by it are still inoperative, while others have been constituted only after years of delay. This is the case in the first place of the regional institution, with the exception of four regions (Sicily, Sardinia, the Aosta Valley and Trentino-Alto Adige), all of which had been constituted by 1949; secondly, the institution of popular initiative and the referendum in matters of legislation; and thirdly the Constitutional Court and the Superior Council of Magistrature, which were constituted only in 1956 after over eight years of delay.

The technical reason for these delays has been the need to draft new enabling legislation, which the Constituent Assembly had demanded from the deputy-legislators. These are necessary more specifically for the regulation of the new institutions and their functioning. In reality, the reasons for this non-implementation are of a political nature.

In the case of the Constitutional Court and the Supreme Council of Magistrature, the government and the parties of the majority have delayed their establishment as long as possible in order not to be deprived of important instruments of power, such as for instance the Fascist police laws, which the court should have abolished—although this did occur later. The failure to set up the other institutions —legislation by popular initiative, the popular referendum and the regional administration by regular statute—can be

186

explained by the majority's preoccupation with denying an advantage to the Social-Communists.

In particular in the case of the institution of regional administration, by far the most important, the parties in power wanted to prevent the regions where the Social-Communists have a majority of the votes (Emilia-Romagna, Toscana, Umbria) from falling under their control.

The failure to implement these provisions of the constitution, and particularly the regional statute, has for years been the subject of long and heated wrangles. The extreme left has had a distinct advantage in this debate, inasmuch as it can pose as the defender of constitutional legality.

CHAPTER 8

A TURNING POINT IN ITALIAN POST-WAR POLITICS: THE POLITICAL ELECTIONS OF APRIL 1948

When the manifestations which the Social-Communists had fomented in the autumn of 1947, in their attempt to cause the fall of the government, had gradually quieted down, the entire effort of the left became concentrated on the preparations for the political elections, which were the most important ones to take place since the war.

With the failure of mass action the electoral consultation scheduled for April 1948 presented the left with its last opportunity to interrupt or possibly reverse the process of consolidation of the fourth De Gasperi Government which was well under way after Social Democrats and Republicans had joined the government. On the governmental level the balance of forces was by now altered in favor of the center parties, but this change remained to be endorsed by the electorate. If the outcome should be favorable to the DC and its new allies, it would usher in a period of political stability, and the process of reconstruction and economic recovery would proceed with new vigor along the lines that had already been traced. On the other hand, a victory of the left would bring a return to the period of uncertainty and immobilism that had existed before the fourth De Gasperi Government, made even more dangerous by the continually increasing international tension.

The preparations for the electoral campaign were intensive and the involvement of the parties was commensurate with the issues at stake. At the end of January the constitution of the "Democratic Popular Front" was officially announced. It had proved its worth in the administrative elections in Rome in 1946 and 1947. The Popular Front was an electoral alliance between the Communist and Socialist Parties, who were to present themselves to the electorate as a single party with a single list of candidates. This decision was taken by the two parties in the hope of obtaining a relative majority on a joint ballot, which would have permitted one of their leaders to claim the premiership in case of victory.

The creation of the "Front" had in fact the effect of clarifying the alignment of the opposing forces to the voters and of dramatizing their conflicts. In addition the constitution of the "Front" caused further defections from the PSI. Some of its opponents, including leaders like Ivan Matteo Lombardo, left Nenni's party and together with Saragat's Social Democrats formed a common electoral list *Unità Socialista.*

The Christian Democrats, Social Democrats and Republicans were aligned against the Social-Communist bloc. Although there was no formal electoral or post-electoral alliance between them, they nevertheless presented themselves to the electorate as members of a coalition. Despite the differences in the political traditions that they represented, their cooperation in the government, though of recent date, demonstrated a basic similarity of programs and aims. The two conservative parties, the Liberals and the remaining elements of the *Uomo Qualunque* Party, then in the process of disintegration, made an alliance within the framework of the so-called National Bloc. Various monarchist groups and the MSI, which after its organizational drive in the past years presented itself for the first time to the voters, made up the extreme right. Both of these groups lacked an original program of their own, and frequently borrowed, though without much coherence, the programs of others. Their major attraction was their ardent anti-Communism and their general appeal to the values of the past. Monarchism and Fascism, though discredited by history, still exercised a considerable appeal to those who during the twenty years of Fascist rule enjoyed a privileged status, or to some of the younger people, who not having had the direct experience of Fascism, were lured by its exaltation of an epoch of great ideals and patriotic values. These were irrational manifestations aroused by a romantic attachment to the past; the followers of these parties, especially the neo-Fascists, were nicknamed "the nostalgic ones" by the public at large.

Despite the number of political parties involved, it became quite evident as soon as the electoral campaign got under way that the contest would be almost exclusively between the Popular Front and Christian Democracy. The other parties inevitably were relegated to secondary positions.

A fundamental tactic of DC propaganda was to appeal directly to the electorate, in an attempt to induce it to give the party all its votes, in preference to the smaller parties which had no possibility of effectively opposing the Social-Communists. Communism was the enemy to be defeated; only a mass party such as Christian Democracy, representing the values of the Catholic Church and of Western civilization, could save the country from Communism; consequently, the votes that were cast for other parties, even if they were members of the democratic alignment, were lost votes in the effort to contain Communism.

In the course of the close electoral campaign, Communists and Christians Democrats exhausted the entire range of polemic arguments. The Social-Communists concentrated most of their propaganda efforts on two themes—the subservience of the DC to the Vatican and to the United States. The DC exploited the fears of the middle classes of a Communist victory, in view of the close party ties with Moscow, and the religious sentiment existing on all social levels and especially strong among the female voters. The help of the Church, especially through the activities of the lower clergy, in this connection proved to be most important.

THE ISSUES AT STAKE

The anti-Communist campaign, which had started in the summer and autumn of 1947, reached its highest pitch during the months preceding April 1948. Directly or indirectly, foreign political issues dominated internal issues. The gradual absorption of the East European countries into the Communist camp and the methods by which this was achieved, the increasing Soviet military buildup on the Western borders, these were all elements that aided the propaganda efforts of the democratic parties. They demonstrated graphically the reality of the choice facing the voter: that it was a choice not only between two parties and two programs, but between two opposed concepts of government, between two worlds with different and antagonistic values. In addition the DC succeeded in convincing a large part of the electorate that this was the most important of all the elections that had been held and that if a clear condemnation of Communism were not forthcoming, it might be the last time this would be possible. To illustrate this thesis, Czechoslovakia was pointed to as an example of what can happen when a Communist Party, though in the minority, succeeds in seizing power and installs a so-called People's Democracy by means of a coup d'etat. The tactics employed by the Czechoslovak Communists, it was said, could be applied by the PCI in the event of a Communist victory. The analogy was not too convincing since the Italian Communists could not have relied, as the Czechoslovak Communists had, on the support of the Red Army; in fact, if they had tried to take power by violent means, they would have certainly

191

provoked the military intervention of the Western powers. Nevertheless the Czechoslovak coup d'etat, which had taken place less than two months earlier, profoundly impressed public opinion and certainly influenced the vote.

The electoral battle was heated, and it was followed with active interest by the United States and the Soviet Union. The importance of the elections transcended national boundaries, since its results would necessarily affect the equilibrium of the opposing blocs. It was quite clear that a victory of the democratic parties would tie Italy to the Western bloc, while a Social-Communist success would have pushed the nation toward a neutralist role in foreign policy, a preliminary to the country's slipping gradually into the Soviet camp.

The campaign effort of the democratic parties was therefore abundantly supported by financial aid from the other side of the Atlantic, while the PCI received help through the Cominform, which had been recently established. In the U.S.A. Italo-Americans were encouraged to write to their relatives, urging them to vote for democracy and against Communism.

The prospect of new economic aid from the Marshall Plan, which had been announced in June 1947, also made a considerable impression on the public and was received with enthusiasm by the DC, while the Social-Communists rejected it as "an imperialist attempt to enslave the country." The aid was necessary in order to continue the country's economic consolidation and to help in solving problems endemic to Italian society, such as unemployment and the impoverished south. The recognition of these necessities could not be without weight on the vote of those who, although they rejected political ties with one or the other of the two blocs, recognized the essential need to find solutions to the many social problems still in suspense and to raise the standard of living.

The Anglo-Franco-American tripartite declaration on Trieste also exerted an important influence on the elections. The three Western powers, having arrived at the conclusion

192

that it was impossible to choose a governor for the Free Territory, committed themselves to act in favor of a return of the city of Trieste to Italian sovereignty. The announcement was made at a particularly well chosen time, at the beginning of March; it eventually reinforced the position of the De Gasperi Government and was widely exploited by the democratic parties in the course of the campaign. Since the April election was to decide not only on an internal course, but also determine the international position of the country, it was easy to demonstrate, by pointing to the tripartite declaration, who Italy's friends were.

THE RESULTS

The elections took place in an orderly fashion without incidents, despite the heated tenor of the campaign. The participation was extremely high, one of the highest yet observed in a democratic country. From 89 per cent of eligible voters registered in the preceding election (June 2, 1946, at the time of the Institutional Referendum and the elections to the Constituent Assembly), the figure rose to 92 per cent. It was evident that the electorate fully realized the decisive importance of its vote.

The high percentage of voters could also be attributed to the efforts of the parties, especially the democratic parties. It was certain that the left, aided by its organizational structure and the control it exercized over its adherents and sympathizers, but even more so by the deep political involvement of the masses, galvanized by class warfare, would exploit its electoral potential down to the last vote. For that reason, the parties of the center and the DC in particular used all their resources and efforts in mobilizing those moderate elements among the electorate who, due to indifference or protest, chose to remain on the margin of political life. The high percentage of those voting—the figures for which were announced after the closing of the polls—indicated that the center parties had succeeded in their aims; as a result the prognostications of the returns

193

which had been uncertain during the better part of the campaign, at the last moment favored them. The final results were announced two days later, surpassing by far the predictions. The anticipated victory of the DC was transformed into a triumph. The party's vote had risen from approximately 8,000,000 in 1946 to 12,712,562, corresponding to 48.4 per cent of all votes cast. The Socialist and the Communist Parties, who on two separate ballots had received, respectively, 4,758,129 and 4,356,686 votes in 1946, totaled 8,137,047 for the joint list of the Popular Front, a loss of almost a million votes.

An overall look at the electoral results will permit a more complete analysis.

Parties	Votes Cast	Per Cent	Seats Chamber	Seats Senate
Democratic People's Front for Freedom, Peace and Work (Social-Communists)	8,137,047	31.0	183	72
Socialist Unity (Social Democrats)	1,858,346	7.1	33	8
Republican Party	652,477	2.5	9	3
Christian Democracy	12,712,562	48.4	304	131
National Bloc (PLI and Uomo Qual.)	1,004,889	3.8	19	7
Monarchist Party	729,174	2.8	14	3
Ital. Social Movement	526,670	2.0	6	—
Other parties	598,985	—		9

The most striking result of the balloting was the gains of the Christian Democrats, who in comparison with the preceding elections gained an additional five million votes. The DC's increase in strength was due to the high percentage of voters and to the losses sustained by all the other parties, from the Republicans to the *Uomo Qualunque* Party, with the sole exception of the Social Democrats. Compared with the results in 1946, the Republicans fell from 4.5 per cent to 2.5 per cent, the Liberal Party and the Qualunquists, united in the National Bloc, totaled only 3.8 per cent, while in the preceding elections they had won 6.8 per cent and 5.3 per cent respectively, with a total of 2,770,058. votes.

Why did some parties, particularly those who based their campaign on a political program similar to the DC, with a similar anti-Communist position, sustain such losses? The effort to concentrate the votes on a major party, as the most powerful bulwark against Social-Communism, would explain this phenomenon. It proved that one of the electoral arguments most frequently used by the DC—not to disperse the votes—had borne fruit. Only the Social Democrats did not suffer the general loss of votes that all the minor parties experienced; they even won a modest success. They not only harvested the dissident and auto-nomist Socialist votes, the votes of those who had followed Saragat after he had split away, but also those who favored the formation of a third force, and there were quite a number of them, who though anti-Communist preferred in internal politics to exercise a role of maintaining a balance between the Social-Communists and the Christian Democrats. The hopes of the supporters of a third force, however, did not last long; the vote for the Social Democrats in the 1953 elections, after four years of quadripartite government, was to be considerably reduced.

Considering the split in the Socialist Party that occurred in January 1947, the April 1948 election did not represent, despite the loss of one million votes, an important regression of the extreme left as compared with preceding elections. The losses it had sustained in northern Italy, where the Social-Democrats had strong positions, were compensated for in part by the progress it made in the South.

However, there is no doubt that in general political terms the "Popular Front," which was expected to gain strength, was defeated in the election of April 1948. Since revolutionary action had become inconceivable, considering the international situation, the left's only prospect was a long and wearing period of opposition.

Another important indication of the lineup within the extreme left was the upset in the equilibrium between Socialists and Communists, which was established in 1946. The extreme left voters shifted to the Communists, as proved by the Communist gain in preferencial votes. They sent 131 deputies to parliament, compared with 52 Socialist deputies. The loss in strength of the Socialists with regard to their allies was bound to increase and was to become one of the most important reasons pushing them, after 1953, to reconsider their own political positions.

THE FIFTH DE GASPERI GOVERNMENT

The victory of the democratic parties was greeted with satisfaction in all the Western European countries and the United States. It was interpreted not only as a victory for democracy in Italy but even as an event of importance for Europe, considering that it broke a series of continuous successes of international Communism. It had the effect of reviving the confidence of all the democratic peoples of Europe in their capacity to resist Communist pressure.

The DC with its 304 deputies in the Chamber held the absolute majority, while in the Senate it had a relative majority with 131 out of 237 seats. The DC would have been capable therefore, with the support of some independent votes in the Senate, to govern alone. De Gasperi, however, proving great foresight, preferred to reestablish the quadripartite alliance with the PRI, PLI and the Social Democrats. This was a fair appraisal of the will of the democratic electorate, which had in the emergency situation chosen the DC to defeat Communism.

Another important consideration which may have influenced De Gasperi to align himself in the government with the other democratic parties was the possibility of limiting the Catholic integralism of certain groups inside

196

and outside the DC, by the presence of political forces with non-confessional character, such as the Social Democrats, Republicans and Liberals. The constitution of such an equilibrium of forces was characteristic of De Gasperi's moderate leanings; though a devout Catholic, he was opposed to all manifestations of intransigent confessionalism, considering them a threat to the leading role of the DC and of the broad national representation assumed by the Catholic party after the war.

In accordance with custom, a few days after the elections .De Gasperi handed his resignation to the new President of the Republic, Luigi Einaudi, the economist who had saved the lira and who had been elected to the presidency on May 11th. De Gasperi was then asked to form a new government, which he presented on May 23rd, in which all four coalition center parties were represented. Thus the quadripartite experiment, which had started in December 1947, and which for a number of years was to assure the stability of the country, was resumed.

14.

PART THREE

The years of quadripartite government, 1948-1953

CHAPTER 1

CONTRASTS WITHIN THE COALITION

The five-year period, extending from the 1948 to the 1953 elections, is commonly known as the period of the "four-party coalition" (*quadripartito*) that is, a governmental experiment based on a large majority, comprising the four center parties: Christian Democracy, the Socialist Party of Italian Workers (Social Democrats) the Liberal and the Republican parties.

After three years of difficult combinations, the alliance of the four moderate democratic parties, cemented by the Social-Communist defeat, appeared to provide the ideal solution for government stability. It was believed that it would be able to guarantee a long period of relative internal peace, which would aid the consolidation of the institutional structures of the young Italian democracy and the national economy. In reality, even the quadripartite formula, despite its relatively long duration, proved only a transitory political solution. After 1953, when the first signs of crisis appeared, a period began in which many attempts were made to revalorize and relaunch the formula. They all failed and condemned the country to long years of immobilism, an obvious sign that the political experience of 1948-1953 was tied to specific conditions and its limits circumscribed.

The limitations of the quadripartite formula were multiple, the most evident one from the beginning being the coexistence within the same majority of forces openly progressive and eager for a renewal, the left Catholics and

201

the Social Democrats, with those who were clearly conservative, the Liberal Party and right-wing currents in the DC. Although the Social Democrats had abandoned many of their early Marxist positions, they demanded a gradual enlargement of the powers of the state in the economic field; this increase of power was to be brought about through a program of reforms, which included nationalization of the key industries. Finally, they envisaged the institution by the state of a permanent form of planned economy, which would, however, respect the fundamental liberties of the democratic processes. The left-wing Catholics not only accepted the basic principles of this program, they had even arrived at more radical solutions. The Liberals and the conservative tendency within the DC took exactly the opposite view; they presented themselves to the public as the most ardent defenders of free enterprise and private initiative. According to the conservative Catholics and Liberals, the function of the state was to guarantee social and political order, to secure respect of the fundamental liberties, and to carry out a flexible and efficient administration. They acknowledged the state's right to engage in certain marginal economic activities (railroad and maritime transport, public works, such as roads, acqueducts and bridges), but they conceived of this activity as directed exclusively toward the creation of more favourable conditions for the evolution and development of private initiative. In reality, these policies were conceived in defense of the privileges of large industry and the landowners.

These conflicting positions came into focus over the question of the agrarian reform. The reform was supported by the Republicans, Social Democrats and the majority of the Demo-Christians, but it was opposed by the right-wing current inside the DC. The Liberals assumed an openly critical attitude, which led to their withdrawal from the government and their refusal to participate in all the subsequent De Gasperi Governments. However, although the members of the four-party coalition were divided by ideological and programmatic questions, their common alliance against the Communist menace generally proved stronger than the causes of division.

It is difficult to understand the quadripartite coalition without keeping in mind the atmosphere of international tension of these years. This was the period of the height of the cold war. Soviet pressure on the Western borders was increasing steadily, causing new alliances among the various nations and new alignments of forces. The anti-Communist struggle dominated the international scene and had immediate repercussions on the internal political situation in various countries. It forced the parties to disregard their divergencies and ideological conflicts and to subordinate them to the necessity of constituting a common front against Communist infiltration. The result was a clear lineup of forces, excluding intermediate positions, and led to unnatural alliances.

A political formula other than the quadripartite would have been difficult to bring about in these years and could not have guaranteed the political stability necessary to the country. A campaign in favor of a democratic Third Force, comprising Republicans, Social Democrats and Liberals, which could serve as a wedge between the DC and the Social-Communists, was carried on for some time but had only a passing success among some groups of intellectuals of the democratic left. An agreement between Republicans, Social Democrats and Liberals, outside of the possibility of any success in carrying out a common program, because of their ideological differences, would have in reality weakened the anti-Communist front. In addition, it would have been very difficult for these parties to differentiate themselves from the DC since the DC, because of a number of tendencies within it, ranging from the progressive left to the conservative right, encompassed a wide arc in Italian political life. The only common difference with the DC was the lay character of the three parties as opposed to the confessionalism of the DC, which at the time when the Catholic influence in the country was growing, had become especially accentuated. Anti-clericalism, however, did not hold sufficient attractiveness as a political cause: it could not have had enough appeal to the masses, and these parties in any case would have been limited to the role of a political minority.

The strong influence of the conflict between the Soviet Union and the United States on the internal political situation in Italy has been mentioned earlier. When the Italian Government accepted Marshall Plan aid in the summer of 1947, it made a most important choice, which anticipated a number of other decisions. This choice expressed the will of the country to fall in line with the Western powers in the struggle against Communism. As has been indicated, the electoral campaign in 1948 evolved around the issue of Communism and anti-Communism, and the success of the DC was essentially a triumph against Communism and for the values of Western civilization. The adherence of Italy to the Atlantic Pact occurred in 1949; it was the natural consequence of the choice made by the government in 1947 and approved by the popular vote of April 18, 1948.

It was logical that quadripartite rule represented a valid political formula at a period of powerful internal and international tension. Anti-Communism, which was shared by all the coalition partners, and De Gasperi's ability to mediate between the most varying political tendencies were the two forces that sustained the four-party government during the five years of its existence. The gradual decrease of internal tension, the stabilization of the international situation into an "equilibrium between powerless powers," and finally De Gasperi's death shook the alliance and led to its gradual but inevitable break-up.

QUADRIPARTITE RULE AND THE MINOR PARTIES:
LIBERALS AND SOCIAL DEMOCRATS

Even during the high point of the quadripartite rule, contradictions between the parties that participated in it were manifest. Both the Social Democrats and the Liberals withdrew their representatives from the government fairly soon, although they consistently supported the government in Parliament. The Social Democrats were the first to reassume their independence of action, thereby causing a government reshuffle in December 1949. They participated again in De Gasperi's sixth government in January 1950, but left it again some time later, after which they remained without any government responsibility for a number of years. The attitude of the Social Democrats was influenced in a decisive way by the complex vicissitudes of the movement toward Socialist reunification.

After the split of the Socialist Party, in January 1947, the left-wing tendency inside the PSDI and the right-wing tendency of the PSI persevered in an effort to reunite the two sister parties, but this possibility soon proved quite remote.

The 28th Congress of the PSI, held in Florence in May 1949, concluded with a new victory for the "fusionists," that is, the tendency favoring close collaboration with the Communists. This restatement of Socialist extremism resulted in a further loss of independence from the Communists, and made any hopes of reunification even more chimeric. The immediate consequence of the PSI Congress was a further split. The splinter group led by Giuseppe Romita, though anti-Soviet, equally opposed participation in the government coalition, being against the policies of rearmament and membership in the Atlantic Pact, in line with the traditional Socialist hostility to military alliances. The Romita group intended to act as a mediating force between the PSI and the PSLI, but when it appeared that this attempt was doomed to failure because of the hardening of the respective positions, Romita directed his effort to preparing the ground for a merger of all the anti-Communist Socialist forces. This was to take place in 1951, after further splits had occurred both within the PSI and the PSLI. The secessionists converged in the Socialist Unified Party PSU (*Partito Socialista Unificato*), a new formation created by Romita as rallying ground for dissidents from both Socialist parties, who were equally opposed to collaboration in the Popular Front and with the quadripartite coalition. Finally, in March 1951, the leaderships of PSLI and of PSU reached an agreement on a fusion, and the new party definitely assumed the name of Italian Socialist Democratic Party (PSDI: *Partito Socialista Democratico Italiano*), which has remained unchanged up to the present.

The fusion of the two groups was accomplished on the basis of reciprocal concessions. The PSLI agreed to withdraw its representatives from the government and the PSU accepted the Atlantic policy. The pressure of dissident Socialist groups thus represented an element of considerable uncertainty in the relationship between the PSLI and the government. Every step toward reunification between the various Social Democratic groups corresponded to a hardening of the PSLI position within the government, until its final withdrawal in 1951.

The collaboration of the Liberals was equally uncertain. In January 1950 they rejected an invitation by De Gasperi to participate in his sixth cabinet, whose formation had become necessary as a result of the resignation of the PSLI ministers and by the Prime Minister's decision to make important personnel changes in various government departments. The government reshuffle indicated that De Gasperi and the DC had decided to proceed with greater speed in instituting reforms, now that the problems of reconstruction had been overcome. These the DC was obliged to carry out in order to realize its program commitments. The most important of the projected reforms was the agrarian reform. It had been planned since 1947, and it envisaged a considerable expropriation, though indemnified, of large landed properties (*latifondo*) that were poorly cultivated and sometimes completely neglected by their owners and their distribution to landless peasant families. The reform, which will be dealt with in more detail, was viewed in conservative circles as a revolutionary measure, and the Liberal Party, which by then had openly assumed their representation, had no other choice but to dissociate itself from the government. After repeated delays the government demonstrated its intention to commit itself to carry out this important measure.

Nevertheless, both the Liberals and the Social Democrats, though at different times they had withdrawn their representatives from the government, still gave it their support in Parliament.

The most faithful of the three parties allied with the DC turned out to be the small Republican Party, which under the leadership of Randolfo Pacciardi remained in the government without interruption until the political elections of 1953.

In conclusion, three De Gasperi Governments succeeded each other between 1948 and 1953. The first one lasted from May 1948 (PSLI, PRI, PLI and DC), to Dec. 1949, the second, in which the Liberals did not participate, from January 1950 until July 1951, and finally, the third, from July 1951 until the political election of 1953 (DC and PRI). These governments were different versions of the same governing formula, and the forces upon which they relied, remained, except for some brief interruptions, the same for the entire duration of the legislature.

THE TENDENCIES WITHIN THE DC

One of the circumstances that contributed most to the continuance of the quadripartite coalition in the years 1948-1953 was the uninterrupted presence of Alcide De Gasperi at the government's helm. De Gasperi was obliged to exercise all his seasoned abilities as a statesman in order to hold together the heterogeneous forces that supported his middle-of-the-road program. His role as mediator was not limited to the parties of his coalition but extended as well to the various tendencies within his own party. In this additional respect, his task was even more time-consuming and wearing.

As was true of the *Partito Popolare*, predecessor of the

DC, the party represented a wide range of political positions, from a socialist left to a reactionary and monarchist extreme right. The coexistence within the same party of forces that were so diverse was made possible by the party's close ties with the Catholic Church, whose influence on it, and consequently on the government in this period, developed to the extent that it encroached on the independence of the state itself.

It was inevitable that the different forces soon organized into tendencies, with their own organizational hierarchies, press organs and activist groups. Each attempted to prevail upon the others and extend its influence within the government branches and in the party directorate, in order to orient it according to its own principles and programs.

Considering the number, strength, and the historic reasons for the existence of these currents, any attempt to eradicate them and lead the party back to a unified platform would have been in vain. From a tactical point of view, a unified program would not even have been desirable, in view of the fact that its many varying political positions provided the DC with the possibility of presenting itself as a progressive and a conservative party at the same time. This could be translated into considerable electoral advantage for the party, toward which popular as well as bourgeois votes converged. On the other hand, the necessarily conflicting activity of the various tendencies severely tried party unity; in order to prevent a schism, which would have had disastrous consequences in the country, De Gasperi was compelled continuously to mediate among the various tendencies and develop a circumspect and moderate governmental program, keeping a middle road between the extremist wings of the party. This policy, which caused discontent among both left- and right-wing elements, was possible while the center, which represented the party majority, remained under the strong leadership of De Gasperi and while his leadership was indisputable.

At least five tendencies could be distinguished within the DC during the years of the quadripartite government; some

208

are difficult to characterize from the point of view of both ideology and program, being tied as they were to the power positions of the DC leaders, whose ideas they reflected. Others, although they recognized the authority of a "leader," based their action within the party on a precise doctrine and political line, elaborated through study groups, discussions and meetings.

The most important nucleus of the party supported the centrist policies of De Gasperi. The greater part of the old guard, such as Attilio Piccioni and Mario Scelba, who had been activists in the pre-Fascist *Partito Popolare*, belonged to this group. These men, immediately after the fall of Fascism, had become the natural heirs of the old *Partito Popolare* and were the principal organizers of the new Christian Democracy. Their program was the official program of the party, but its reformist orientation was gradually weakened due to the necessity to mediate between the various antagonistic tendencies within and outside the party and to retain the support of the Church and moderate public opinion. The ideological motivations that had originally inspired De Gasperi's center positions were gradually abandoned and reduced to a technique to maintain party unity and assure the party's success at the polls.

The extreme right wing of the party was represented by about 70 deputies and senators (out of a total of 435 in the Chamber and Senate), some of whom held monarchist views and represented the economic interests of the most important conservative groups. They were very close to the Vatican, and frequently affiliated with the "Catholic Action." For a few years, after 1951, they were known as *vespisti*, because of their habit of meeting at the *Vespa*[1] Club in Rome. As an ideological vehicle they espoused rabid anti-Communism and were systematically hostile to any reformist initiatives of the party. They opposed the measures for agrarian reform and the increase in local autonomies, two traditional aspects of the Catholic political program.

---

[1] The name of a famous motor scooter.

The party's left wing was made up of three groups. One was headed by the future President of the Republic, Giovanni Gronchi; one was composed of trade-unionists, and a third was grouped around the review *Cronache Sociali*. This latter was the most lively tendency, because of its intellectual contribution and the seriousness of its aims; its members were called *Dossettiani*, after the name of their leader, Giuseppe Dossetti, professor of church law at the Catholic University in Milan.

Originally, the first two groups formed one tendency, under the leadership of Giovanni Gronchi, who, as early as the time of the *Partito Popolare*, had been a trade-union organizer. Later on the trade-unionists separated from the group, concentrating their efforts on increasing the independence of the Catholic trade-union movement from the party.

Both groups, those around Gronchi and the trade-unionists, fought for reformist policies, administrative decentralization, the strengthening of local administrative autonomies, the land reform, and a major role to be taken by the state in the economy, including the nationalization of some of the key industries. The final aim of these reforms, which was approved by the entire Demo-Christian left, was the establishment of greater social equality, a more just distribution of the national wealth between all classes and a greater participation on the part of all the popular classes in the government of the state. This was a program that came very close to the Socialist positions. Gronchi was also one of the first leaders of the DC to envisage the necessity of an alliance between Catholics and the Nenni Socialists, according to the governmental formula later to be called the "opening to the left." After the 1953 election and the failure of numerous attempts to reestablish the quadripartite combination, this solution appeared as the only formula that could assure a greater measure of stability to the country.

The Dossetti tendency of the DC was the most representative among the currents of the left. It included the youngest and most politically educated elements of the party;

almost all, with the exception of a few leaders, were formed politically in the last years of the war, or in the period immediately following it. They brought a dedication and seriousness into party politics which however were frequently suffocated by rigid and intransigent orthodoxy.

Although the political program of the Dossetti group was the same as the programs of the other left-wing currents, it was distinguished by its more profound analysis of social problems and its conviction of the necessity for a closer tie-in between political activities and the social doctrine of the Church—between Catholic morality and political action. The ties between this group and certain sectors of the militant Church were very close, particularly with young priests, who, motivated by a Christian and progressive spirit, engaged in welfare and educational work in direct contact with the masses of workers and peasants. The Dossetti integralism was destined eventually to collide with the moderate and conciliatory position of De Gasperi, who though close to the Church pursued a policy of broad collaboration with laic (non-confessional) elements. Dossetti and his followers were accused by both De Gasperi and the right of indulging in abstractions and of having little practical political sense. Dossetti's ill health and the necessity for him to undergo a period of rest, in addition to the pressures from the right, compelled him to retire from political life in 1951.[1]

After Dossetti's retirement, Giorgio La Pira and Amintore Fanfani, both professors at the Catholic University in Milan, became leaders of this tendency. La Pira rapidly acquired great popularity because of his passionate defense of the poor and humble and because of the extreme simplicity of his ways. A complex personality, he oscillates between evangelical mysticism and astute political realism. He became mayor of Florence in 1951, an office

---

[1] After a few years's absence, Dossetti returned to active politics, running for the office of mayor of Bologna in the administrative elections of 1956. He was defeated, not only because of the traditional strength of the CP in that city, but also because of the prevailing reservations about him.

to which he has been reelected twice, in 1956 and in 1960. Fanfani quickly emerged as a first-rate statesman and politician. Active, dynamic, possessing great political finesse and open to compromise solutions, he represented a considerable divergence from Dossetti's original position. Fanfani first accepted an office in De Gasperi's Government and later, after 1953, attempted to succeed him as Prime Minister. The history of the DC is tied to a considerable extent to the name and political action of Fanfani, who became the most important architect of the alliance between Catholics and Socialists, and who was the first to head a government of the "opening to the left."

Dossetti's retirement from politics and the emergence of such personalities as Fanfani changed considerably the character and the aims of this tendency, orienting it toward more direct participation in politics in place of the specific political and religious dedication that was Dossetti's unique contribution. Under the new impetus, the group split into two currents, that of the so-called "Base" and that of the "Democratic Initiative," which, propelled by Fanfani's activism, greatly increased its influence and following. The "Basists" remained for a number of years closer to Dossetti's inspiration and ideas, while the "Democratic Initiative" became completely involved in the struggle for control of the party. Later, however, the "Base" adherents too abandoned their wait-and-see attitude and began to assume positions of responsibility, first in local administrations, then in the government. These groups constituted the most homogeneous and best-trained political leaders which the DC in its twenty years in power was able to provide for the country.

THE PARTIES OF THE EXTREME LEFT

A report, presented in the Central Committee of the Italian Communist Party, attempts to justify the unquestionable defeat of the Social-Communists in the April 1948

212

elections with the following arguments: "The results of April 18th were determined largely by the intervention of foreign imperialism, by religious terrorism, by illicit pressures applied by the state apparatus, and by a large number of astutely organized intrigues. The Demo-Christian 'victory' is a result of the violation of the electoral freedom of the Italian people." These and similar accusations indicated the evident embarrassment of the leadership of the largest left-wing party in explaining to their own electorate the battle they had lost after they had made many bold forecasts on the eve of the elections, predicting the victory of the People's Bloc.

The same embarrassment and signs of disorientation were clearly manifest within the ranks of the PSI, judging from the interventions and discussion that took place at the party's twenty-seventh Congress, held in Genoa in June 1948 in order to clarify the reasons for the electoral defeat. The secretary of the party at the time, Lelio Basso, granted that "the April 1948 elections must be considered as one of the general aspects of the reflux of the working and democratic class movement in the entire capitalist world, under the impact of a vigorous counter-offensive of conservative forces." This was a realistic appraisal of the situation; nevertheless for a few years longer the Socialist leaders avoided deducing from it the implications that a new policy was warranted. On the contrary, the final motion of this Congress, as well as of the following one held in Florence in May 1949, reaffirmed the alliance with the Communist Party.

In an attempt to camouflage the crisis of confidence which had developed inside the two parties as a result of the electoral defeat, and also to distract the attention of the masses, the extreme left, almost immediately following the elections, transferred its activity to the trade-union level, instigating a series of agitations, strikes and street mani-festations. These were not intended as a prelude to a revolutionary effort, now that lawful action had irremediably failed; it was merely a tactical diversion. The possibility of violent action with a view to the conquest of power was

213

more than ever outside the plans of the PCI. The events following the attempt on Palmiro Togliatti's life confirm this.

In an atmosphere of considerable tension, on July 14th, 1948 a fanatically nationalist Sicilian student, Antonio Pallante, fired four revolver shots at Togliatti, the PCI leader, wounding him seriously. The reaction of the masses throughout Italy was immediate. The workers in the large cities spontaneously moved into the streets. A general strike was proclaimed, the major industries in Turin were occupied by workers, and road blocks were put up rapidly in Genoa, Turin and Milan. Armed workers' militia were quickly organized and equipped with weapons, which had been well hidden since the partisan resistance. One word from the party directorate would have been enough to transform the street demonstrations into an armed insurrection. But the word was not given, the PCI leaders themselves undertook the task of pacifying the masses, and after a few days normal conditions were reestablished.

The most visible and immediate consequence of the July 14th episodes, which were a quite open threat to the state and which had occurred after a long series of strikes and agitations, whose basic objectives were also of a political nature, was the break in trade-union unity between the three mass parties. From 1944 to 1949 one trade-union organization, the Italian General Confederation of Labor (CGIL: *Confederazione Generale Italiana del Lavoro*) had represented all workers of whatever political orientation, from the Communists to the Catholics. But the preeminence of the PCI within the CGIL and its systematic utilization of the organization for political purposes, in organizing strikes and agitations in support of PCI policies, had aroused protests and uneasiness among the other political currents. The July 14th strike offered a long-awaited opportunity for the Catholics; they left the CGIL and founded the Italian Confederation of Trade Unions (CISL: *Confederazione Italiana dei Sindacati Lavoratori*). The Social Democrats followed soon after and founded in March 1950 their own trade-union organization, the Italian Union of

Labor (UIL: *Unione Italiana del Lavoro*). Thus the profound conflict, which existed on the political level between the parties of the extreme left and the parties of progressive democracy and the moderates, was broadened, as was inevitable, to embrace the trade unions.

In a long-term perspective, the consequences of the July 14th quasi-insurrection were of the utmost importance to the future of the left-wing parties. Now that the state had been strengthened, any violent action aimed at the conquest of power would result in failure and would cause the disappearance of the PCI from the political scene for many years, but the refusal of the party leaders to transform the spontaneous mass movement, inspired by the attempt against Togliatti, into an insurrection revealed to the masses and to their adversaries the powerlessness of the Communist Party, and the obvious contradiction existing between the threats of revolution that the party had for years brandished at the Italian bourgeoisie and its real capacity for action.

Thus, in a few months, the PCI suffered two major defeats, which, although it was not immediately manifest, had a profound influence on the party's future. It would still gain other successes, such as that in the 1953 elections, whose results can be explained by a special situation which shall be dealt with later, but the gradual elimination of all possibilities for the conquest of power was to condemn it to a long period of stagnation. After 1948 the Communist Party was for many years left with no other hope but the victory of international Communism in the struggle between the two great-power blocs. As the manifestations of the cold war between the West and the East became increasingly harsh, Communist leaders were induced to believe that a decisive confrontation was practically at hand and that the victory of the USSR in Europe would in a brief time also upset the Italian internal situation. In the years from 1949 to 1951, the Communist Party oriented its political action in this sense, taking positions that were more and more differentiated from those of the PSI. It concentrated its efforts both inside and outside Parliament on overall opposition, whose main objective was to combat the determined pro-Western foreign policies of the centrist De Gasperi Governments. As they had in the case of the Marshall Plan, the Communists organized campaigns against Italy joining the Atlantic Pact, against rearmament and against the establishment of American bases in Italy. Nevertheless, even these efforts proved sterile within a short period, when it became clear that the conflict between the great powers remained far from any resolution for a long time to come. Faced with these realities, even the prospects of a "global" solution, which would eventually put Italian Communism in power, appeared unrealistic. In any event the doctrine of competitive coexistence finally prolonged indefinitely this evolution. The political crisis which inevitably followed the realization of this fact, together with the ideological crisis that had been provoked by de-Stalinization and by the Hungarian revolt of November 1956, forced the PCI on the defensive in the attempt to maintain its power positions within the local administrations as well as its electoral strength.

CHAPTER 2

ECONOMIC PROGRAM AND SOCIAL REFORMS OF THE QUADRIPARTITE COALITION

The period from 1948 to 1953, that is, the years of the quadripartite coalition, was particularly marked by advances in the economic field. Governmental stability, relative social peace, which had been achieved as a result of the unequivocal vote of April 18, 1948, and, above all, the anti-inflationary policies of the Minister of Finance, Luigi Einaudi—which since the end of 1948 had met with undoubted success—had encouraged the state and private initiative to adopt new programs of improvements and economic expansion.

The index of industrial production in 1954 indicated an increment of 71 per cent as compared with that of the year 1938, the pre-war year in which production had reached its highest peak. Considering that approximately three years (1945-1948) were needed to repair war damages and to reach the pre-war level of production, the further increase of 71 per cent was attained in less than six years. On the basis of statistical data published by the Central Office of Statistics, it was evident that increases in production had been made in all industrial sectors. The progress was especially rapid in some fields, such as petro-chemical production. Thanks to important reserves of methane gas, which had been discovered in the Po Valley in 1946, and its intensive exploitation undertaken by the state enterprise

Italian General Oil Company (AGIP: *Azienda Generale Italiana Petroli*)[1] the production of petro-chemicals in 1954 was approximately 150 times that of 1938. Increases above the average were realized equally in chemical, mechanical, electrical and metallurgical industries.

These production increases and those realized in the years to follow were in an important part due to the benefits of the Marshall Plan. From April 1948 until December 1952 about $1,515 million were injected into the Italian economy by the ERP (European Recovery Program) program, as the Marshall Plan was officially called. One-fifth of this amount was utilized for the acquisition of machinery, predominantly industrial in kind. These goods were resold to private business and the proceeds from the sales amounting to about 664 billion lire constituted a fund called "countervalue fund" that the government destined for further public work investments. The Italian Government used them partly in industry, partly in agriculture, construction and in public utility works, predominantly within the framework of the plan for the development of the South.

The history of government interventions in the economy of the country in the years 1948-1953 merits special mention because of their economic importance, as well as their political significance. Reconstruction having been completed, the buying power of the lira stabilized and the political situation consolidated, the country expected that the government would now begin to face some of the "basic" problems inherent in the economic and social structure of the country.

The duties of a truly democratic government could not be limited to the establishment of a parliamentarian and multi-party system. Problems that dated back to the achievement of Italian unity and, with the exception of some timid attempts at solutions, that had been postponed by all the successive governments and regimes had to be faced with determination and resolved. This was an unconditional

---

[1] In 1952 AGIP was incorporated into ENI (see pp. 233 and 300).

necessity if the popular masses who were still under extreme left-wing influence were to be won over to the cause of democracy and if the support were to be kept of those who had voted against Communism on April 18th in condemnation of its methods and spirit, although they shared some of the Communist Party's demands for social justice. The commitments made by the government parties could not be put off any longer; they had been too widely affirmed and the country's expectation was too great.

THE LAND REFORM

Various instances of the occupation of uncultivated, or semi-cultivated lands, which had occurred in Sicily and in other areas of Southern Italy had prompted the government to act. De Gasperi, supported by the center and left-wings of the DC and despite the open opposition of the conservative forces inside and outside of his party, decided to present two projects for land reform laws, which had been by then for several years under study and in the process of formulation. The first was the law for the Sila, named after a zone in Calabria, which was the object of the reform. It had been approved by the Council of Ministers on November 15, 1949. It was voted by Parliament, although with a few amendments, and became law on May 15, 1950. The second project for a law (the so-called *stralcio* law) envisaged a program of reforms on a much broader range than the first one, but with narrower limits than the project originally envisaged; it was presented to Parliament on March 17, 1950, and enacted on October 21st.

The territories that came under the reform comprised a total of 585,485 hectares.[1] In each territory an autonomous agency was established to carry out the complicated processes of expropriation, subdivision and distribution. The data

---

[1] one hectare = 2.4711 acres. The country's total of cultivated land is 20,958,500 hectares.

concerning expropriation in the various territories are the following (in hectares):

	Hectares Expropriated
Po Valley (Romagna)	45,697
Maremma and Fucino (Tuscany, Lazio)	207,406
Apulia and Lucania	199,368
Calabria	11,342
Sila (Calabria)	73,274
Sicily	45,915
Sardinia	2,582

Taking into account another 60,000 hectares that had been acquired by the land reform agencies, either through exchanges or by direct acquisitions, the total came near to 700,000 hectares envisaged by the *stralcio* law. This figure does not include the major part of the territories subject to expropriation in Sicily (approximately 200,000 hectares), because the execution of the reform in Sicily was not entrusted to the national government but to a specialized agency, constituted for that purpose by the Sicilian Regional Government.

The criteria according to which expropriations were carried out varied in the two laws. According to the first law, covering the Sila region where the territories were sufficiently homogeneous, both in quality and output, properties exceeding 300 hectares were subject to expropriation. In the areas subject to the *stralcio* law, whose character varied considerably from region to region, a different criterion was applied. The criteria of expropriation of any land unit varied according to its total output by the unit, or output per hectare. The *stralcio* law, contrary to the Sila law, did not stipulate any limits to exemptions beyond which the mechanism of expropriation would become operative; though it did stipulate that so-called model farm properties should be excluded from expropriation, that is, farms managed with modern techniques, in which labor was considerably mechanized and the productivity very high.

Compensation was paid for the expropriated properties

to the legitimate owners according to average market prices. The expropriated land was then distributed by means of a *tirage a sort* or drawing lots to peasant families who applied for it. After a period of two years, the recipients were to begin to pay yearly installments of about $25 for a period of 30 years, after which they definitely acquired ownership of the land.

Fifty per cent of the distributed property was constituted by complete farm properties (each on the average of ten hectares), considered sufficient to maintain an entire family; the other 50 per cent was subdivided into fractions (2½ hectares each), which were assigned to peasants who were already proprietors of small pieces of land or who were engaged in some other activity. A total of 109,103[1] families benefited from the land reforms and of those, about three-fourths lived in the South.

The function of the land reform agencies, however, was not limited to the expropriation and distribution of land. Large parts of the terrains subject to expropriation were in such poor condition that they required a major effort to improve, demanding considerable technical means and know-how and important financial investments. For that reason the agencies became involved in the massive work of clearing and irrigation and primarily in the continuing work of technical assistance. The program of construction of farmhouses, to provide housing for the families of the recipients of land, was especially important. Since the reform was introduced, the various agencies have spent a total of about 300 billion lire, of which more than one third has gone for the construction of farmhouses, 70 billion for clearing the land and preparing the soil, 33 billion for the acquisition of machinery, which was lent to the recipients; the remainder was spent for road work, schools, agricultural

---

[1] The social status of the families which benefited from land assignment is the following:

small proprietors	7.6 %
sharecroppers	40.4 %
agricultural laborers	52 %

villages and technical assistance. Judging from the amounts invested, the reform effort of the De Gasperi Government was considerable, doubtless superior to any similar work done in the country previously. Nevertheless the problems of injecting new vitality into, and providing new incentives for, Italian agriculture, and the basic modification of its structure are far from being resolved, nor has the land reform made a decisive contribution toward their solution.

Those who formulated the plan for the reform in the years between 1947 and 1949, and De Gasperi who decided to carry it out, intended the reform to attain two fundamental objectives. One was political—to win over permanently and decisively a broad section of the agricultural population to democracy. Considering the conditions of life among agricultural workers, it was understandable that they were vulnerable to the enticements of extremist political parties.

The Communists on the one hand encouraged them to rebel, and the neo-Fascists and right-wing elements exploited their ignorance, increasing their isolation from and diffidence toward the government and retarding their participation in democratic political life. The authors of the reform thought that by creating a class of small landowners, who along with the land were given property to defend, the new democratic state could be consolidated and this new class would have interest in supporting the state against the attacks of Communism.

The other objective was economic. The reclamation of great land properties and of terrain with poor but extensive cultivation was expected to increase agricultural production and create new prosperity.

Both hypotheses, though valid in theory, seem not to have worked out in practice. The peasant populations who have benefited from the land reform have not significantly changed their political attitude from one of protest, as is evidenced by the electoral results in the land-reform zones. The left-wing parties all too often have had the opportunity to minimize the benefits of the reform and to criticize the methods of its implementation (poor land, difficult to cultivate and with a low output, lack of technical assistance, housing constructed with cheap materials, etc.), and to exploit the jealousies and rivalries which inevitably sprang up among those who had received the land. The benefits accruing from increased production have also been below expectations as well as the return for the capital invested.

The criticism, voiced by politically disinterested observers, of the principles and methods employed to carry out the reform explains in part at least the failure to realize both the political and economic objectives.

The reform, which had been retarded a number of years, was too limited in scope to influence profoundly the political attitudes of a large strata of workers. Since there are approximately six million landless agricultural workers (farm workers and tenant farmers) in Italy, a far greater number than the number of those who benefited from the land reform, it is easy to understand its limited impact. From a strictly economic point of view, the reform failed largely because the expropriated terrains were broken up into too small fractions. This is in contrast to the current trend in modern agricultural economy, which is to regroup small productive units into great or medium-size enterprises. The ever-increasing mechanization in agriculture and the continuing need to introduce both new techniques of production and methods of industrialized production are difficult to reconcile with the existence of small property, exploited on the basis of a family economy. It should also be added that the reform program had not been accompanied by an adequate educational program, not only technical instruction but primarily civic, aimed at raising the agricultural population in the most depressed areas out of a condition of profound divorce from society, so that they might become conscious of their rights and their duties as citizens.

Whatever the evaluation of the success or failure of the land reform, after more than a dozen years in practice, some of the basic problems that it was designed to resolve still occupy the attention of the government, and they have become even more pressing with the disequilibrium that has developed between industry and agriculture as a result of the exceptional industrial growth of the last years. One of the most serious effects of this imbalance is the gradual depopulation of the land, which poses in most urgent terms the need for further government intervention in this sector. In the face of these new problems, solutions of the land-reform type appear to be clearly outdated.

THE QUESTION OF THE SOUTH

At almost the same time that the land reform was under consideration, another fundamental problem had to be faced; that was the development of the South. The land reform concerned more specifically the southern regions and represented an important contribution to the solution of the social and economic problems of this part of the country, but the southern question was of such magnitude and complexity that it required a much greater effort, both in the search for solutions and in the use of the means necessary to carry them out.

The southern problem resulted from the deep cleavage between the economic and social conditions in the provinces of Southern Italy and those in the North and North-Central Italy. In order to resolve the problem and to fill the gap between the two parts of the country the South would have to be raised to the same standard of living and level of progress as the rest of the country.

The socio-political complex of the South corresponds more or less to its geographic divisions. It comprises all of the regions south of the line Rome-Pescara, including the islands and more specifically the regions of the Abruzzi, Molise, Campania, Apulia, Basilicata, Calabria, Sicily and Sardinia. The land surface of these regions is 12,303,763 hectares, corresponding to 42 per cent of the entire Italian peninsula. According to the 1951 census, there were 17,643,318 inhabitants living in the South, that is, 37.43 per cent of the Italian population.

224

These figures, though general, give a sufficiently clear idea of the immensity of the problem. A solution of the southern question would concern over one-third of the Italian people and almost one-half of the national territory.

The literature on the southern question, particularly that of recent date, is of such size that to analyze in specific detail all aspects of the southern question would take up much time and space. The discussion here is limited to underlining those problems that appear essential to an understanding of the essence of the question. The comparative data that follow point up the contrast between the southern and the northern provinces. (The statistics are for the year 1951, unless otherwise indicated):

	South	North-Central Italy
Live birth in excess of stillborn in communities over 100,000 inhabitants (1952)	40,585	20,429
Income per capita (Italy: 100)	58.2	126.1
Consumption of electric power per capita in kwh.	153.1	683.1
Consumption of meat per capita in kg. (Italy 13.4)	7.6	17.1
Number of destitute families (in thousands)—(From the parliamentary investigation on poverty, 1952-1953)	1,160.1	1957.0
Persons per room of habitations (Italy: 1.39)	1.86	1.21
Average income per hectare in thousands of lire (Italy: 265)	230	290
Industrial workers	709,788	3,456,466
Nominal capital of industrial stockholding corporations (in millions of lire)	242.5	30,636.5
Unemployed registered with the labor office in 1952	820,456 (39.6)	1,252,953 (60.4)
Illiterates per 100 inhabitants over 6 years of age (1948)	24.3	5.7

	South	North-Central Italy
Number of radios (1952)	906,515	3,321,094
Underoccupation in agriculture by thousands of days (1952)	359,944.9	351,961.5

Source: SVIMEZ

These data give some of the basic facts. The deep gap between the level of the southern provinces and the other areas in Italy is most clearly manifest in the difference in income and consumption and in the scarcity of industries, the southern area being predominantly based on agricultural and tertiary activities, together with the absence of capital concentrations, which in a society such as the Italian with a predominantly capitalistic structure necessarily wield political influence.

The unemployment (a phenomenon that was in the process of being gradually eliminated by 1963) was about equal in South and North. Underemployment in agriculture[1] is much higher in the southern provinces. This fact is tied to the greater poverty of the soil, and the organizational deficiencies typical of a primitive system of tenancy. Furthermore, the level of culture appears extremely low, considering the high percentage of illiterates, a phenomenon which weighs heavily not only in the present situation but also represents a serious mortgage on any possibility for future development.

On the basis of these figures and summary considerations, it is evident that the South is a strongly depressed area, with a level that is frequently below the level of the poorest regions of southern Europe. However, these figures cannot show the state of material and moral destitution of the

---

[1] Data relative to unemployment in agriculture have been selected since agriculture was by far the most prevalent economic activity in the South in the years referred to in the data, and of major importance to the entire country.

226

southern populations. Hundreds of thousands of people live in primitive conditions, particularly in Calabria and Lucania, the poorest regions. People and animals live together in narrow, unhealthy houses that are more like stables than homes. They lack the most elementary hygienic precautions. Great sectors of the population are undernourished. Their ignorance, superstition, and prejudice are difficult to eradicate because they have almost no relationship with any form of social or political activity.

The reality of the human condition in Southern Italy is dramatically portrayed in the extensive literature on the southern question, from Guido Dorso to Giustino Fortunato, from Carlo Levi to Danilo Dolci (to name only a few among them).

This reality has its roots in historic and economic factors both ancient and of recent origin.

HISTORIC ANTECEDENTS

The poverty of the soil, which once was very fertile,[1] the difficulties of access and communications, the shortage of water courses, particularly if compared to the fertile plains and the navigable streams of the North, are the paramount explanation for the natural conditions of poverty of the South. To the natural differences between South and North should be added the historical and cultural considerations to give a fully rounded picture. While the central and northern regions of Italy remained in contact in the course of the centuries with the centers of European culture, actively participating, sometimes in a determining way, in the process of its formation, the southern areas were subjected to the

---

[1] Definite but limited examples of the fertility of the soil in antiquity still exist; the country around Naples, the area of the Gargano in Apulia, and the coastal stretches in Sicily are still rich and valuable areas of agricultural production.

long and exploitive Spanish domination and remained outside of the general currents until the end of the last century.

The unification of Italy brought the South back into contact with the rest of Europe, but no immediate advantages were derived from it for the area; in fact, in some ways it aggravated the existing uneasy situation. The efforts undertaken by the Italian Government to bring the independent nation up to the level of the major European countries (public works, communications, army, administrative organization) caused an increase in the tax burden, as the result of which the South was further weakened and impoverished. The inhabitants of Milan or Florence, though they often lamented the taxes imposed by the new government, still had a much superior capacity to pay them than the average inhabitant of the South, for whom the levy of the same tax frequently meant hunger or ruin. In addition, the process of industrialization, which had been undertaken in the North, was frequently carried out at the expense of agriculture, which at that time was practically the sole economic activity of the South. For example, in 1887, in order to protect the young industries of the North from foreign competition, the government increased customs tariffs, thus provoking a retaliatory increase in French customs on Italian products. This customs war was doubly ruinous to the South. It resulted in considerably damaging its agriculture and it compelled the southerners to pay higher prices for the products of national industries.

The result of the policies of the new Italian governments was that at the end of the century the disequilibrium between North and South had deepened and had created bitterness and resentment among the southern populations. The relationship between the two Italys have since been profoundly influenced by this situation. The Southerners accused the Rome governments of being under the influence of the Piedmontese (later of the Milanese) and of treating the South as an exploiter does a conquered land. The Northerners reproached the Southerners for being a dead weight on the nation, imputing to them lack of initiative, corruption in local

228

administrations, and deploring their state of backwardness. The reciprocal lack of understanding between North and South, by no means a phenomenon limited to Italy, still continues nourished as much by psychological and habitual attitudes as by economic and political contrasts.

The progressive impoverishment of the South, which at the same time had a very high and constantly growing birthrate, was one of the main reasons to account for the mass emigration toward North and South America that began at the end of the last century. In the years 1876 to 1913, more than seven million Italians emigrated across the Atlantic; about four million of them came from the southern provinces.

The attempts to aid the South undertaken by the government before World War I were invariably insufficient and badly managed. Public works programs, such as bridges, roads, railroads and schools that were built in great numbers after the achievement of Italian unity could not solve the problem. The South took advantage of these measures, but in reality nothing was done to eliminate the fundamental causes of its backwardness, and since the progress in the South was much slower than in the rest of Italy, the disequilibrium worsened and the problem became even more acute. The Fascist regime of Mussolini, though following a course similar to that of the preceding governments, undertook a greater effort, especially during its first ten years in power. It increased the extent of public works, undertook important melioration and irrigation works, and it attempted to give a new impetus to agriculture in its basic production (the battle for wheat). But Mussolini also failed to accomplish the basic objective, which he had never seriously considered in any case—that of closing the gap between North and South. The southern problem could be solved only by a long-term, sustained effort and the dictator preferred to spend public money in military adventures in Africa and Spain, drawing heavily on the human reserves of the South, who were enticed to enroll in the "volunteer

229

troops" by the promise of enlistment premiums and allowances.

Thus, after World War II, the new Italian democracy inherited an old and heavy problem, which because of changed political conditions demanded a rapid final solution. The pressure of the extreme left-wing parties, which saw in the South great possibilities to proselytize; public opinion, which without distinction of political allegiance had by now become sensitive to the human and social aspects of the problem; the summons from abroad; and the international importance which the problem of underdeveloped areas had taken—all contributed to making the resolution of the southern question an unavoidable and urgent commitment.

THE "CASSA DEL MEZZOGIORNO"

Thanks to the discussions, studies and programs of more than half a century and modern research on economic development techniques, the way in which the problem of the economic development of the South should be tackled had become more clear. Only by a long-term effort in the form of a series of coordinated interventions with the employment of important capital could the problem be brought to a satisfactory solution. This effort had to be directed in the first place toward the creation of infrastructures, such as a communications network, acqueducts, irrigation installations, land reclamation, power plants and the formation of a specialized manpower, which would create the conditions for a further industrialization. After the creation of the infrastructures with public financing the industrialization was to be left to private initiative, which was to appeal to local savings, but mainly to capital from the northern industries, which were to be persuaded to invest by the offer of an advantageous credit policy and fiscal exemptions. According to this scheme, a logical cooperation between state intervention and private initiative, in line with the classical principles of a laissez-faire economy, would have

230

been established. If this solution had not succeeded, more rigorously planned solutions inevitably would have to be adopted.

Proceeding along this line, the quadripartite coalition, five years after the war, established a project which envisaged a long-term plan of investments. The corresponding law was approved by all parties (with the sole exception of the extreme left, which belittled the government plan, calling it insufficient). It was presented to Parliament on March 10, 1950, and enacted four months later, in August of the same year. The plan was partially modified by various legal dispositions, stipulating the establishment of an agency to be called the "Fund for extraordinary public utility works in the South," which later on was simply called the "Fund for the South" (*Cassa del Mezzogiorno*). The agency was allocated a huge number of tasks, whose aim, to be coordinated organically, was to change the natural environment of the underdeveloped areas usefully, regulating the rivers, stopping erosion of the land, reclaiming swampy areas, constructing roads, acqueducts, agricultural villages, stables for cattle, industrial installations for the use of local agricultural products, etc. A good part of these projects were intended to improve agriculture, and had been conceived in support of the land reform. Furthermore, the agency was to function as a credit institution, to service agricultural and industrial private initiative, anticipating the amounts necessary for carrying out these projects, all of which had been previously approved.

The financial basis of the plan was constituted by a fund of 1,280 billion lire, to be spent in twelve years; later on, in 1955, another 204 billion lire were added to finance through the agency special projects in Calabria. Further additions were made in 1957 and 1959, to reach a total of more than 2,000 billion lire.

Considering the need to operate swiftly, in accordance with a long-term plan, the agency was given special autonomy, and its organization was made flexible, exceptionally so for a state organization. The management and control was

231

placed in a committee of Ministers, made up of the economic and financial department heads. This committee was given the task of elaborating general plans for the activities of the agency, and of approving every year the overall projects to be realized.

From the time it started to function, in 1951, until June 30, 1963 the agency approved 234,889 projects at a value of 2,050 billion lire; out of these, 15,298 projects at a value of about 1,394 billion lire concerned public works, 219,591 projects valued at 665 billion lire were presented by private economic operators. The work completed by June 30, 1963, amounted to a value of 1,450 billion lire, corresponding to a total of 316 million work days.

In general the *Cassa del Mezzogiorno* has worked swiftly. It has achieved a visible transformation, and through an important program of works, it has contributed to the absorption of unemployment. The increase of buying power and a higher standard of consumption, which could be registered in the South since 1955, was its first tangible result.[1]

But along with these positive achievements, there has been criticism of the agency's activities. In particular it has been accused of having aimed at outwardly visible results, that is, those that could be exploited politically, of having spent huge amounts in sectors where a later emigration has reduced the utility of the projects to nil and, in general, of not having taken sufficiently into account the real needs of the industrialization process that was to follow. In this sense, it would appear that the original orientation of the agency was particularly subject to criticism, because it had concentrated a better part of the expenditures in the agricultural sector.[2]

The establishment of the agency represents only one aspect, though the most important one, of the government

---

[1] The per capita income in the South increased 56 per cent between 1951 and 1959; in the North the increase was 65.8 per cent.

[1] To finance projects in the agricultural sector, often in support of the Land Reform (253.7 billions), the Cassa spent a total 602.9 billion lire.

measures to aid the South. Tax exemptions, loans and credit facilities have been utilized on a wide scale with the aim of attracting private capital investments to the South. The policy of incentives had already been started in 1947 by the offer of a tax exemption for ten years on liquid assets and profits originating from investments in the South. Other fiscal exemptions have been granted, new institutes of agricultural and industrial credit have been created, and the government has asked those already existing to increase their range of credit in the southern regions, so that they could cover part of the interest and participate in the possible risks.

The list of measures of this type is too long to be dealt with here. It is enough to point out that, according to the conclusions reached by the most qualified observers of southern economy, thanks to government policies, the possibilities offered to private investors have been numerous and varied, and the credits, particularly in the last years, have been abundant and with very favorable conditions.

However, though the industrial development in the South has proceeded at a more accelerated pace than in the past (the level of employment in the industrial sector increased by 28 per cent in the years 1951-1959), it cannot be said that private capital investments have lived up to expectations. This was demonstrated by the existence of credits which had been destined for private investors but had remained unused because of the lack of applications, or because of the inconsistencies of the projects presented. On the other hand, the commitments of the agencies controlled by the state have been considerable; both the IRI and the ENI[1] have earmarked a part of their investments for very considerable industrial complexes situated in southern regions. Furthermore, as was to be foreseen, private initiative developed in a fairly disorderly fashion, being distributed over a vast geographic area, instead of concentrating in the

[1] *Ente Nazionale Idrocarburi* (The National Petrochemical Corporation) the state monopoly for the exploitation of the national petrochemical oil resources.

most favorable local areas. For that reason industrial development as a chain reaction was not forthcoming, since certain industries should have created preconditions for other industries to emerge. In order to correct this tendency to dispersion, there emerged a need to channel this industrial development. "Development Consortia" (*Consorzi di Sviluppo*) were created for the areas in which it appeared that the prospects for a concentrated industrial development existed. These Consortia were established with the participation of local agencies (municipalities, provinces, chambers of commerce) and given broad powers in matters of expropriations and the financial and technical capacity to take measures in view of great projects for structural transformation, which would meet the particular requirements of development plans. Some provinces have been declared "zones of industrial development" (Brindisi, Taranto), while others are preparing to assume this character. It would seem obvious that if this system should continue to develop as it has, new forms of collaboration between private and public initiative would need to be tried.

Today, thirteen years after the initiation of this major plan for the development of the South, it is still impossible to draw up a balance sheet of the prospects that private and public action have opened up in this part of Italy. The exceptional economic development, which was registered in the years 1959-1962, considerably modified the nature of the problem of the South. "The economic miracle," though it involved the entire peninsula, was none the less more concentrated in the industrial northern regions, and had prompted hundreds of thousands of southern workers to migrate North, depopulating entire regions and causing the greatest internal migration experienced since the days of Italian unity. This new situation, which could not have been foreseen at the time that the plans for the rebirth of the South were drawn up, together with the experiences of the years 1950-1961, would suggest that the elaboration of a new policy for the South is warranted. It is generally thought that

234

it will have to envisage more precise and better coordinated forms of state intervention.

The land reform and the establishment of the *Cassa per il Mezzogiorno* were the major reform measures taken by De Gasperi during the years of the quadripartite coalition. Others, though they involved less important expenditures, but were equally designed to improve living conditions in the country, were a series of laws to foster reforestation (known as the Fanfani Law, after the Minister who proposed it), whose main aim was the employment of jobless and unqualified manpower, various measures for the clearing and transformation of landed property, and the INA-CASA plan, which envisaged a broad program of construction of low-income housing. The taxation reform, or Vanoni reform, named after the Minister who authored it, also dates back to this period. It established a more functional and modern system of tax assessments in establishing tax exemptions for broad categories of low-income classes, increasing the personal income taxes of the moneyed classes and making them progressive, and making the distribution of the taxation burden, both direct and indirect, more equitable.

FOREIGN POLICY: THE ATLANTIC PACT AND EUROPEAN UNIFICATION

Although the Peace Treaty had left the question of the Italian colonies and the painful problem of Trieste unresolved, with its signing Italy was finally able to enter independently the realm of international relations and formulate its own foreign policy. The extent of the country's scope of activity was, however, restricted by the worsening of the international situation, which caused defense problems to become of paramount importance. The cold war had by now reached its zenith, and the two opposed blocs had become clearly delineated. Italy, just as all the other European countries, was expected to make a choice. There were historical, cultural and political considerations, that gave rise to two alternative courses for Italian foreign policy: to join the Western bloc by accepting the economic and defense aid that the United States was preparing to propose, or to take a position of neutrality and disengagement from the two great-power blocs.

The neutralist position was widely espoused by the general public in 1946 and 1947 for different reasons: the most common was the natural reaction to the painful experiences of the war, memories of which were still vivid. Among some sectors of the public, neutralism was a reaction of protest to the clauses of the Peace Treaty, a protest characterized by the desire for a dignified, if dangerous, isolation. There was furthermore the "ideological" neutralism of those (mainly groups of anti-Fascist intellectuals from the democratic left) who, examining critically the traditional policy of intervention that had led the country to participate in two world wars, demanded that Italy refrain from any commitments in the form of alliances, in order to dedicate all the country's energies to moral and civic reconstruction. With the intensification of the cold war and the increase of Soviet pressure and that of international Communism, the neutralist positions became increasingly weaker. Italy did not dispose of sufficient power even to undertake its own defense: its frontiers had been demilitarized by the Peace Treaty and its armed forces were little more than symbolic; thus the country was at the mercy of any aggression, however minor. Furthermore, the difficulties of economic reconstruction, upon which the existence of democracy depended to a large extent, was such that they could not be overcome without major foreign aid, which inevitably implied a political commitment. To these political considerations, ideological and religious motives should be added, which in this struggle between the two great-power blocs entailed an unequivocal alignment of the country on the side of the West. In the course of the years 1947-1948 all of these factors effected a gradual change in the orientation of a part of public opinion. In no period before had problems of foreign policy

236

been projected with greater urgency to the Italians, and at no time had the relationship between foreign and internal policy been so close.

As the cold war became manifest in such developments as the establishment of the Cominform (September 1947) and the Czechoslovak coup d'etat (February 1948), the impossibility of maintaining positions of neutralism such as those espoused in Italy appeared clear, inasmuch as neutralism would have opened the way to Communism. Italian acceptance of the Marshall Plan (July 1947) implied a political choice, considering the terms of the plan and conceived as it was as a means of resistance to Communism. The political election of April 18, 1948 endorsed this choice by a large majority of votes.

Foreign policy considerations played an exceptional part in the electoral platforms; the majority of the parties of the government coalition took a clear position with respect to international affairs.

Italy's adherence to the Atlantic Pact, which followed in April 1949, was a natural consequence of the acceptance of the Marshall Plan and the results of the 1948 elections. The Atlantic Pact was the key to De Gasperi's foreign policy, which he promoted with conviction and perseverance.

For a number of years, beginning in 1948, Italian foreign policy could be considered and evaluated exclusively in the function of the Atlantic Pact. The extreme left-wing opposition was, of course, opposed; it accused the parties in the government of leading the country toward a new war and demanded a neutralist policy, for obvious tactical aims. For De Gasperi and the supporters of the four-party alliance the Atlantic Pact was an exclusive commitment which could not be renounced. Italian adherence to NATO, which for the majority of the public signified above all an alliance with the United States, was definitive. American governing circles themselves recognized that Italy at that moment was one of the closest and most faithful allies of the United States. The military commitments, which had been assumed in consequence of the Atlantic Pact, were on the whole observed, although they entailed serious financial sacrifice for a country as poor as Italy, which was also involved in a major program of economic revival. Special items of the budget, totaling 250 billion lire in three years, were approved in addition to the regular military budgets, which in 1953 reached 618 billion lire, that is, 23 per cent of all government expenditures. The government was committed to the reconstitution and modernization of the armed forces, and in 1953 Italy succeeded in constituting twelve full divisions, two of which were armored. It also reconstituted naval bases, airports, and improved the navy and aviation though strictly within the limits of a strategy based on defense.

Another important aspect of foreign policy for Italy was European unification. De Gasperi and Carlo Sforza, his Minister of Foreign Affairs, were undoubtedly the Italian leaders who gave the greatest impetus to the cause of a united Europe in the years from 1947 to 1952. Their contribution equals that of other eminent European leaders like Robert Schumann, Henri Spaak and Konrad Adenauer.

De Gasperi conceived of a policy of European unification as a natural complement to the Atlantic policy, and he rejected the interpretations of those who saw in the future European federation a third force between the two great-power blocs and an alternative to the Atlantic policy. The adherence of Italy to the OEEC (Organization for European Economic Cooperation), the central organization for the implementation of the Marshall Plan, represented, for De Gasperi, the first act of a united Europe policy, inasmuch as the first economic collaboration between the European countries was realized through the OEEC and served as a prelude to future integration.

In May 1949 the establishment of the Council of Europe was agreed upon by 15 European nations in London, among them Italy. It was to be a kind of European assembly with consultative functions; in the following years many of the most important problems relating to the organization of the new European institutions were to be aired by it. The Council of Europe, however, is still in the preparatory phase as part of the machinery in the unification process. Before reaching the executive phase, some basic questions regarding constitutional structures have to be resolved. In particular, the problem of the type of union which will be created must be agreed upon: confederation or federal union. In the event that a federation is chosen, the various states would have to be assimilated within the common organism or, as the most enthusiastic proponents of the European idea have proposed, a super-state would have to be constituted in which the national states would be required to relinquish completely their own sovereignty. Italy's adherence to the policy of European integration has been unequivocal from the start; the Italian representatives have always been in the forefront in demanding and supporting the most advanced proposals, and each time these proposals have encountered the opposition of other European partners, the Italians have served as mediators to find a compromise.

The first concrete step toward European federation was accomplished with the establishment of the Coal and Steel Community, the draft treaty for which was presented by the French Foreign Minister, Robert Schumann, in April 1951. The Schumann Plan envisaged that the integration process would start in the economic field to lead in stages to political unification when the doubts and reservations of many governments had been overcome. The Schumann Plan represented a most important first step, but what appeared more important in the mind of De Gasperi and others in favor of integration was the establishment of organisms that could begin within a short time to approach the problem of political integration. To this end, in the autumn of 1952, Italy and France proposed that the Coal and Steel Community be entrusted with the preparation of a project for a European constitution.

At this point the process of integration was interrupted, which was to have grave consequences for the future of Europe. The proposal to constitute an integrated European army (the European Defense Community, EDC), made by the French Prime Minister René Pleven, met with strong oppo-

239

sition in France and to a lesser degree also in Italy. Powerful opposition to De Gasperi's policy was manifest in Italy from the right as well as from the Social-Communists. The opposition to the European army reflected negatively on the project for a European constitution, which remained permanently suspended, notwithstanding the periodic efforts of the supporters of European unity to revive it.

In the years to follow, even after De Gasperi's death, the questions of European integration were reopened and Italy again demonstrated its will to collaborate. But by then it seemed clear that the process of European unification would have a much longer gestation period than that originally envisaged, due to changes in the international situation.

In the years immediately following the war, the economic difficulties and the necessity to resist Soviet pressure gave a powerful impetus to European unification. However, when the most difficult times were overcome and the European nations had resumed greater freedom of action, integration gradually lost urgency and immediacy, and the process was definitely transposed from the political to the economic realm. The Common Market, which was constituted in 1957 and has proved to be the most efficient means to achieve the economic advancement of the six member nations, clearly indicates this new orientation.

CHAPTER 3

NEW POLITICAL ORIENTATIONS

THE BALANCE SHEET OF THE FOUR-PARTY ALLIANCE

The internal political situation in the spring of 1951 was considerably changed as compared with that two years earlier, prior to the beginning of the four-party experiment. The parties participating in the government were by now only two (the Republicans and the Demo-Christians) of the original four. The Social Democrats and Liberals had left the government coalition, although they continued to support the De Gasperi Cabinet in Parliament. The quadripartite formula had begun clearly to manifest its inadequacy, not as much on the parliamentary level (the DC could still count on a majority with a reasonable margin) as on the general political level. The economic situation of the country was quite favorable if the starting base for reconstruction is borne in mind; a satisfactory stability had been achieved both in the political and economic fields; the Communist danger had become less imminent than it had appeared in 1946, 1947; the defenses of the state had been reinforced; the currency was stable and production was on the increase. However, if from an analysis of the actual situation one proceeds to an examination of long-term prospects, the picture altered. After long hesitation and under pressure from the democratic left the government embarked on an effort to solve the basic problems of the country, but the reforms that had already

241

been introduced (land reform, and *Cassa del Mezzogiorno*) seemed to many, and in reality were, inadequate to attain the goals envisaged. They had grown out of too many compromises to be truly efficient instruments. They could have appreciable effects on certain sectors, but they could not determine fundamental transformations or bring about solutions. Problems such as the educational one and unemployment had not been faced squarely. The 1952 census showed that there were 5 million illiterates in Italy. In 1953, 2,480,520 persons were registered with employment agencies, representing an increase of unemployment by 1.1 per cent as compared to the average of the preceding years, starting with 1947.

The parliamentary investigation of poverty and unemployment, which in the years 1952-53 was carried out by the Vigorelli Commission, revealed that the standard of living of the majority of Italians was still extremely low as compared to European standards. 11.7 per cent of Italian families were declared to be in a condition of utter destitution and almost as many to be needy, while 65.7 per cent were living in "modest" conditions. The investigation showed that 232,000 families lived in cellars, attics or warehouses; 92,000 in caves or shacks; and that the major part of the homes declared habitable were devoid of a minimum of hygienic installations.

The economic policy of the government was visibly influenced by the interests of great capital. Few efforts were undertaken to enlarge the basis of the participation of the people in political life. The result was that many institutions envisaged by the constitution (the popular referendum, regional autonomy, the Constitutional Court) still remained unimplemented, because the right obstructed the laws that would have rendered these provisions operative. Today the administration of the four-party alliance can be judged on the basis of facts not available at the time of its existence. From these it is quite apparent that much of the energy and time of those who then were in power, first of all De Gasperi, were consumed in the attempt to maintain an equilibrium between the demands of the progressives and the intransigent opposition of the conservatives, and when certain measures could not be put off any longer, they were subject to such compromise as to denature their substance.

Although conditions of living had improved considerably in the last three years, dissatisfaction and discontent with the government was growing in many quarters. It was more a nebulous state of mind than an attitude of concrete protest. The democratic left was dissatisfied because of the inadequacy of the reformist solutions and because of the heavy-handed methods of Scelba's (Minister of Interior) police in handling the frequent demonstrations of popular protest. It was known that most of these manifestations were organized directly or indirectly through the trade unions who depended on the Communist Party. That labor conflicts were exploited for political motives was condemned, but nevertheless the readiness with which the police charged the demonstrators or made use of rubber truncheons prompted reactions of protest among the genuinely democratic public.

The right and the conservatives on the other hand felt betrayed by the DC and De Gasperi, for whom they had voted on April 18th. The land reform, though carried out on a limited basis, had not only hurt the interests of a few thousand large landed proprietors but had attacked the prestige and power of the entire economic right.

A growing opposition with regard to De Gasperi's foreign policy was also developing, commonly shared by right and left. The Prime Minister was accused of having abandoned an independent national policy by linking it to the Atlantic Alliance and above all to the United States. To the wounded national pride was joined the preoccupation over the increasing military expenditures, which had become necessary in order to achieve the rearmament imposed by adherence to the Atlantic Pact.

The considerable intrusion of the church into public life was a cause of widespread protest in all non-clerical political circles; even the Demo-Christians themselves were frequently embarrassed by it. Another source of popular

243

discontent against the DC, amply exploited by the left-wing parties, was the excessive attachment to power, manifested by the Demo-Christian ruling circles, which necessarily led to government corruption and favoritism. Thus the expression *sottogoverno*[1] was coined, which was meant as a sarcastic reference to the plethora of jobs and well-paid public functions, advantages reserved almost exclusively to those belonging to the majority party.

All of these causes for criticism and complaint were exaggerated and exploited by the propaganda of the extreme left, which, having put aside any intention by this time of taking revolutionary action, had no weapon left but a systematic and corrosive long-term opposition.

Gradually opposition against Church encroachments developed even within the DC, though at election time the support of the Church, being one of the conditions for success at the polls, was actively sought.

The extreme right as well fully exploited the errors of the government and the disillusionment in the country, dwelling on its own preoccupations with economic and foreign policy.

The first indication that the attitude of a part of the public was changing came at the time of the administrative elections, which were held in two ballotings in the spring of 1951 and 1952. Although the DC succeeded in winning important city administrations from the Social-Communists, such as that of Turin and Florence, traditionally strongholds of the extreme left, and Venice, it lost nevertheless almost four million votes as compared to the political elections of April 1948, dropping from 48.5 to 35.9 per cent. The Communists sustained some sporadic losses, while the Nenni Socialists realized considerable progress contrary to all expectations.

The other parties of the government majority, Republi-

---

[1] An expression which referred to the corruption and nepotism in the majority party which grew out of its power positions in the government.

244

cans and Liberals, suffered considerable losses, while the Social Democrats, as a result of the recent Socialist reunification, won a certain measure of success. The most striking results were the votes obtained by the extreme right-wing parties, Monarchists and neo-Fascists, the latter having trebled their vote, especially in the South.

Although administrative elections had been traditionally less favorable to the DC, the results demonstrated general discontent, especially the conservative reaction to the land reform. This in substance was the significance of the transfer of DC votes to a certain extent to the Liberals and to the Monarchist and neo-Fascist right.

MONARCHISTS AND NEO-FASCISTS

Following the disappearance of the *Uomo Qualunque* Party from the political scene, as a result of its electoral defeat on April 18, 1948, the representation of the interests and the political positions of the conservative right had been taken over by the Monarchist Party and by the Italian Social Movement. The former was headed by Alfredo Covelli and Achille Lauro, a well-known Neapolitan shipowner and principal leader of the movement. The party was formed after the institutional referendum of June 2, 1946, with the aim of organizing a political movement among the voters who had cast their ballots for the monarchy. The party's political platform was the restoration of the monarchy, an objective that it proclaimed officially even after the constitution had entered into law. The constitution and specifically Article 139 stipulated that the republican form of govern-ment was guaranteed against any possibility of a constitutional amendment. Thus, since the possibility of a restoration was excluded, the aim of the Monarchists lay outside constitutional legality. Nevertheless, the Monarchist Party continued to campaign for a return to the monarchy, since this aim continued to provide its main political attraction for some of the conservative nobility and certain popular classes in Naples, Palermo, Foggia and other particularly depressed zones of the South who formed the backbone of the Monarchist electorate. The poorer classes, who respected the institution of monarchy, as a result of a long feudal and absolutist past, and who had little political awareness or education, acted contrary to their own interests. The orientation of the Monarchist Party was in fact downright reactionary, particularly with regard to social problems, which it envisaged solving by paternalistic concessions. It was thus a party based on minorities that had once been privileged, and on the political ignorance of certain strata of the southern proletariat. The reasons for the recent success of the Neo-Fascist Party, the Italian Social Movement (MSI, *Movimento Sociale Italiano*), which emerged for the first time on April 18, 1948, were not vastly different.

In the period immediately following the liberation a party that renewed the programs and ideals of the past regime could have no success, due to recent experience of partisan struggle, the action of Republican Fascism on the side of the Germans, and the violently anti-Fascist spirit which then pervaded the entire country. The new constitution prohibits (Clause XII) the reconstitution in any form whatsoever of the old Fascist Party. Nevertheless, as time passed and the solidarity between anti-Fascist parties gradually frittered away and the political struggle between Communism and anti-Communism intensified, some ex-Fascist groups reappeared in public life. They were guided by a few leaders of limited political stature, who had held secondary positions either during the twenty years of Fascism or after July 25th, in the Social Republic. In the beginning, the intransigent elements who had lived through the experience of the Social Republic and whose following was mostly in the North prevailed in the party. Later on, after a series of violent internal conflicts, the progressives were pushed aside and moderate elements of southern origin, in favor of collaboration with the Monarchist Party, prevailed. In this way the MSI acquired the more natural physiognomy of a conservative party, grouping elements of the petit and middle bourgeoisie, southern landowners, small shopkeepers as well as some of the younger students (the party accepts inscriptions from the age of fourteen) who had had no direct experience with Fascism. The protests and criticism both in Italy and abroad that accompanied the first appearances of neo-Fascism dissipated quite soon when it became clear that the MSI could count on only a limited following and was not a threat to the democratic institutions. The new movement lacked both leaders of national stature and a clear political program, which, in answer to the trend of the times, would have enabled them to gather a broader following in the country. Both the MSI and the Monarchists appealed to the general discontent and the excitability of the electorate. The residues of nationalism, rabid anti-Communism and the nostalgia of some who looked upon the twenty years of the Mussolini regime as the good old days, largely explained the limited success of the Fascist movement.

From time to time the most extremist groups, composed mostly of teenagers, organized manifestations of a Fascist character, such as reunions with black shirts and pennants or acts of rowdyism and violence against political adversaries. Such manifestations, however, were rare and were promptly curtailed by the intervention of the police and by the anti-Fascist public. As this type of manifestation worked against the movement's own purpose, they were soon abandoned by the more realistic elements of the party. These hoped, and their calculations turned out to be correct, that in the atmosphere of dissatisfaction with the government, which was increasing after 1951, the party would find fertile soil for the realization of further progress if it stayed within the limits of legality. These elements, among whom were Augusto De Marsanich, Secretary of the party, and Filippo Anfuso, a former Fascist ambassador, attempted to give the MSI a veneer of respectability. They modeled the organization on the pattern of the democratic parties and succeeded in gaining the support of a daily paper, *Il Secolo* of Rome. They attempted with very limited success to organize in July

247

1952 their own trade union, the CISNAL (*Confederazione Italiana dei Sindacati Nazionali Lavoratori*: Italian Confederation of National Unions) and received permission, which up to now had been denied them, to hold their first party congress.

All these efforts bore fruit in the political elections of 1953.

CHAPTER 4

THE 1953 ELECTIONS

THE "FRAUDULENT LAW"

The administrative elections held in 1951 and 1952 had alerted the government parties to the switch in the attitude of the electorate. Though they confirmed the basic orientation of the Italian voters to be democratic and pro-Western, they showed that the factors that had brought about the overwhelming electoral victory of the DC over Social-Communism had been in large part overtaken by events and that it would be unrealistic to expect the same results to reoccur. The DC was to remain by far the strongest party, but, even joined together with the other minor parties, it would have difficulty in maintaining an absolute majority. Government stability, which, despite frequent conflicts among members of the government coalition, had in substance been maintained since 1949, was clearly threatened and along with it the quadripartite formula, which had been the basis of this stability.

It should be kept in mind that De Gasperi's political program was tied to the quadripartite coalition in the future, as it had been in the past. The Demo-Christian leader thought that a moderate policy of mediation between the progressive positions of the left and the conservative positions of the democratic right was the only possible policy, not

249

only for the DC, an interclass and extremely heterogeneous party, but for the country as a whole. In the five years which had come to an end, the Catholic statesmen had succeeded in imposing along fundamental lines a sufficiently organic political program. But this had been achieved in the face of unforeseen difficulties and opposition, which had been all the more worrisome if one considers the overwhelming electoral victory of 1948, which had given the DC its parliamentary strength and prestige. For that reason a poor electoral showing or, as was to be expected, further losses of the government parties would cause a particularly difficult parliamentary situation. The four parties would have a very narrow margin of majority and would be compelled to look for support among other political formations, either on the extreme left or on the extreme right. This would in turn weaken the already unstable equilibrium between Social Democrats and Liberals and would most probably create a crisis within the DC itself, reviving the conflicts among its tendencies. These unfavorable prospects led to the unfortunate proposition for the modification of the electoral law, in such a fashion as to assure the government party by a legislative trick its margin of a parliamentary majority, which the electorate seemed unwilling to give them.

The new law proposed for the elections to the Chamber of Deputies (the old electoral law for the Senate would remain in force) a system that combined the proportional and majority systems, based on two particulars:

1) The alliance of two or several parties;

2) The attribution of a premium of majority to the party or group of allied parties that totaled over 50.1 per cent.

The premium of majority would have permitted the allied parties to gain a total of 385 seats (later reduced to 380), corresponding to 65 per cent of the entire Chamber.

Thus, if the four government parties had allied themselves at the polls, as De Gasperi had planned, they would have won over 50.1 per cent of the votes, a result which

250

seemed easy to achieve. They would then have received 65 per cent of the available seats in Parliament, at the expense, it was understood, of the other parties. A majority of 65 per cent represented a safe margin for any government; with it the quadripartite coalition would have been out of any danger. De Gasperi's preoccupations with government stability displayed political acumen but they inevitably conflicted with the basic principles of democracy and, in particular, with the rigidly proportionalist system traditionally accepted by the Italian electorate.

The proposal for this law was no sooner presented to Parliament than it encountered the most violent protests on the part of the opposition and caused considerable confusion among the members of the government majority due to benefit from it. The opposition accused the government of a plot against democracy and of an attempt to achieve absolute power. In defending itself, the government stated that according to the law any group of allied parties, including those of the opposition, could benefit by the premium of majority, and that the law in fact reinforced the small parties. thus claiming it upheld the genuinely democratic principle of the defense of minorities. The first argument could easily be countered, in that in the given political situation no group of parties outside of the government coalition could have conceivably captured 50.1 per cent of the votes, unless the Social-Communists had become allied with the Fascists and Monarchists, an absurd hypothesis. To the second argument —that the law protected minor parties—it could be objected that it protected only those belonging to the government coalition, inasmuch as the others would suffer from it.

The objections of the opposition were difficult to refute and they acquired even greater weight when seven deputies from one of the majority parties, the PSDI, in contrast with the official position of their own party, openly declared themselves against the law and publicly denounced its anti-democratic nature. The seven, among whom were such outstanding personalities as the Florentine lawyer Piero Calamandrei, were suspended from their functions in the party; they then decided to resign and form a new political group, the *Unità Popolare* (Popular Unity), which would present its own candidates and conduct its own electoral campaign in open and determined opposition against the electoral law.

The discussion of the projected law continued in an atmosphere of tension which extended from Parliament to the entire country. After its approval by the Chamber, the law went to the Senate where the government could count on an even narrower majority; there the attacks of the opposition reached their highest pitch. Senate members indulged in lengthy speeches, presenting numerous amendments in an evident attempt to drag out the discussion of the law and to prevent its approval in due time. This debate degenerated into actual scuffles between groups of opposing deputies, and frequently the Aula of the Senate was transformed into a boxing ring. However, since the government majority was clear in both Chamber and Senate, the new electoral law was approved on March 29th. Parliamentary obstructionism, organized by the opposition, although it failed in its original aim, succeeded in another no less important aim—in exposing the government and the government coalition parties as endeavoring to reinforce and protract their own power by illegal means. The electoral law was effectively dubbed the "fraudulent law" (*legge truffa*), and the discontent, already widespread in the country, acquired a new, more specific justification.

ELECTORAL CAMPAIGN

The electoral campaign, which was conducted most energetically by the opposition, put the government parties on the defensive. It developed around a series of issues involving both foreign and domestic policy, but the prime targets were the land reform and the "fraudulent law." The left engaged in propaganda directed at the grass roots level, especially in the areas where the land reform was in process, minimizing the efforts of the government and the benefits to the landless peasants. The propaganda of the right-wing parties echoed the left in accusing the DC of an attack against private property. The same parallelism between extreme right and extreme left propaganda existed also in matters of foreign policy. While the Social-Communists accused the government of having enslaved the country to American policy and of carrying out a policy bound to involve the country in a third world war, the Monarchists and neo-Fascists, although claiming to accept the Atlantic policy, accused De Gasperi of having renounced an independent foreign policy in favor of following blindly the United States. All this criticism came at a particularly unfavorable moment for the government, since in view of indications that international tension was easing (one of the weather vanes was Churchill's speech in Locarno in May 1953), the public began to question whether the rearmament effort, undertaken by the government at huge cost and sacrifice, had not then become unnecessary.

Facing the well-organized campaign of the left, the DC lacked the aggressive imagination it had demonstrated during the preceding campaign in 1948. It built its own case on the economic benefits resulting from reconstruction and the reform measures, continuing to warn of the danger of Communism and stressing the fact that the DC was the only party which, because of its strength and ideology, could effectively counter it. It justified the Atlantic Alliance as the only policy able to guarantee the nation's security against the continuing threats of the Soviet Union. Taking cognizance of the changed mood of the country, however, it refrained from extolling the direct ties with the United States, a position which until a few years previously had been considered a sure one to win electoral success. Another indication that the Italian public was revising its foreign policy attitude was the strongly negative reaction to a speech by the American Ambassador, Mrs. Clare Booth Luce, in which she inferred that unpleasant consequences for Italo-American collaboration would result if the election favoured extreme left or extreme right-wing parties. This open intervention

253

in Italian politics was widely exploited by the opposition and damaged the cause it was intended to defend.

In general, however, foreign policy, contrary to the 1948 elections, played a secondary role by comparison with internal problems. In addition the stress given the Communist danger impressed the public less than in 1948; the atmosphere in the country was no longer as tense as it had been in 1946-1948, years in which the extremist forces exercised real psychological pressure on the country. Although Communism was organizationally still very strong, it had lost much of its original revolutionary fervor. All of these factors prevented the DC from being able to exploit the same issues as successfully as they had in 1948; thus it could be anticipated with certainty that the party would suffer some loss of strength, although it was also certain that the allied parties would, according to the new electoral law, benefit from the majority premium, since it was assumed that they would get over 50 per cent of the vote. For that reason it was a great surprise to the entire country, and especially in government circles, when the voting did not bear out these expectations.

THE RESULTS

Elections to the House of Representatives

Parties	Votes Polled	Seats
PCI	6,120,709	143
PSI	3,441,014	75
PSDI	1,222,057	19
PRI	438,149	5
DC	10,834,466	216
PLI	815,929	14
PNM	1,854,850	40
MSI	1,579,880	29
Others	693,505	4

The results of the election, which took place on June 7th for the Chamber of Deputies, gave the allied government parties, the DC, PSDI, PRI and PLI, about 49.85 per cent.

57,000 votes were lacking to achieve the percentage necessary to qualify for the majority premium. The "fraudulent law," which had cost the government so much remained inoperative, and the seats in the Chamber were distributed according to the old, proportional electoral law. In the Senate,[1] the elections to which were held according to the old law, the results ironically were more favorable to the government parties, who totaled 50.2 per cent.

The inoperativeness of the new electoral law was not the only surprise of the elections. The electoral success of the left[1] and especially of the PCI was way beyond expectations; it polled the greatest number of votes since 1946. No less striking was the success of the Monarchist Party, which, as compared to 1948, trebled its votes and seats. The MSI won approximately a million votes more than it had in the elections two years previously. All the government parties, together with the DC, suffered appreciable losses; particularly the PSDI, which went down from 1,800,000 votes in 1948 (increased by 0.5 per cent in 1951-1952) to 1,222,957. The *Unità Popolare*, the group of dissident Social Democrats who had resigned because of their opposition to the "fraudulent law," won 171,099 votes, which were insufficient to keep the party alive; it disbanded shortly afterward. But the votes cast for this group were a factor in the failure of the government parties to attain the 50.1 per cent required by the law.

THE SEARCH FOR A NEW MAJORITY

The electoral results were interpreted in various ways, as normally happens under such circumstances; everyone attempted either to enhance his own victory or to cover up

---

[1] Although the constitution stipulated a six-year term for the Senate, compared to five years for the Chamber, the Senate had been dissolved in April by the President of the Republic, who had taken advantage of his powers in accordance with Article 88 of the constitution.

[1] Contrary to the 1948 elections, the PSI and PCI presented separate lists.

his lack of success. However, it was difficult to disregard some of the indications that emerged most clearly from the results, such as the reinforcement of the extremes and the displacement toward the left of some of the democratic and progressive voters. The Communist Party increased its votes at the expense of the PSI, which profited in turn by votes that had formerly gone to the Social Democrats. Within the DC the left-wing current emerged relatively reinforced, notwithstanding the losses of the party as a whole. The results clearly condemned the reformist policy of the quadripartite alliance, which because of the way it had been carried out had antagonized the conservatives, who saw in the reform an attack against private property, as well as the progressives, who judged it to be too gradual and limited. It was indicative of the importance that the reforms had in the minds of the voters that the major losses of the government parties and the major gains of the opposition, especially the Communist opposition, occurred in the southern regions, the main area to be affected by the land reform. The electoral law proposed by De Gasperi was also rejected by the major part of the voters, as was clearly apparent from the results.

The conclusions to be drawn from the vote could not help but influence the formation of the new government and the search for a new majority. De Gasperi presented the resignation of his seventh cabinet, as was customary in constitutional practice, but also because the electoral results had changed considerably the composition of Parliament. Despite its losses, the DC remained by far the strongest party, and responsibility again fell to it to constitute a new government. The President of the Republic again chose De Gasperi to head it, although the DC leader's prestige had been considerably diminished since he was considered the person most responsible for the unfortunate electoral law. De Gasperi accepted the nomination and undertook long and arduous consultations in search of the best governmental formula. The quadripartite coalition, which De Gasperi, loyal to his beliefs, attempted at first to revive, could have been adopted, although its plurality was critically reduced

256

(to five votes), but the Social Democrats opposed it. The Social Democrats' left wing reproached the party leadership with having accepted the "fraudulent law" and in general of having in recent years gone along with the government coalition. The formation of a Christian Democratic government that would include the Liberals and Monarchists, though possible from a parliamentary point of view, was rejected by De Gasperi because the DC, by collaborating with conservative forces, would have been compromised, since it had defined itself during the quadripartite years as an eminently center party, and its internal equilibrium would have been disturbed. There was therefore no solution left but a one-party government, composed exclusively of Demo-Christians who would attempt to achieve the necessary parliamentary majority on the basis of a moderate program acceptable both to certain elements of the right and of the democratic left (Republicans and centrist currents among the Social Democrats). This was another way of reconstituting the quadripartite alliance, avoiding any preceding agreement with the parties and appealing directly to the sense of responsibility of the members of Parliament individually. The power of the party directorates, however, and the dependency of the deputies and senators on their leaderships —one of the most characteristic aspects of post-war Italian politics—precluded the success of such an attempt. On July 28th, when the new government presented itself to the Chamber for a vote of confidence, it was defeated. The Communists, Socialists, Monarchists, and neo-Fascists voted against it, while the Social Democrats and Liberals abstained. This vote put an end to a long series of De Gasperi Cabinets whose succession had been uninterrupted since 1945, and it practically marked the end of the political career of the Demo-Christian leader.

De Gasperi's failure to constitute his eighth government gave rise to a new formula for a governmental alignment that was destined to influence profoundly the political events that followed. The suggestion came from Pietro Nenni, the leader of the Socialist Party, who during the debate in the

257

Chamber following the presentation of De Gasperi's eighth government announced the availability of his own party for a government "opening to the left" (*apertura a sinistra*).

The expression was to have an important future: it envisaged the enlargement of the government majority toward the left-wing parties and including the Socialist Party. More important, it manifested the desire of the Socialist Party to follow a different policy · from the one it had pursued up to now, in particular one that was independent of the Communist Party.

This was not the first time that there had been mention of "an opening to the left." The proposal had already been advanced during the electoral campaign. It represented a gradual evolution that had taken place within the Socialist Party since the 1948 elections. The idea of an "opening to the left" was considered on the side in the consultation for the formation of a new government as an alternative to a one-party government, and it was supported by left-wing Demo-Christians and Social Democrats. De Gasperi first took it into consideration, then discarded it. The participation of the Socialists in a new majority was judged to be premature, at the least, by the veteran DC leader. There were too many obstacles: the direct ties that still existed between the Socialists and the Communists and the opposition of the majority of the DC; but the main stumbling block was the difference in foreign policy between De Gasperi's still resolute Atlantic stand and the declared neutralism of the Socialists. For seven years the two parties had been engaged in a relentless struggle; a sudden reversal of positions would have dangerously disoriented the public. If such an evolution was inevitable, as some people affirmed, its realization would have to be prepared gradually and patiently. Nevertheless, the "opening to the left" was from then on considered a concrete though remote possibility. During the long period of incertitude and government insecurity that followed the failure of the eighth De Gasperi Cabinet, the formula of the "opening to the left" slowly matured until it imposed itself as the only alternative solution.

PART FOUR

From the four-party coalition to the opening to the left

CHAPTER 1

"1953-1958: DIFFICULT BUT NOT STERILE YEARS"

The second legislature, which extended from the elections in 1953 to those in May 1958, coincides with one of the most difficult periods of Italian political life, as has been generally conceded, though with emphasis on different aspects, by both the majority and the opposition.

On the eve of the political elections of 1958 Amintore Fanfani, then Secretary of the DC, published a volume of political speeches "1953-1958. Difficult but Not Sterile Years." His example was followed by Pietro Nenni, the Secretary of the PSI, whose parliamentary speeches appeared under the title: "A legislature which failed 1953-1958." Both titles express judgements that bear witness to the critical situation of Italian politics in these years. From the point of view of government activity, the judgement of the Socialist leader is substantially valid. The exhausting search for a parliamentary majority and the precarious position of those that were constituted from time to time with great effort almost brought to a standstill the reformist activity undertaken by De Gasperi in the preceding legislature (1949-1953). It was natural that governments based on limited majorities sometimes kept in power through the abstention of extreme right-wing parties, could not undertake broad measures for economic progress and social reform. For the most part the legislative activity carried out by the government during this period fell into the category of ordinary administration, although individual laws were significant affir-

261

mations of government responsibility; these reinforced the position of the state in the economy and created some of the conditions for a policy of social planning. Laws such as the ones regulating the exploitation of hydrocarbons, the nationalization of telephones, and the creation of a Ministry of State Participations reinforced the position of the state in the economy and created some of the conditions for a policy of economic planning which was later to represent one of the main points of the "opening to the left" program.

Fanfani's judgement that these years were not "sterile" is equally valid, if one changes the focus of attention from the government to the activities of the parties. The evolution and the displacement of political forces, which occurred within the parties, especially within the DC and the PSI, justifies Fanfani's observation.

As has been demonstrated earlier it is useless, in the Italian parliamentary system, to seek a government majority in Parliament if it has not been previously made possible through an agreement among the parties. The 1953 elections dealt the four-party coalition a severe blow and revealed the necessity for a new majority which would support a new policy: this could come into being only as a result of new party combinations and alliances. The years from 1953 to 1958, "difficult but not sterile," saw the necessary preparation for the inclusion of new forces in the majority, thus marking a gradual transition to a new political formula.

The evolution of the international situation made an important contribution to the formulation of this new policy, as well as certain events which represented a change in the policies of the Socialist countries. Stalin's death, the 20th Congress of the CPSU (Communist Party of the Soviet Union), the Hungarian Revolution, and the general decrease of tension accelerated important changes of opinion within the major parties and contributed to the creation of new relations among them. An examination of foreign political events is therefore indispensable to an analysis of certain developments in internal politics, a factor that had already emerged in the years preceding 1953; that is, the close relationship in Italian post-war politics between international events and the internal situation.

The period of 1953-1958 was at the level of government and parliamentary activity a period of immobilism. At the level of the political parties, it was on the other hand a period of gradual evolution. But in the economic sphere the years following 1953 were to bring the most positive results. The economic development was intensive in every sector and in particular in industry, whose indices of production increased continually. The revenue increased, exports increased until they exceeded imports (1958), and along with these the reserves of hard currency. Certain basic problems still remained unsolved, that of unemployment and of the South, but the groundwork was being laid so that at least on the level of strictly economic solutions these problems too would gradually become less burdensome.

The period 1953-1958 was thus full of contradictions. The government crises succeeded one another with such frequency and the problem of obtaining a parliamentary majority appeared so difficult to solve that the solidity of the political institutions as such seemed to be in danger. On the other hand, the life of the parties was intensive and productive in a long-term sense, and in the economic field the exceptional progress that in the years following 1958 was to be called the "Italian miracle" was in its initial phase.

THE GOVERNMENTS

From July 1953 to June 1956 six governments succeeded each other at the helm of the country. They were:

Government	Participating Parties	Date of Formation	Duration (in days)
De Gasperi	DC	July 16, 1953	17
Pella	DC	Aug. 17, 1953	142
Fanfani	DC	Jan. 17, 1954	14
Scelba	DC, PSDI, PLI	Feb. 10, 1954	497
Segni	DC, PSDI, PLI	July 7, 1955	669
Zoli	DC	May 16, 1957	398

The two government formulas that were tried in these years were the so-called *monocolore* (monocolor), that is, a government constituted by one party alone, the DC, with the parliamentary support of other political forces, and re-editions of the four-party alliance, whose reconstitution was attempted persistently. But neither one turned out to be adequate. The monocolor solution compelled the DC to accept the support of the Monarchists and Neo-Fascists, as in the cases of the Pella and Zoli Cabinets, critically disturbing the internal equilibrium between the right and the left within the DC, which was fundamental for so hetero-geneous a party. The relaunching of the "quadripartite" coalition, which was first tried by Scelba and then by Segni, also turned out to be unproductive and temporary, because of the reluctance of the Social Democrats and Republi-cans to support a government formula that had been clearly rejected by the results of the 1953 elections, and also because of increasing opposition within the DC itself. The difficulties encountered in these attempts demonstrated clearly to what extent the period of the quadripartite coalition, which had been tied to a different international and internal situation and had benefited from the prestige and mediating ability of De Gasperi, had by now outlived itself.

That the period to follow the 1953 electoral consultation would be especially difficult was evident from the start. The summer of 1953 was entirely taken up with attempts to form a new government.

After the failure of the above-mentioned Monocolor government experiment, sponsored by De Gasperi, the at-tempt to reconstitute the quadripartite coalition, undertaken by Attilio Piccioni, one of the most influential leaders of the DC, also failed because of the opposition of the Social Democrats. The negative results of De Gasperi's and Pic-cioni's efforts provoked sharp conflicts among the tendencies within the DC, whose most important leaders—Guido Gonel-la, then Secretary of the Party, an able man with a limited personal following, Fanfani, leader of the left, and Scelba, persistent supporter of the quadripartite system—were fighting

264

to succeed De Gasperi. Since the country needed a government, the absence of which was beginning to be reflected even in normal administrative activity, the idea gradually asserted itself that a way out of the deadlocked situation could only be the constitution of a business cabinet, that is, a government that was not politically qualified and was limited to administrative tasks until a new agreement had been reached between the parties and a new majority had been formed on the basis of a precise political platform.

The formation of the business government was entrusted to Giuseppe Pella by the President of the Republic. Pella was a Demo-Christian politician with no following among the currents inside the party but with close relations with the industrial and financial interests of the North. Pella formed a government of technicians (he was himself an industrialist and economist), composed exclusively of Demo-Christian ministers and a few independent experts. When the new Prime Minister presented his cabinet to Parliament to obtain its vote of confidence, he insisted on the temporary character of his experiment and outlined a program of administrative measures, which excluded any long-term policy of reform and upheld the traditional orientation of foreign policy, although his tone seemed to indicate a position of greater independence with regard to the Western allies and to the United States in particular. The obvious aim of this new attitude was to please the right-wing parties, which, although faithful to an Atlantic policy, openly criticized the excessive submissiveness of the government in the past. The Pella Government obtained an unusually large majority. The Demo-Christians, Republicans, Monarchists and Liberals voted in favor; the Social Democrats and neo-Fascists abstained; and the Socialists and Communists voted against it.

A few days after its formation attention in government circles was unexpectedly and dramatically turned to the Trieste question, which had been left unsolved by the Peace Treaty. This was to give the Pella Government a political cause that the Prime Minister had so aptly avoided in his speech of investiture to Parliament.

265

After the three-power declaration (U.S.A., Great Britain and France), made on the eve of the political elections in 1948, in which the return of Trieste to Italy was pledged, the problem of the Italian borders with Yugoslavia continued to remain unresolved. The Italian Government reminded the allies, especially the United States, several times of the promise, but following the Soviet-Yugoslav break and Yugoslavia's exit from the Cominform, the Western powers, hoping to attract Tito into their camp, assumed a cautious attitude and appeared unwilling to implement for the time being their commitment to Italy.

In the Free Territory of Trieste the situation was as follows: Zone A, which included Trieste and a strip of territory west of the city, totaling 86 square miles, with a population of 302,200 inhabitants (of which 239,200 were Italians and 63,000 Slovenians), remained under Anglo-American military administration; and Zone B, east of Trieste, comprising 199 square miles, with 73,000 inhabitants, predominantly Slovenians, was under Yugoslav military administration. As the years passed, Zone A became more and more assimilated with Italy, as a result of a series of administrative agreements between the Italian Government and the allied powers,[1] while in Zone B an intense process of denationalization of the remaining Italian communities was under way.

In a speech in Rome on September 13, 1953, Pella advanced the proposal that a plebiscite be held in both zones of the Free Territory of Trieste, making it understood that a rapid solution to this question would considerably facilitate the ratification of the treaty on the European Defense Community (EDC), which was encountering the opposition of the right-wing parties and conservative public opinion.

---

[1] The currency, the administrative structure, the political system were Italian. Italy also had contributed important financial aid which had helped to reconstruct the Triestine economy.

This served as a warning to the allies, and especially to the United States, which had frequently exercised pressure to have the EDC treaty ratified, since the reinforcement of the Western defense system depended upon it. Pella made it plain that the country was tired of waiting for the "payment of the Trieste bill of exchange." This was, of course, a tactical expedient to put pressure in turn on the allies, but as a result, in the mind of a certain sector of the public, Pella had assumed a more energetic attitude in the defense of national interests and his personal position was therefore reinforced. The conservative press, that is, the majority of the Italian press, received the Prime Minister's firm statement favorably, bearing out the growing dissatisfaction with the pro-Western orientation that up to now had been pursued without question.

The allied governments answered Pella's proposal in a bipartite declaration, which stated that they were willing to hand over the entire territory occupied by Anglo-American troops to Italian administration. This meant for all practical purposes a return of Trieste to Italy within a short time. The response to the announcement was enthusiastic. Patriotic manifestations took place all over the country, and the prestige of Pella, the effectiveness of whose policy was borne out by the allied response, increased even more with the public.

On October 10th and 11th, Marshal Tito reacted violently to the bipartite declaration, warning that Yugoslavia would consider the occupation of Zone A by Italian troops as an act of aggression. In the course of the month of October the tension between Italy and Yugoslavia increased, and the allied powers were subjected to strong pressures from both sides. Manifestations against the British and American Embassies took place in Belgrade, while in Trieste, during a heated demonstration in favor of reunification with Italy on November 6th, the local police, who depended on the allied military government, opened fire on the crowd, killing six demonstrators and wounding sixty. Following this episode, the attitude of important segments of the Italian public toward the allies became openly hostile; the U.S.A. and Great Britain were accused of playing a double game. In Rome popular manifestations were organized in front of the British Embassy.[1] The Italian Government strongly protested to the allied authorities, who, in their anxiety to avoid new episodes, refused Pella permission to go to Trieste to participate at the funeral of the victims and the Italian journalists permission to visit the wounded in the hospitals. In consequence of the allied hardening of attitude and a new refusal by Tito to accept the proposals contained in the note of October 8th, Pella mobilized two divisions and sent them to the border area of Gorizia. The Italian measure was immediately followed by Yugoslav counter measures.

Following these events, which were less threatening than they appeared, inasmuch as they were steps taken for prestige reasons in support of the two governments' respective policies, the allied powers resumed the initiative, proposing a conference between the interested governments. This proposal was rejected by the Yugoslavs, because of the conditions stipulated by Pella, who demanded that the negotiations should take the tripartite declaration of October 8th as a point of departure. Nonetheless the proposal put an end to incidents and reduced the tension between the two governments. In consequence, a few days later, both the Italian and the Yugoslav troops were withdrawn from the borders and the year ended in a calmer atmosphere, although the Trieste problem was left unsolved. A solution was reached a few months later with the partition of the Free Territory of Trieste. Zone A and the city of Trieste, with a few rectifications to satisfy Yugoslavia, were transferred to Italy, which in exchange definitely renounced its rights to Zone B.

The Trieste episode gave considerable ·strength to the Pella Government and assured him of the support of the right-wing parties, which manifestly approved "the tough

---

[1] The allied military commander in Trieste, John Winterton, was a British general.

line" adopted by the Prime Minister. The energetic attitude assumed by Pella with regard to the allied governments, his frequent references to "patriotic values," his decision to mobilize the armed forces had inspired in the country a temporary return of nationalist sentiment that played into the hands of the Monarchists and Neo-Fascists, traditionally the defenders of national values and "a strong state." Pella's policies became independent of the DC, a fact which dangerously undermined the supremacy of the party over the government, and were viewed within the DC with suspicion and concern. The personal following and popularity which Pella had gained threatened to prolong indefinitely the government, which the DC leaders had intended only as a transitional government. It was also feared that the closer ties established with the right-wing parties would eventually change the equilibrium of the various currents within the party and arouse the hostility of the Social Democrats and Republicans, with whose aid the DC leaders still hoped to be able to reconstitute the quadripartite coalition. Finally, there was concern over the effect that Pella's attitude could have on the relations between Italy and the United States. The DC, faithful to De Gasperi's line, continued to base its foreign policy on close friendship with the United States.

The reservations to the Pella Government, expressed more frequently and openly among the centrist elements, the strongest in the DC and represented by men such as De Gasperi and Scelba, and the left, which opposed Pella for ideological reasons, soon brought matters to a head. At the beginning of January 1954 the party secretariat vetoed a government reshuffle, which Pella had proposed and which involved appointing a new Minister of Agriculture, Aldisio, a member of the conservative wing of the DC supported by the Monarchists. The party veto was unofficial and theoretically the government was not bound by it, but it represented an unequivocal condemnation by the party, an action that could have been followed by a vote of non-confidence in Parliament. Consequently, Pella was compelled to resign.

CHAPTER 2

RETURN TO THE QUADRIPARTITE COALITION

THE SCELBA GOVERNMENT

Pella was succeeded by Fanfani, the leader of the "Democratic Initiative" current, which from its original left-wing position was in the process of evolving toward the center. He was carrying out within the party a mediating function that would have permitted him to inherit De Gasperi's role and the secretaryship of the party[1]. He was designated by the President of the Republic, on the insistence of the party, to form a new government in which all the DC currents would be represented. Parliament, however, refused its vote of confidence and the Fanfani Cabinet fell only two weeks after its formation. The right and the left-wing parties voted against, the Liberals abstained, and the DC and the Republicans voted in favor.

The reasons for this negative vote were for the most part political (Fanfani's program was realistic and well-conceived) and resulted from the lack of confidence the parties had in Fanfani, one of the most controversial figures in Italian political life. His past sympathies for Fascist corporatism antagonized the democratic left, which followed his transformist maneuvers with suspicion. And his progressive

---

[1] Fanfani was in fact elected to this position in June 1954.

270

views made him suspect to the right. His defeat prompted Fanfani to concentrate his efforts inside the party on improving its organization to enable him to get control, an objective that he achieved within a short space of time.

The failure of Pella's business government and Fanfani's attempt to form a Demo-Christian monocolor government encouraged the DC leaders to return to the quadripartite formula. The chance was given to Scelba, one of the most convinced supporters of this formula.

The coalition of the years 1948-1953 was revived, although with difficulties and a certain reluctance on the part of the minor parties, whose adherence had to be negotiated by the DC and obtained for a considerable price. The Social Democrats agreed to enter the new government in exchange for the vice-premiership for Saragat, their leader, and the promise that the government would enact a series of social laws, which were included in its program. The Liberals were given two especially coveted ministries: Public Education which bolstered the PLI in its traditional role of defender of lay education against Catholic confessionalism, and the Ministry of Industry, which assured a laissez-faire orientation of the country's economy. The Republicans remained outside of the government but assured it their parliamentary support.

The Scelba Government began its activities in an atmosphere of relative optimism. The Social Democrats voiced their satisfaction with the social laws, which the government was preparing to enact and which established medical assistance to pensioners, insurance assistance to the peasants and the expansion of the construction program for low-cost housing. The right, despite its negative vote, received favorably the announcement of anti-Communist measures, which Scelba had on purpose included in his program. These measures were aimed at limiting Communist Party penetration into the organs of administration, the Army, etc., and at reducing its extensive participation in commercial activities, whereby the PCI collected the better part of the funds required for its financing.

271

The extreme left-wing parties reacted with extreme violence to the new government. The Communists found their *bête noire* in the new Prime Minister, whose energetic police measures taken while he was Minister of the Interior, in 1947-1948, had started the decline of the agitation activity of the Social-Communists and the trade unions that were tied to them. In the new cabinet Scelba reserved for himself, along with the premiership, the Ministry of the Interior, in order to insure the continuance of the systematic effort to contain and reduce the strength of the PCI. Scelba's program therefore seriously menaced the PCI's power positions. In the hope of blocking the government initiative, the party hastened to counter-attack through the CGIL, the Communist-dominated trade union, proclaiming a series of strikes and manifestations with clearly political objectives.

The propaganda offensive of the left was facilitated by a series of scandals which broke out in the first months of the Scelba Government, seriously impairing its prestige with the public. The first was the death of the bandit Gaspare Pisciotta, which occurred under mysterious circumstances in a jail in Palermo.[1] But the most spectacular scandal was without doubt the so-called Montesi affair. It started with the mysterious death of a young woman, Wilma Montesi, which had probably been caused by an excessive dose of narcotics during an orgy held in a hunting lodge near Rome. The case dragged on for three years arousing, especially in its early stages, the morbid interest of the public which was fully exploited by the left-wing parties.

The whole affair ended in 1957 with the acquittal of the

---

[1] Pisciotta was a lieutenant of the famous Sicilian bandit Salvatore Giuliano; he had maintained during his trial that he had killed Giuliano in agreement with the police, while the official version was that Giuliano had been killed by the *carabinieri*. The opposition press was ready to exploit Pisciotta's declarations, which were damaging to the government; and since Scelba had been Minister of Interior at the time (four years earlier) that Giuliano was killed, an attempt was made to indicate his political responsibility in this affair.

main defendants, among them Gianpiero Piccioni, son of Scelba's Foreign Minister, and Ugo Montagna, a pseudo marquis, very well known in the Roman demi-monde. But the early investigations had revealed a whole web of favoritism, collusions and abuses which put the Demo-Christian ruling class and some sectors of the state administration in the worst possible light.

The Scelba Government experienced further difficulties due to the ratification of the EDC Treaty, which was opposed by some Demo-Christian and Social Democratic parliamentarians who feared a German military resurrection, and by the extreme right for nationalistic reasons. The stability of the government would have been put to a severe test by a parliamentary debate on the ratification of the treaty, but the rejection of EDC by the French Parliament saved the government this embarrassment. The French refusal to ratify the treaty definitely eliminated the project for a European army, causing a serious crisis in the process of European unification and in particular putting an end to the attempts for political integration.

THE VANONI PLAN

The most significant government activity in the last months of 1954 evolved around the passing of a series of social laws ranging from social insurance for peasant farmers to the requalification of unemployed manpower; a long term plan for the construction of low-cost housing and school buildings was likewise enacted. But the reformist zeal, which was much publicized during the planning stage, spent itself on these and on a number of other minor measures, leaving the great, fundamental problems untouched. A "Ten-Year Plan for the Development of Occupation and Revenue," the so-called Vanoni Plan, named after the economist and Demo-Christian statesman who had elaborated it, was presented in December 1954. The conflicts and opposition that it engendered in the most conservative circles of the DC prevented it from being more than partially applied, which finally nullified its essential aims.

The plan called for an increase in the investments of the national income from 20.5% to 25.4% over a ten-year period, to be achieved through an economic policy of austerity and by inviting foreign capital investments, a 5% yearly increase in the national income, and the creation of a total of four million new jobs, which would permit the absorption of the existing unemployment and the new labor force. One of the essential premises of the plan, whose final aim was the achievement of a better distribution of the national wealth, was government intervention in those sectors in which private initiative was likely to be insufficient because of the lack of a profit incentive. Again, political conditions and the pressure of powerful private economic groups imposed the principle, as it had earlier with regard to the reconstruction policies, that government action should not be substituted for private initiative, that the latter would be sufficient to achieve the planned rhythm of economic development. Because of these pressures, government intervention was insufficient and the exceptional economic development, which began in 1954, evolved in a disorderly fashion with national income in the period 1954-58 increased by about 5.2% per year, above that envisaged by the Vanoni plan. But this income was far from being evenly distributed, with the result that the already existing lack of balance worsened. The proof was in the continuing unemployment at a constant level of about 2,000,000 persons a year, while the workers' real salaries only increased from 123 to 128.[1]

The government headed by Scelba and those that followed, of Segni and Zoli, in 1955 and 1957, were all responsible for the failure of the plan. Nevertheless it remained a symbol of the government's good intentions as well as an index of conflicts within the DC between the progressive current, which had enthusiastically supported it, and the conservative current, which had sabotaged it.

---

[1] 1948 = 100.

274

Another serious setback to the government's reputation in the field of social reform was caused by a compromise agreement to revise the law on land contracts, that is, the law regulating the termination of contracts for tenant farmers by landed proprietors. The termination of a contract was tied to a "just cause" clause, a formula which stipulated the few cases in which a tenant farmer could be evicted from the land. The Liberal Party, representing the landowners' interests, insisted that the "just cause" stipulation be abolished, which would leave the tenant farmers with little means of legal recourse vis-à-vis the landowners. The draft of the law, which the Scelba Government was preparing to present to Parliament, included a compromise favorable to the landowners, in order to get Liberal support in Parliament. This further yielding by the government to conservative pressure met with the protest of the Republicans, who decided to join the opposition, and of the Social Democratic and Demo-Christian left.

The compromise on the land contracts weakened the Scelba Government further by reducing its majority, and, far from solving the problem, kept it alive in the exchange of bitter polemics that followed in subsequent years.

Other conflicts developed between the majority parties with regard to various other important measures under discussion, such as the reform of the IRI (Institute of Industrial Reconstruction), the regional organization (that is, regional administrative and political decentralization, which, according to the Constitution, was to be effected by the establishment of autonomous regional governments), and finally the law on mineral resources, the importance of which was enhanced by recent discoveries of methane gas in the Po Valley. The problem to be resolved was whether these methane and oil resources should be exploited directly by a state monopoly, or whether the right to exploitation would be granted private companies. The interests involved were important enough for some leading American oil companies to show active interest in obtaining the right of exploitation.

It became clear that the Scelba Government would be unable to solve these major questions, having lost its initial drive and being almost immobilized by its policy of trying to maintain a balance between the progressive and conservative forces within the government coalition.

CHAPTER 3

NEW ORIENTATIONS WITHIN THE PARTIES

THE LIBERAL PARTY

The conflict between the right and left tendencies had always existed within the quadripartite coalition, even during its heyday (1948-1953), representing one of the basic limitations of this political formula, but the internal and international situation in those years and De Gasperi's mediating abilities had assured relative political stability. De Gasperi's death, which occurred on August 18, 1954, outside of the deep sorrow it caused the country, further weakened the Scelba Government, which had been supported by De Gasperi's authority. In addition, the distance between progressives and conservatives inside the coalition tended to widen, thus increasing the Prime Minister's difficulties. At the end of 1954 the entire political alignment was in motion. The displacement of forces was in process especially in the Liberal, Demo-Christian and Socialist Parties, which were to be determining factors in the coming years. In the spring of 1954 Giovanni Malagodi was elected secretary of the Liberal Party; an able and energetic man, he was known to be linked with the economic ruling class and to the big monopolistic groups of the North. Malagodi's secretaryship—he still held the position in 1963—ushered in a new period in the history of the party.

In the post-war years the old Liberal Party had followed

277

a substantially conservative line; its policies for reconstruction followed old laissez-faire patterns. An all-out supporter of private initiative, it always rejected any proposal aiming at the increase of state powers of intervention in economic matters. However, this orientation was not undisputed. Inside the party, alongside a conservative majority tied to the industrial and agrarian interests, was an active and fighting minority which conceived the tasks of the Liberal Party as having two objectives: the defense of laic values and upholding the liberty of the state against the invasion of Catholic confessionalism and the increasing influence of the Church; and active participation in a reform program that would gradually eliminate the profound social and geographical disequilibrium and build a free and modern society. Although the Liberals of the progressive tendency were also defenders of private initiative, they were willing to sacrifice it wherever it did not recognize the tasks and interests of a modern and democratic society.

The coexistence of these two tendencies kept the party divided and in conflict for many years, weakening its political action but exercising at the same time an equilibrating function.

The accession of Malagodi to the secretaryship of the party marked the end of the progressive influence: the defense of the interests of the "economic right" against any policy of reform and state intervention henceforth constituted the essential aim of the party. The departure of the progressive Liberals at the end of 1955, who left the Liberal Party and founded the Radical Party, was the immediate and inevitable consequence of the party's new orientation. The Radical Party had a short life as a political formation (for all practical purposes, it ceased to exist in 1962), but it made important contributions to the study and discussion of the program of the new center-left coalition which in these years was in the process of formation.[1] An analogical dis-

---

[1] Not disposing of an organizational apparatus and a representation in Parliament, and having a limited membership, the PR acted more as a

placement toward the right occurred in the *Confindustria*.

In recent years the Italian captains of industry, encouraged by an ever more advantageous economic situation, have been adopting new and more dynamic patterns of industrial management. The increase of investments (about 65 per cent in the period between 1950-1959) resulted both in a higher level of mechanization and in a considerable increase in labor productivity, which during the same period rose by 100 per cent. This evolution had deep repercussions on the industrial enterprises themselves. By instituting a policy of higher salaries and major incentives for the working class elite, together with new means of pressure and intimidation, industrial management succeeded, especially in the more important combines, in reducing considerably the strength of the extreme left-wing trade union movement, which was linked to concepts and methods of struggle which by then were outdated. In the elections for the internal commissions,[1] held in April 1955 at the Fiat works, the CGIL receded from 60 per cent (1954) to 38 per cent, with a loss of over 15,000 votes; similar results occurred in other enterprises. Encouraged by this setback to the Communist trade unions, the industrialists decided to broaden and intensify their action of political pressure through the *Confindustria*.

The change in orientation provoked a change of the industrial leadership. The former president, Angelo Costa, a man of moderate views, was replaced by Alighiero De Micheli, president of the *Assolombarda*[2] (Business Association of Lombardy), a younger and more dynamic man, who was expected to intervene more directly in the political life of the country. The policies of the Liberal Party and the action

---

pressure group than as a party. Its activity evolved mainly around study groups, congresses on particular problems of political life and the columns of two weeklies, *Il Mondo* and *L'Espresso*. Thanks to a considerable number of intellectuals, experts and technicians who adhered to it, the Radical Party developed an important role as a stimulus to research, which benefited the entire democratic left.

[1] The internal commissions are representative organs for the defense of the workers with regard to management.

[2] The most influential regional branch of the *Confindustria*.

279

of *Confindustria* in the following years became more and more integrated and directed toward the same objectives.

The displacement of the Liberals toward the right could not be without influence on the equilibrium of the forces represented in the government, all the more since it corresponded at the same time to a considerable increase in the weight and political influence of the left-wing currents within the DC.

CHRISTIAN DEMOCRATIC AND SOCIALIST PARTIES

The DC Congress, which was held in Naples at the end of June 1954, was concluded with a major strengthening of the "democratic initiative" current and with the election of Fanfani, its leader, to the secretaryship of the party. The victory of "democratic initiative," the most important of the left DC currents, signified the beginning of a process of renewal within the Catholic ruling group, first inside the party and later at the level of government, and consequently a revision of the course followed up to then by the party. This change, which was not unexpected, was realized only after long preparation undertaken in the preceding years. In Naples the DC ceased to be a centrist party, which it had been during the entire De Gasperi period, and laid the basis for a new policy oriented to the left. Though it continued to be, as it had in the past, a party which drew its membership from all social classes, the DC, in competition with the other left-wing democratic parties, committed itself to a policy of safeguarding the rights of the working class and of improving its living conditions.

Such a program could be realized, however, only with the support of new forces and new parties. After the Liberal Party had become clearly identified with the conservative right, the DC needed new allies, in addition to the Republicans and Social-Democrats, whose combined strength could not provide strong enough parliamentary support to allow the DC to undertake major social reforms.

280

Thus it began to watch with ever growing interest the slow evolution going on within the Socialist Party.

The results of the PSI Congress, held in Turin from March 31 to April 2, 1955, encouraged this interest. In a speech, which caused a considerable stir in the entire country, the leader of the PSI repeated the invitation for a policy of "an opening to the left," affirming that his party was ready for an experiment of collaboration with the Catholics.

Nenni's renewed offer and the increased influence of the left-wing current of the DC appeared to open new possibilities for a center-left majority. Consequently, the government's position, which was now considerably weakened, due both to intrinsic factors and to the political shifts that had taken place within the coalition parties, in the PLI and in the DC, became even more precarious.

The request for a "clarification" (which in parliamentary language is equivalent to a request for the fall of the government) became more insistent, and only the trip of Prime Minister Scelba to the United States, which had been planned earlier, put off the crisis. After his return from Washington, on April 8th, the attacks against the government were resumed with renewed intensity.

THE ELECTION OF PRESIDENT GRONCHI AND THE OPENING OF THE CRISIS

A further element intervened which, in the government's weakened position, definitely decided its fate. The seven-year-term of the first President of the Republic, Luigi Einaudi, was about to come to an end. Since Einaudi refused to run for a second term, the problem of the succession to the highest office in the state was opened. Considering the political importance of the choice, the antagonisms between the parties of the majority were immediately unloosed. If they had been united, they could very well have decided the election by their own strength. As it turned out, on the contrary, the election of the new president was the episode that gave the government the *coup de grace*.

The official candidate of the DC and of the government, Cesare Merzagora, President of the Senate, of conservative tendency, did not succeed in obtaining the necessary majority because a part of the Demo-Christian deputies, disregarding party discipline, refused to vote for him. Instead, Giovanni Gronchi, who represented the left-wing current of the DC, was elected. A large majority was formed around him. This majority included the Communists and Socialists who had presented Gronchi's candidature with the precise intention of embarrassing the government, because he was considered too far to the left. As Gronchi's victory became apparent, the center and the right of the DC, who had openly fought him, were compelled against their will to vote for him in the final ballot[1] in order not to make the election of the president dependent on the Communist votes. The defeat suffered by the government appeared clear and all the more serious, because, according to general opinion, Gronchi was one of the first convinced proponents of an agreement between Socialists and Catholics which stood at the base of the "opening to the left." After a last attempt by Scelba to reinforce the coalition through a government reshuffle, which failed because of the Republicans' refusal to participate, the crisis was inevitable. On June 22, 1955, Scelba handed in his resignation to the President of the Republic, whose election he had so bitterly opposed.

Following Gronchi's election and the resignation of the Scelba Government the internal crisis in the DC deepened. The party was divided into three main currents: the left led by Fanfani, the party secretary, who though reinforced by his victory at the congress in Naples still did not possess sufficient forces to impose his own social program on the whole party; the center, constantly fluctuating between right and left-wing positions, under the leadership of the so-called

---

[1] According to Art. 83 of the Constitution "The presidential election takes place by secret ballot with a majority of two thirds of both Houses assembled in a joint session. After the third ballot an absolute majority is sufficient."

"notables," that is, influential men, each having a personal following though insufficient for the formation of a new current; and the right, headed by Giulio Andreotti and Pella, which was linked to the clergy and large industry.

Considering this state of internal division and conflict within the party, it appeared difficult to undertake a revolutionary operation of the scope of an entente between Socialists and Catholics, which would have resulted in a reversal of alliances and could have caused a serious crisis inside the DC, jeopardizing its unity. On the other hand, a seriously reformist policy could not have been carried out without Nenni's Socialist Party, whose numerical support in Parliament was indispensable in order to counterbalance the inevitable opposition of the Liberal Party and to establish a wide majority in favor of the government. For that reason, after many explorations and conversations between the leaders of both parties, the DC was compelled to postpone the experiment of an "opening to the left." Too many Demo-Christians, even from the left-wing current, voiced serious doubts. The objections were that the Socialist Party was still too closely linked to the Communists, after the many years of popular-front orientation; that the autonomist current inside the PSI, in favor of breaking the ties with the Communists, was still not sufficiently strong to carry with it the entire party in a policy of collaboration with the Catholics. The 20th Congress of the Soviet Communist Party, the policy of the "thaw," of a relaxation of tension, inaugurated by Khrushchev, and the Hungarian Revolution were to give the decisive push in the process of disinvolvement from the Communists.

THE SEGNI GOVERNMENT

The "opening to the left" presupposed a gradual orientation of the left wing of the PSI and the right wing of the DC toward positions held in common by the Nenni autonomists and the progressive Catholics. It was expected that

283

such a confluence would only take place after several pending issues between the two parties had been cleared. This would obviously have required time and long negotiations. Before a complete understanding could be reached only transitional governments with limited political tasks and with a limited program could be constituted. They would open a political truce-period during which the possibilities for the new majority would be explored. It was with this in mind that the government headed by Antonio Segni[1] was formed in June 1955. It was not representative of any of the three major currents within the DC. Segni, though a DC "notable," was acceptable to the Demo-Christian left wing, because of his participation in the land reform.

A moderate, temperate man, he enjoyed the confidence of the right as well. He was the man best suited to mediate between the various DC currents, whose differences had become increasingly intense. The transitional character of the Segni Government and the lack of alternative solutions, made possible, despite opposition, a return to the quadripartite formula, which had appeared irremediably finished in the last months of the Scelba Government. For that reason, after long negotiations to gain support for the government outside of the DC, the Liberals and the Social-Democrats decided to join the majority. The Republicans kept aloof, waiting to judge the government according to the program which it would present.

The Segni Government stayed in power for almost two years, until May 12, 1957. The two years were not especially productive on the level of government activity, although some important problems, which had already come up under the Scelba Government, matured in this period. For the most part during the period of the Segni Government, in particular the "unforgettable year 1956," the attention of the public, and even more so that of the parties, was focused on international events.

---

[1] Antonio Segni, professor of Agriculture at the University of Rome, formerly a Minister of Agriculture in various cabinets, is one of the authors of the land reform. He was elected President of the Republic in May, 1962.

CHAPTER 4

HISTORICAL AND POLITICAL JUSTIFICATIONS
OF THE OPENING TO THE LEFT

THE WORKING CLASSES AND THE STATE

The crisis of the Scelba Government officially opened the debate on the "opening to the left," which up to that time had been a subject of discussion among the various political currents of the democratic left. The fact that the quadripartite formula had failed turned the attention of the DC and the public as a whole to the problem of enlarging and consolidating the government majority with the participation of other forces. Considering the position of the parties, which reflected the political tendencies in the country, such a broadening could be achieved only through an accord of Socialists and Catholics. On the other hand, the formation of a new majority was merely one aspect of an historical and political consideration of much greater magnitude: the participation of the working class masses in the political life of the country.

From 1947, the year which marked the end of government cooperation between the three mass parties (the DC, PCI and PSI), the gulf between the working masses and the state had become progressively greater.

The 1948 election blocked the Communist march to power, but also created a profound break between the working class, organized and controlled by the extreme left-wing parties, and the rest of the country under DC guidance.

After the defeat of 1948 the PCI was left with no other

prospect but a long-term action, undertaken on all levels, aimed at undermining democratic institutions: in Parliament, the trade unions, in intellectual circles, in the factories and among the poorest proletariat in the South, who were still politically unaware and among whom the Communists hoped to gain many adherents. In this effort to organize the opposition against the majority in power the PCI had achieved considerable success. Due to its enormous financial means, its discipline, and the ingenuity of its propaganda, the party succeeded in creating a state within a state and in freezing almost 35 per cent of the Italian electorate in an attitude of systematic and intransigent opposition.

The recovery of these masses and their inclusion into the active life of the Italian state was considered the most urgent problem of the democratic political parties. Since 1950, the left currents of the parties of the majority and in particularly that of the DC had become increasingly aware of the problem. This was a political group composed of young elements, who had been formed in the anti-Fascist struggle and in the emotional atmosphere of the postwar period. They assumed a critical attitude toward the old leadership of the DC and of its centrist orientation, whose ineptitude they openly denounced; that is, their inability to carry out a broad program of social reforms which would give the working classes not only a higher standard of living but also complete equality of rights with all other citizens. The influence which the privileged strata had excercised on the governments after the war had given weight to the Communist theory of class struggle and had contributed to the deepening of the gulf between the state and the working class, thus playing into the hands of the Communist Party. If this alienation were to continue, it would be impossible to achieve a genuine democracy in Italy a democracy which would not only be reflected in its institutions, but also in its social and economic relations. Furthermore Italian society would always remain under the potential danger of anti-democratic coups as a result of the constant pressures to which the government was subjected from both right and left extremists.

For that reason it was necessary to bridge the gap and break through the isolation of the masses, to remedy the injustices which had been done to them and to give them the feeling that they belonged in a society as full members and not as second-class citizens.

The problem of the "inclusion of the masses into the state," as it became known in political language in the years following the 1953 elections, became the essential problem of the democratic left-wing parties and currents. The most outstanding formulation, an historic pronouncement, was the message addressed to the country by President Giovanni Gronchi soon after his taking of office. Gronchi's message produced an enormous impact. It was a courageous overture to the working classes, a clear reminder to the government that it was time to carry out a broad program of reforms and an admonition to the privileged classes and vested interests not to hinder a new attempt to bring about a political and social renewal.

THE AUTONOMIST TENDENCIES WITHIN THE PSI

The currents of the democratic left counted on the Socialist Party for the achievement of the tasks that lay ahead. For historical and ideological reasons the PSI could provide a better guarantee for a long-term agreement on a program which could resolve the social problems of the country within the framework of democratic principles.

Even during the popular-front period, a strong tendency had remained within the PSI in favor of maintaining the party's autonomy with regard to the Communist Party. It advocated the development of an independent Socialist policy in view of providing the working class with an alternative (hence the expression, "socialist alternative," which had been coined to define a similar policy).

As early as the summer of 1948, in the course of the Socialist congress, held at Genoa to evaluate the reasons for the electoral defeat of April 18th and future prospects,

287

the objective considerations that would justify a policy of a "socialist alternative" had emerged. It appeared clearly from an analysis of the future outlook of the party made by the leaders of the autonomist currents (Riccardo Lombardi, Giuseppe Romita, Giovanni Pieraccini), that if the party intended to carry out a policy that would benefit the working classes, it had to disengage itself from the political line followed by the Communists. After the defeat of April 1948 and its renunciation of revolutionary action, the Communist Party had no prospects for the near future; it therefore could have no other course in effect than to isolate the working classes in a sterile opposition. The only possible policy that could secure immediate benefits for the working classes, in the last analysis, was then a policy of reformism in the classical style, which would accept without reserve and implement democratic political institutions. But in 1948 the outlook for a policy of social demands and conquests did not appear favorable.

The victorious majority, following its electoral success of 1948, had stiffened its own positions, and the Italian bourgeoisie, which by now had become more secure, having passed unharmed through the "great fear" immediately after the war, was not disposed to make many concessions to the working classes. For these reasons, but above all due to the fear that to take a line independent of the Communist line might imperil working-class unity, the Socialist Party continued, although with growing reservations, the policy of collaboration with the PCI.

But as time went on, the alliance with the PCI became increasingly uncomfortable for the Socialists. It is enough to compare the electoral results achieved by both parties between 1946 and 1953, to understand why:

	PSI	PCI
1946	4,758,129 (20.7%)	4,356,686 (18.9%)
1948	8,137,047	
1953	3,441,305 (12.7%)	6,121,922 (22.6%)

Between 1946 and 1953 the PSI lost more than a million and a half votes, while the PCI gained almost 2 million votes. If the increase in the electorate is taken into account, and the percentages of the figures are compared, the losses of the PSI increased (falling from 20.7 per cent to 12.7 per cent); even considering the inevitable losses as a result of the Socialist split in 1947, and the subsequent formation of the Social-Democratic Party, the losses of the PSI in absolute terms remained considerable. They were caused in large part by the shift of votes from the PSI to its Communist ally. This may be demonstrated by an analysis of the results of the 1948[1] elections (in which both parties presented a joint list of the popular front), as well as from subsequent studies.

The comparison appeared even more unfavorable on the organizational level. The PCI, due to the means for action at its disposal and the better training of its leaders and officials in the techniques of modern political struggle, was corroding the positions of the Socialists even in areas where the PSI had traditionally enjoyed great prestige. It also extended its influence and control in one of the currents of the PSI, the left current, whose leaders (Tullio Vecchietti, Vittorio Foa, Emilio Lussu) were closely linked to the PCI. In the joint trade union, the CGIL, whose apparatus was entirely in the hands of the Communists, the situation was still more unfavorable to the PSI.

Hence, the results of the Unity of Action Pact, which had tied the two parties in a close alliance for several years, were anything but positive for the Socialist Party, which witnessed the gradual decrease of its influence among the working-class masses. There can be no doubt that this was one of the reasons which prompted the Socialist leadership to develop a new policy and to accentuate the need for differentiation between itself and its ally. That was why the

---

[1] The ground lost by the PSI to the PCI appears, despite the single joint list, in the calculation of the preferential votes, which were obtained by Socialist and Communist candidates.

campaign for the 1953 election was conducted by the PSI on the platform of the "Socialist alternative," which, although not in open opposition to the PCI, nevertheless competed with it and represented the logical shift in the passage to the policy of the "opening to the left." The electoral results, which were favorable to the candidates belonging to the autonomist current of the PSI, encouraged Nenni to insist with greater emphasis on this new orientation.

The Socialist leader, in July 1953, clearly enunciated the concept of an "opening to the left," affirming the availability of his party for the formation of a new majority. Speaking in the Chamber during the debate on De Gasperi's eighth cabinet, which was rejected a few days later, Nenni declared that for his party "the Socialist alternative was postulated on an opening to the left of the majority and the government with the inclusion of the working class masses in the democratic and republican state; it envisaged a policy aimed at the infusion of democratic principles into the laws and customs of our country, guarantees of freedom, economic reforms, which are written into the Constitution... Our answer as to the possibility of an opening to the left is affirmative; that means that we consider in the actual situation that there is an objective possibility of an opening to the left."

The conditions under which the Socialists were ready to support a government of an "opening to the left" were enumerated by Nenni for the first time in his speech in July 1953: the abrogation of the electoral law (the possibilities of an agreement on this point were discounted); a request for the enactment of laws to implement the Constitution (especially the laws concerning regional autonomy); the reform of land contracts, the nationalization of industries operating as monopolies (but in reality the Socialists would have been satisfied with the nationalization of electric power, at least in the first phase), and a new educational policy of equal opportunity for all.

These demands were not exorbitant and could easily be conciliated with the programs of the Social Democrats, Republicans and the left-wing of the Demo-Christians. They were nevertheless ahead of the political climate at the time and of the disposition of forces within the three parties themselves, particularly within the DC, where the right and center currents were still stronger than the left current, despite its recent progress. Two major obstacles were in the way of a rapid realization of an opening to the left, and explain its very long period of gestation. The first was the Socialists' continued collaboration with the Communists in the trade unions and in local administrations where Socialists and Communists joined to form majorities or together constituted the opposition. The second was the position of the PSI in matters of foreign policy.

The Socialist and Communist Parties had been associated for many years in opposition to the foreign policy of the center party coalition: together they rejected the Marshall Plan, even though inside the PSI there were many members who advocated accepting its aid; they conducted a common propaganda campaign against the Atlantic alliance and against rearmament. This joint action had finally convinced the public and even informed observers that no difference existed between the positions of the two parties, inasmuch as neutralism and opposition to military pacts, which had been a standard political theme of the Socialists from the end of the last century, coincided with the Communist position of open support for the Soviet Union.

However, with the evolution of the international situation and the reduction of tension between the two great-power blocs, the real divergencies between the two parties began to become openly manifest. When the immediate danger of a global conflict appeared to have receded, the Socialists no longer felt bound by a policy of class unity and assumed an increasingly independent attitude.

The Atlantic alliance was no longer condemned, as it had been in the years 1949-1951 as an instrument of aggression; in addition, within the Western world, political positions were becoming more differentiated, and the Socialists were ready to recognize this fact. By now an agreement, even in matters of foreign policy, with the Catholics, who in the last few years had manifested tendencies toward making an effort for world peace and favoring a foreign policy aimed at easing international tension, appeared to be within the realm of possibility. The Socialists no longer demanded the renunciation of military pacts, but rather a policy which would promote peace and rapprochement between the great powers.

According to Nenni, the choice of a new foreign policy for the Socialists was "no longer posed in terms of acceptance or of hostility to the Atlantic Alliance, but between what "I call Atlantic die-hardism and the tendency now represented by London to put an end to the cold war with a peace without victors or defeated."

The Socialist attitude became more conciliatory in 1955 in the atmosphere of the so-called "Spirit of Geneva." But the most significant influence on the Socialist Party position was the 20th Congress of the CPSU (Communist Party of the Soviet Union) and the Hungarian Revolution.

THE 20TH CONGRESS OF THE CPSU AND THE HUNGARIAN REVOLUTION

Both events had highly important repercussions on the attitudes of the extreme left-wing parties in Italy. They not only nearly caused the outbreak of a crisis within the PCI, which had been latent for years, but also profoundly affected the relationship between the Socialists and Communists. While the crisis within the PCI was quickly brought under control, since it endangered the unity of the party, the relationship with the Socialists was irremediably marred.

The 20th Congress of the CPSU (February 1956), Khrushchev's denunciation of the cult of personality and subsequent episodes, such as the rehabilitation of some well-known victims of Stalinism, and the dissolution of the Cominform, aroused doubts and caused disorientation among the PCI members and sympathizers.

The administrative elections, held in June 1956, were

marked by considerable losses for the Communists, in particular in centers such as Turin, Milan and Genoa, where the PCI had been traditionally strong. While the Communist leadership was able to limit the negative effects of the Congress revelations within the party ranks during the first months following the Congress, the publication of Khrushchev's secret speech by the U.S. State Department provoked serious ferment and demands for clarification. In order to soften its consequences and to prevent the development of a new rebellion within certain sectors of the party's rank and file, Togliatti, in an interview given to a left-wing cultural review, *Nuovi Argomenti*, interpreted the recent events in the Soviet bloc as the beginning of a new course for the Western Communist Parties. Togliatti affirmed these events, indicated there was no longer a necessity for the Soviet Union to play a guiding role and that every Communist Party would be free to follow its own course, that is, the course that would be considered best adapted to the historical conditions of the country. This unprejudiced thesis of so-called "polycentrism" could have been extremely dangerous to the unity of the party. In fact, Togliatti's ideological concessions, made necessary because of the danger of an internal revolt, after having been called to order by the Russians, remained a dead letter and the political life within the party continued to develop along the officially established lines. During the whole summer of 1956 the party assumed a cautious attitude of expectation with regard to further evidences of de-Stalinization. The difficulties that had arisen as a result of the Twenty-Second Congress of the CPSU seemed to be gradually subsiding when, at the end of October 1956, the dramatic Hungarian popular insurrection against the regime of the Stalinist Matthias Rakosi and his replacement by Imre Nagy took place.

The crisis precipitated within the party by the Hungarian revolution was even more serious than the preceding one. It not only shook the rank and file but the leadership strata as well, as evidenced by the contradictory interpretations of the events given by responsible party chiefs. There appeared

293

to be no official line to explain the events. The line supported by *Unità*, the PCI daily, was that a counter revolution, backed by reactionaries, had taken place; it was obviously in contradiction, however, with the news carried by pro-Communist papers coming from the Hungarian capital.

Even the Communist-controlled trade union, CGIL, disavowed the *Unità* thesis, and adopted an attitude of solidarity with the insurrectionists, while an important group of Communist intellectuals signed a manifesto of protest against the party leadership. The protests, which came in from all over the country, the hostile attitude of the rank-and-file, threatened grave consequences for the integrity of the party. But further developments in the situation enabled the Communist leader to retake the initiative and again control the crisis.

One was the Anglo-French attack against Suez which in part diverted the attention of the public and presented the Communists with the opportunity to make the same accusations of aggression and imperialism against the Western powers that had been leveled against the USSR for its intervention in Hungary. The other was the decision of the Hungarian Prime Minister, Imre Nagy, to withdraw Hungary from the Warsaw Pact and to authorize the formation of other political parties in the country outside of the Communist Party. This enabled the leadership of the PCI to renew the charge of a "counterrevolution" and thereby justify the second armed Russian intervention, which in a few days defeated the insurrectionists. The Soviet intervention was presented as a painful necessity in defense against an attempt to restore a reactionary regime, an attempt, which, had it expanded to other East-European countries, would have presented a danger for the Communist revolution and could have provoked the third world war. Thus proclaiming a state of emergency and appealing to the discipline of the party in the name of the highest aims of peace and the revolution, the PCI was able to quell dissidence and deviationism.

As a consequence of the Hungarian Revolution the PCI lost the support of a considerable number of its members (about 300,000), among whom were some of its most articulate elements, especially intellectuals, whose support the party had always valued highly for prestige reasons; but due to the evolution of events and the discipline of its members, the leadership managed to safeguard party unity. The political elections in 1958, which resulted in only minor losses for the party, showed that the crisis, at least from the most evident consequences, definitely had been overcome.

SOCIALIST REACTIONS

Neverthless, the Twentieth Congress, the Khrushchev report and the Hungarian insurrection had caused a serious break between the Communists and the Socialists. In a series of articles in *Avanti*, the Socialist daily, Nenni defined the position of his party with regard to the Twentieth Congress. In them he condemned not only Stalin's tyranny, but leveled a more broad criticism against a regime which allowed a similar tyranny.

The violent polemics between Socialist and Communist leaders over the interpretations of the Hungarian revolt were augmented by manifestations of indignation and condemnations among the Socialist rank-and-file. Nenni declared in the Chamber: "We condemn without reticence the Soviet intervention in Hungary, as it manifested itself in the first and even more so in the dramatic last phase of the Hungarian uprising." A few days later the Socialist leader returned the Stalin prize he had received in 1953.

Despite numerous and unequivocal affirmations of its position, the PSI did not attempt to profit from the crisis within the PCI and persuade its members and sympathizers to join the Socialist ranks; it was unable or unwilling to carry its action to this logical end. Its uncertainties and the deficiency of its organization were still too great; and the PSI was not encouraged by the other democratic parties, who attempted to profit from the Communist crisis by engaging in

295

propaganda offensives. These, however, rather than harming, served the PCI, in that they prompted the Communist followers to close ranks around the party.

Only a powerful Socialist movement could have profited from the disorientation caused by the Hungarian uprising and have broken the political monopoly of the PCI among vast sections of the working classes. The negotiations, which took place between Nenni and Saragat, to examine the possibilities of a reunification of the PSI and the PSDI, in the summer of 1956 (so-called meeting of Pralognan, from the name of the alpine village where it took place), almost ten years after the Socialist split, had awakened great hopes. The constitution of a strong unified Socialist Party could have isolated the PCI and gradually reduced its importance. But neither Nenni, still hampered by a strong pro-Communist minority inside his party, nor Saragat, whose party had lost much of its initial reformist zeal in the course of so many years of participation in the government and feared it would lose its identity in association with the more numerous PSI, had the courage to take a decision, which could have become of historic importance.

A few months after the Hungarian revolution, in February 1957, the Socialist Party held its 32nd Congress in Venice. It marked a further separation from the Communists. Nenni's speech to the Congress delegates, outside of giving a substantially different interpretation of the Twentieth Congress of the CPSU and of the Hungarian revolt from that of the Communists, also affirmed the PSI's full acceptance of the democratic parliamentary method. "When we say democracy, we not only mean an aim but also a method with which we intend to inspire our practice," Nenni stated, "renouncing, so far as we are concerned, the appeal to violence... When we say democracy, we express our loyalty to universal suffrage, in Parliament, to the multiplicity of parties, that is, to the representative system, which has in the republican Constitution its basic charter and in which we see a sufficient guarantee for the working class to develop its struggle for power."

The Congress of Venice ended in a success for Nenni's and the autonomists' theses, but at the same time it reconfirmed the contradictions existing within the party. The final motion, presented by Nenni, which constituted a distinct differentiation of the PSI from the PCI, was approved unanimously. But immediately following, the vote to elect the directorate of the party, which should have concretely reflected the decisions of the congress, gave the *carristi* as the PSI leftwingers were called, who favored a policy of collaboration with the PCI, an unexpectedly high number of representatives in the party directorate. As a clear result of the Congress there remained a declaration of principles, of unquestionable political importance; this demonstrated the great extent to which the separation of the PSI from the PCI was by now irreversible. Nevertheless, the way toward a more positive and rapid development remained, for the time being at least, blocked.

The history of the party during the years that paved the way for the "opening to the left" was full of these contradictions. On the one hand there was a majority, as yet not strong enough, which demonstrated the clear will to proceed toward a new policy; on the other hand, a powerful minority, which intended to maintain the party's allegiance to the popular front policy, and which attempted to retard and impede the process of disengagement.

Thus, alongside the official Socialist statements denouncing the Unity of Action Pact, which had tied the Socialists to the Communists since 1934, and a concrete situation in which the two parties entered into open competition, during the electoral campaign of 1958, mutual sympathies persisted as well as close collaboration in the provincial and local self-governments, in the trade unions, in the agricultural cooperatives, and in cultural circles.

The opponents of the "opening to the left" policy denounced the continuance of these relations, accused the Socialists of duplicity, and construed the policy as a new tactic of the left for the conquest of power. In reality, after the first phase, the separation of the two parties was necessarily slow; for the Socialists the process meant the reversal of a long-standing political tendency, cemented by many battles fought together. The problem, after so many years of intransigent opposition, was to convince the working classes that this position was sterile and produced the contrary results. A similar process went on within the DC; its progressive groups attempted to convince the moderate tendencies within the party that an alliance with the PSI was the only means to achieve government stability and the necessary condition for a policy of reforms. Both these processes were bound to be full of incertitude and difficulties.

CHAPTER 5

TOWARD THE POLITICAL ELECTIONS OF 1958

THE SEGNI GOVERNMENT: INTERNAL POLICY

During the two years of the Segni Government, the political debate evolved in the main around the problem of land contracts, which dealt with relations between tenant farmers and proprietors. This question which had been drawn out for years, had been tackled by the preceding Scelba Govenment.[1] Immediately after Scelba's fall the protests and demands for revision that had accompanied Scelba's agreement with the Liberals were renewed. The opponents were the Republicans, Social Democrats and the left-wing currents of the DC, who, preoccupied with the discontent in the rural areas, feared that it would be exploited by the Communists. Their protests induced the government to study new solutions which were presented to the Parliament, in January 1957. After heated debates, which on February 28th even caused the PRI withdrawal from the majority, a new compromise was reached in April. The new project of law set forth the specific reasons which would enable the proprietor of the land to appeal to the "just cause," in order to evict a tenant from the land, increasing them from the original four to six.[2] This solution, although it improved the law,

---

[1] See page 276.   t
[2] This compromise was not final. The discussion on the land contracts went on under the succeeding governments until, in 1958, due to the impossibility to reach agreement, the Fanfani Government definitely abandoned

which had been passed under the Scelba Government, remained contrary to the interests of the peasants since it weakened their bargaining position vis à vis the proprietors. On the other hand, the government intended with this provision to counteract the growing disinterest of small and medium proprietors in agricultural activity. Such economic and political reasons as the low income from agriculture and the growing influence of the extreme left in the farming areas, which made the relations between peasants and proprietors increasingly difficult, provided the basis for this disinterest and of the crisis, which by now had become chronic in Italian agriculture.

In the industrial sector, on the other hand, the government agreed in a much larger measure to the demands of the left currents, consolidating and broadening the already vast public interests. The reorganization of the industrial activities partially or totally controlled by the state was undertaken to coordinate this activity, and a Ministry of State Participations was created in January 1956. The question of the exploitation of petrochemicals, which involved numerous private national and international interests, was resolved in favor of ENI (The National Petrochemical Corporation), the state enterprise for the exploitation of the national petrochemical oil resources; ENI was granted the monopoly to prospect in the Po Valley, particularly rich in methane gas deposits. Thus once again the principle of government intervention in industry was reaffirmed. The concession of the exclusive right to exploit the Po Valley methane and oil resources to ENI was in fact part of the program advocated by the progressive left for the public control of all sources of energy and was to lead, as a final act, to the nationalization of the electric power industries in 1963, one of the most significant acts of the first government of the "opening to the left."

Another important act of the Segni Government was the formation of the Constitutional Court, which after an unjus-

all efforts, which had by then gone on for ten years, to give the problem a new legal framework.

tifiably long delay, finally instituted one of the most important governmental organs provided for by the Constitution. The judges were elected in November and December 1955, and the Court held its first session on April 23, 1956.

NEO-ATLANTISM

The foreign policy of the Segni Government did not substantially differ from the traditional orientation in favor of the Atlantic Alliance and of close cooperation with the United States. If there was change, it mainly concerned the forms this policy took. Yet it was none the less symptomatic of an evolution that was developing on the international level and that was being reflected in internal politics.

After Stalin's death, the changes within the Soviet ruling group and the need of the USSR for a long period of peace in order to assimilate its internal and external conquests, led to a break in the cold war and the reduction of tension between the two great-power blocs. The new situation manifested itself gradually amid many contradictions, but in 1956-57 the "spirit of Geneva"[1] had borne fruit both on the political and, even more so, the psychological level. The Italian public was one of the first in Europe to realize the changed atmosphere, but the majority continued realistically to recognize the need to maintain mutual defense structures and particularly NATO intact. The Segni Government, and the one headed by Zoli that followed in May 1957, pursued policies which on the whole stuck quite closely to the traditional line.

Although Italian foreign policy was by now far from the "Atlantic die-hard" policy of De Gasperi, it was not swayed by pressures from the democratic left-wing currents, which demanded that Italy become actively engaged in a

---

[1] So-called because of the atmosphere of confidence and hope ushered in by the meeting of the heads of state of the four great powers (U.S., U.S.S.R., Great Britain and France) that took place in the Swiss city in July 1955 for the purpose of "reducing international tensions and the consolidation of confidence in the relations between the countries."

301

policy aimed at the reduction of tension, and that the country develop a more independent course with regard to its Atlantic commitments.

It was precisely in these years, however, that a new approach to foreign policy was germinating, of which the general public was barely aware, but which enjoyed considerable support among certain élite groups. The expression "neo-Atlantism" described this new orientation. The circles around President Gronchi were "neo-Atlantic." Young officials of the Ministry of Foreign Affairs, who were close to the secretary of the DC, Amintore Fanfani; the President of ENI, Enrico Mattei; and some elements within the left-wing democratic parties supported the same line. They gave the Atlantic Pact a new interpretation, rejecting it as an exclusively military alliance, and considering it as an instrument of the political and economic collaboration of the Western nations.

Although the Constitution does not stipulate any function of the President in matters of foreign policy, President Gronchi became the most authoritative exponent of "neo-Atlantism". In a speech given to the U.S. Congress during an official visit to Washington, Gronchi affirmed that the Atlantic Pact "did not correspond to the present-day situation... No one can view without anguish or uneasiness the prospects of a world in which peace rests almost exclusively on military strength and on half-finished political entities."

In addition to a new approach in the Atlantic policy, the "neo-Atlantists" demanded that Italy be more active in taking political and economic initiatives, especially with regard to the new nations of the Middle East and the African Mediterranean, with the double aim of aiding these countries to reach a higher standard of civilization and well-being and to find new markets for the products of the national economy. The ENI, which under the impetus of Enrico Mattei was becoming one of the major economic forces in the country, was one agency by which aid to underveloped countries in harmony with Italian interests could be carried out. One of the first and the most typical examples of the use of ENI for political purposes was an agreement reached with Iran for the exploitation of a part of its oil resources. This agreement (Sept. 1957) assumed considerable political importance since it abandoned the fifty-fifty rule traditionally followed in the distribution of the oil profits and gave more favorable conditions to the producer countries, thus breaking the monopoly of the international petroleum cartel to which powerful American and British interests were tied. In the following years, ENI continued to penetrate Near Eastern countries and North Africa, linking specific economic interests with more general political objectives.

Dissent from the cautious line of the government in foreign policy was also expressed by the influential mayor of Florence, Giorgio La Pira, one of the leading personalities of the Demo-Christian left. Through a series of cultural congresses (Conventions for Christian Peace), which were held in Florence and which produced an international response because of the wide participation of scholars, artists and writers, La Pira initiated an appeal for pacifism, inviting all peoples, in particular the Soviet Union and the United States, to settle their differences in a peaceful and friendly fashion. Although many considered La Pira a mystic and utopian, there can be no doubt that some of his initiatives held political weight and found support and sympathy in Catholic and Socialist circles in Italy and abroad.

All these moves, which grew in number in the following years, led eventually to the elaboration of an unofficial foreign policy, which was frequently in contradiction to the official line; they were inspired not only by the change in the international situation, but also by internal political conditions. In preparing the ground for a more flexible foreign policy, the currents of the democratic left attempted to diminish the gap which traditionally separated Nenni's Socialist Party, opposed to the politics of blocs and military pacts, from the position of the government coalition parties. For this reason the activities of these groups made a notable contribution to the "opening to the left," and to the parley between Socialists and Catholics.

After a long pause, which followed the rejection of the European Defense Community (EDC), new initiatives also developed in the field of European unification. The idea of European unity was relaunched with better results in the creation of Euratom and the Common Market, to which the six member countries of the Coal and Steel Pool (France, Germany, Italy, Belgium, the Netherlands and Luxembourg) adhered with the Treaty of Rome on March 27, 1957. The basis for a program of research and realizations in the field of atomic energy was constituted by the former; the program was limited but permitted great development in the future. The Common Market agreement was much more revolutionary. It envisaged the progressive elimination of customs barriers and of all limitations on international exchanges within a period from twelve to fifteen years, thus creating a huge unified market, characterized by the free circulation of agricultural and industrial goods.

When, in July 1957, both treaties, the fruit of long drawn-out negotiations, were presented to the Italian Parliament for ratification, the Communist deputies voted against both, while the Socialist deputies voted in favor of Euratom and abstained from the vote on the Common Market treaty. In abstaining, the Socialists expressed a number of reservations of a political nature, such as, for example, the possibility that certain European monopolistic groups might exercise a predominant influence in the Common Market. At the same time, however, by refusing to follow the Communist line, they demonstrated that they had overcome a number of traditional political prejudices and that they understood the great possibilities of benefit which this project opened up to all Europeans without distinction of class.

The signing of the treaty on the Common Market was the last important act of the Segni Government, which, in its final phase, was showing signs of increasing weakness.

A good part of the program, which had been presented two years earlier, remained unimplemented, and furthermore the government balance, originally oriented toward the left, was shifting to the right, thus ending in the loss of the support of the Republicans and Social Democrats.

On February 28, 1957, in the course of a confidence vote on the government project on the land contracts, the Republicans left the majority and voted against the government. The government was able to continue for another two months with the support of the neo-Fascists and Monarchists, who together had voted for Segni.

By April, the crisis appeared inevitable. The Social Democrats, under the pressure of the Party's left wing and prompted by electoral considerations, took the initiative. In fact, with political elections approaching, for a party that drew its votes from a progressive electorate, such as the PSDI, it would have been dangerous to continue support of the Segni Government, which was by now reduced to carrying on routine business with the parliamentary backing of the right. Following a speech by Saragat against the government, Segni resigned (May 6, 1957).

THE ZOLI GOVERNMENT

The transition government headed by Segni was replaced by a transition government headed by Adone Zoli, which remained in power for little over a year, until the political elections of June 1958. It was the most precarious of all the governments that had followed one another since 1953. The manner in which it was constituted clearly indicated the point which the crisis in the political situation had reached.

The refusal of the Republicans and Social Democrats to assume government responsibilities such a short time before the elections compelled the DC to form a cabinet composed exclusively of Demo-Christians (monocolor). Adone Zoli, a Florentine lawyer well-known for his anti-Fascism, who enjoyed considerable personal prestige but had no particular following within the currents of the DC, was designated to administer the government for the short time until the new Parliament was elected. In the absence of a preconstituted majority, it appeared clear from the start that Zoli would have to appeal to the votes of the right and that hence he would present a program precluding any reforms and limited to purely administrative activities. For that reason, in line with a policy they had followed during the last phase of the Segni Government and in order to end their political isolation, the neo-Fascists and Monarchists decided to support Zoli. The Monarchist and above all the neo-Fascist votes compromised the Zoli Government which came under the attack of both the extreme and democratic left opposition and even of the progressive currents within its own party. At the moment of the vote of confidence the government received from Parliament 305 votes in favor and 255 against. The necessary majority being 281 (half of the votes plus one), Zoli decided to accept Monarchist support rejecting that of the neo-Fascist (24 votes) as "neither necessary nor desirable." But the day after the vote it was ascertained, after a more exact control of the ballots, that the necessary majority was instead 282 (two opposing votes had by mistake been counted as abstentions). Thus the government would have been short one vote, if it refused to accept the neo-Fascist support.

Confronted with this new situation, the Prime Minister, in keeping with the position he had assumed in the matter, handed in his resignation. The President of the Republic, before accepting it, renewed his consultations with the parties. First an independent, Cesare Merzagora, President of the Senate, was charged to form a new government; after the latter had failed, the charge was given Amintore Fanfani. Fanfani too met with insurmountable difficulties; the Republicans and Social Democrats again refused to enter a quadripartite coalition government and conditions for a majority that would include the Socialists did not as yet exist. In addition, a few days earlier, the *Osservatore*

Romano had expressed in an editorial in unmistakable terms the opposition of the Vatican to any maneuver in the way of an "opening to the left." Lacking any alternative President Gronchi refused Zoli's resignation; the latter agreed to withdraw his objections to the neo-Fascist votes and received a new vote of confidence from the chambers.

Within the DC, the solution accepted by Zoli engendered profound discontent. Although it was recognized that Zoli was compelled to act in a "state of necessity," the directing party organs tried a number of times to dissociate the party from the government for electoral considerations, claiming that the Zoli Government could not be considered a true Christian Democratic Government, inasmuch as its program was far from the program the party was preparing to present in the next elections.

Lacking the support of his own party and preoccupied with trying to brush off the neo-Fascists, Zoli was obliged to proceed with the utmost prudence.

Despite its short duration and the conditions under which Zoli was operating, his government nevertheless managed to take a number of important measures. His most notable achievements were: the extension of state control over the national telephone companies, ten-year extension of the Development Agency for the South (*Cassa per il Mezzogiorno*), and an increase in the agency's financing. In addition, the process of implementing the Constitution, which had begun under Segni, was continued with the establishment of the Superior Council of Magistrature,[1] the constitutional organ destined to render the magistrature more independent of the executive. Zoli's major strength lay in the certainty that, in the event of his fall, the President of the Republic would be compelled to dissolve Parliament and call for new elections, an eventuality that all parties feared, in view of their unpreparedness to face the electorate.

During the Zoli Government, the debate on the relations between state and church were resumed with vigour. The

---

[1] See page 182.

problem had been revived as the result of an episode, the case of the bishop of Prato, which for a few weeks was to impassion the public from all walks of life. The bishop of Prato, Monsignor Pietro Fiordelli, had officially branded as "public sinners" and "concubines" a young couple from his diocese, who instead of celebrating their wedding with a religious ceremony had chosen to get married according to the civil procedure stipulated by Italian law. The case arose because the two statutes governing marriage, che canon law and the civil law, were in contradiction.[1] According to the former, civil marriage is nonexistent and consequently Fiordelli's attitude was justified; following the civil law, according to which the marriage was perfectly valid, the bishop's statement amounted to an act of defamation. The case went to court and the bishop was convicted (March 14, 1958) and fined 40,000 lire by the Florence tribunal.

The punishment was nominal, but the question of principle was serious. The polemics between the non-clerical political parties, the Republicans and Radicals, and Catholics became extremely bitter and threatened to move onto the political level. The reaction of the church was violent to the condemnation of the bishop, an unheard of event and therefore quite shocking. Newspapers, Catholic associations, bishops, cardinals and finally the Pope condemned the action of the Florence court; its judges were menaced with excomunication. The Catholic Action newspaper went so far as to compare Fiordelli's conviction to the plight of the bishops in China. The debate was officially closed a year later with the annulment of the sentence by the Florence Court of Appeals, which absolved the bishop by declaring its own jurisdictional incompetence. The episode, however, reopened the serious problem of the relations

---

[1] The Italian law provides for two types of marriage: the religious marriage administered by a minister of the Catholic Church, to which full civil effects are recognized (art. 34 of the Lateran Pacts); and the civil marriage (not recognized by the Catholic Church) administered by the mayor in his functions as a civil official.

between state and church and revived the debate between non-confessional parties and Catholic opinion, thus adding a new motive to the electoral campaign that followed by a few weeks the court's decision.

THE ELECTIONS OF MAY 1958

The months preceding the elections of May 1958 were quiet as compared with earlier electoral compaigns.

The Communists, after the 1956 events, remained on the defensive, preoccupied primarily with maintaining their position rather than improving it. They limited their propaganda to familiar themes, expounded in 1953, that is, condemnation of the Atlantic policy and rearmament, denunciation of Demo-Christian corruption and clerical over-bearing.

The PSI, after the congress of Venice, which had revealed the extent of its internal contradictions, did not campaign openly in favor of the "opening to the left," but, as in the 1953 elections, stressed the "Socialist alternative," leaving the means and mainly the alliances that would have permitted the realization of this alternative up in the air. The autonomist current, however, was particularly active, in the hope of an electoral success that would reinforce the party and make its disengagement from the PCI and the negotiations with the Catholics possible.

The DC, following tradition, avoided committing itself to a precise political orientation, and stressed the economic progress that had been realized in the past years (national revenue in 1953 was 10,193 billion lire, in 1957, it was 13,728 billion), attributing this advance to the experience and success of its administration. The DC attempted to present itself to the voters as the only party capable of guaranteeing the country's well-being, order and effective anti-Communist action. "Progress without adventures" was its most widely used and successful slogan. The DC attempted to reassure that part of the electorate which regarded the

309

projected discussions with the Socialists with diffidence and suspicion.

The results of the elections did not show significant variations (the Italian voter after World War II has demonstrated that he is one of the most consistent in Europe), but they nevertheless indicated some important trends.

Elections to the House of Representatives
May 25, 1958

	Valid votes	Seats in the House
PCI	6,704,706	140
PSI	4,208,111	84
PSDI	1,345,750	22
PRI and Radical Party	405,574	6
DC	12,522,279	273
PLI	1,046,939	17
PMP	776,942	14
PNM	659,865	11
MSI	1,407,913	24
Others	485,554	5
		596

Compared to the preceding elections, the DC won approximately 1,700,000 new votes, that is, taking into account the increase of voters from 40.1 per cent to 42.3 per cent. The dramatic events which in May 1958 brought about the fall of the IVth French Republic and the return of General de Gaulle to power were manifestly to the advantage of the DC. The profound crisis, which was shaking France, influenced moderate opinion in Italy, prompting it, as always in periods of uncertainty and danger to rally around the majority party. This phenomenon demonstrated the attraction exerted by the DC and the confidence it inspired in the moderate electorate, despite the divisions and conflicts which had in recent years become more acute within the party.

The Socialist Party won almost 800,000 new votes, representing about 14.2 per cent of the electorate, as against the previous 12.7 per cent. The Communist Party, despite the crisis it went through as a result of the Hungarian events and the Twentieth Congress, held its position (22.6 per cent in 1953, 22.7 per cent in 1958), surprising many observers, even impartial observers, who had predicted that the party would suffer serious losses.

Among the minor parties, the Social Democrats won about 100,000 new votes, which in view of the numerical increase of the electorate merely meant that they retained their vote of 1953 (4.5 per cent). The Liberals made evident progress, winning 200,000 new votes, advancing from 3 per cent to 3.5 per cent of the electorate and confirming the success of the Malagodi line. The Republicans, despite their courageous policy of opposition and their alliance with the Radicals, lost heavily. The clear regression of the two Monarchist parties, the result of a recent split, showed in the loss of about 500,000 votes (from 6.9 per cent to 4.8 per cent), and the neo-Fascists declined from 5.8 per cent in 1953 to 4.8 per cent.

The victory of the Christian Democratic Party, within which the left-wing current had gained considerable ground, the substantial improvement of the position of the Socialists, the considerable losses sustained by the extreme right-wing parties, and the arresting of the Communist advance, were by themselves positive signs for the future of democracy. On the whole they were significant indications since they opened new possibilities of political combinations and in particular laid the groundwork for a future government of the "opening to the left," which was the only alternative to a continuing deadlock. Despite this, the historic accord between Socialists and Catholics came only in February 1962, almost at the end of the term of legislature and after an extended debate.

PART FIVE

The opening to the left

CHAPTER 1

THE THIRD LEGISLATURE, 1958-1963

The most important event during the third legislature was the constitution of the first government of the "opening to the left." The new majority, which had its foundation in the alliance between the Catholic and Socialist parties, manifested itself for the first time in the confidence vote for the Fanfani Government (the third government of the legislature) on March 10, 1962. Four years had passed since the 1958 elections before this important operation was realized. They were necessary to overcome the last obstinate hurdles of its opponents and to negotiate a program on the basis of which the future dialogue between the two political forces was to take place.

The importance attributed to the program, which after 1960 became the main preoccupation of the parties of the future coalition, and the time and the energies required to elaborate it, indicate the nature and the significance of the operation of the "opening to the left." The problem was not just the formation of a new majority and the preparation of a new program more or less organic of reforms. This could have been the intention of those who adhered to the "opening to the left" after having established that no other alternative existed or who thought that the "opening" would be reduced to an ordinary operation of transformism. But for those who had promoted and obstinately supported it, the "opening" was to represent a turning point in Italian postwar politics,

315

meant to usher in a process of renewal of the structures of Italian society, which had been expected for a long time but never realized.

Since the fall of Fascism, this had been the objective of the political action of the democratic left; the causes and circumstances of its failures have been pointed out. The convergence of Catholics and Socialists represented the sole historical chance for new attempts by the forces of the democratic left to carry out its own program of renewal.

This is the significance of the "opening" from an historical point of view; its meaning on the political level is no less important. The "opening" materialized a dialogue between two parties, which for years had followed different courses in open opposition to each other. On the one hand was the party which for fifteen years had enjoyed the uninterrupted exercise of power and which by now controlled all its levers. Being no longer influenced decisively by those economic groups, which for so many years had determined its orientation, it was ready to concede to the working classes a representative participation in the government of the country. It asked in exchange the renunciation of revolutionary and maximalist aims and the acceptance without reserve of the methods of parliamentary democracy. On the other hand, a party, which represented a part of the popular masses, abandoned a position of sterile waiting and declared it was ready to accept the conditions proposed, and advanced in turn its own. They were prompted by dual objectives: to weaken the heads of the great private economic concentrations and thereby strengthen the powers of the state in the field of national economy, and to increase the participation of the masses in political life with the aim of enhancing their weight in the society and their influence over the government.

THE PROGRAM OF "THE OPENING TO THE LEFT"

The main Socialist requests, in line with these two objectives, were accepted after lengthy discussions and constituted the programmatic points of the government of March 1962. They were: the nationalization of electric power industries; the adoption of economic planning; the implementation of the regional autonomy statute, in accordance with the articles of the Constitution; measures to improve living conditions in rural areas and protect peasant property; and a plan for the eventual democratization of the school system.

The nationalization of the electric power industries was clearly a political objective. Although the official justification given for this measure was to decrease the price of electric current in order to broaden its consumption, the true intention was to take away the control of power sources from private groups. The nationalization of electric power, which followed the establishment of the state monopoly for petroleum and methane gas (ENI) and the commissioning of a public corporation for the production of atomic energy (CNEN), realized by the preceding governments, was part of a pattern aimed at the eventual management of all sources of energy exclusively by the state. It was demanded by the Socialists also in function of the preparation of an economic plan (or programming, as it was called to make the idea more palatable). State control of production and, even more so, of the distribution of power represented an effective instrument, which could have influenced the decisions of private enterprises, directing them in a certain way and coordinating their activity with the programming of state economic operations.

The second objective of the PSI, the broadening of the participation of the working classes in national political life, was inherent in the other points of the program: the enactment of the regional autonomy statute and the democratization of the state schools. The creation of the regions would have resulted in considerable decentralization of political life and the administration. This decentralization was designed to favor the popular parties better organized on the local level and would have undercut the influence of great concentrations of economic power, for it was easier to exercise pressures so long as the decision-making power lay with the central government. In addition, the regional system would develop local government and multiply the representative organs through the creation of councils and communal governments, thus giving the popular masses additional possibilities to enter into political life and reach positions of power.

The benefits of a school system open to all classes was of more long-range consequence. The new school system would enable all meritorious pupils to receive an education at any level; previously the state program of studies still reflected the aristocratic conception of culture and favored students of higher social status who had grown up in a more cultivated environment.[1]

The measure in favor of the peasants, the increase of pensions for certain categories of workers, were demanded by the PSI in order to provide immediate benefits for the working classes.

These were the basic programmatic points which emerged from the lengthy negotiations between the PSI and the DC, and which should have provided the proving ground for the first experiment of collaboration between the two parties. The first center-left government adopted these points in their entirety.

THE OPPOSITION

The natural opponents of this program were the economic right, on the one hand, and the Communists on the other. The former saw in the "opening" program a direct menace to its power positions and privileges. The concessions the DC was preparing to make to the PSI were made at the expense of the classes which up to now had exercized their influence on the government, from which they derived specific benefits. For that reason, the conservative forces

---

[1] The partial elimination of Latin from the high school program was part of the measures for school democratization.

undertook an intensive counter-offensive, through the press, for the most part controlled by the monopolies, through pressure groups and their own representatives within the majority parties and the right-wing parties. At the crucial moment of the struggle the economic right failed to get the support of certain Vatican circles which had represented up to then one of the major obstacles to the "opening to the left."

Following the election of Pope John XXIII, in October 1958, there were clear signs that a basic new evolution was taking place inside the supreme organ of the Catholic Church. During the pontificate of Eugenio Pacelli (Pius XII), in the entire post-war period the ecclesiastic hierarchy had taken an active part in the Italian political developments through its influence on the DC. From the beginning of the pontificate of John XXIII, it was evident that the interventions of the church were neither as frequent nor as insistent as formerly. It appeared clear that, for Pope John, the universal objectives of the church prevailed over its particularistic interests, and that the attitude of intransigence maintained by Pius XII toward the Communist world had been replaced by the recognition of a need to reach a "modus vivendi" between the opposing blocs in order to assure world peace.

The changed attitude of the Vatican had profound repercussions as well on the internal political situation in Italy. The feeling was current that the church would no longer, as it had in the past, obstruct a dialogue between Catholic and Socialist forces. This possibility gave the DC greater freedom in the development of its policy and weakened its conservative currents, which were linked with the clergy and which had been the most zealous spokesmen for church instructions.

The reasons for the Communist opposition to the "opening", which at least in the initial phases, were hidden behind a reserved acquiescence, were more complex. The PCI saw a serious threat to its policy and existence as a major proletarian party in the "opening", since it aspired to become the exclusive representative of the working class. As the result of the dialogue between the Socialists and Catholics, the PCI was definitely losing not only an important ally but it was also running the risk of losing the consensus and sympathies of its own electorate. Between the Communist policy of expectation of the messianic conquest of power, which did not seem to have any prospects, and the Socialist policy, which endeavoured to provide concrete advantages and create new possibilities of immediate progress for the working classes, the latter could eventually prevail and win the support of most workers. Considering the hopes and interests which the dialogue between the PSI and the DC was engendering in certain sectors of the public, an attitude of open hostility on the part of the PCI might have produced disappointment and discontent also among Communist sympathizers. For this reason, and also in order not to burn all its bridges to the Socialist Party, which in case the experiment failed could return to the popular front, the PCI assumed an attitude of benign expectation with regard to the program of the "opening". This attitude, however, would have changed to one of opposition as soon as the implementation of the agreements between Socialists and Demo-Christians ran into difficulties.

Less precise as far as its final objectives and motivations was the attitude of the moderate opinion. Its opposition to the "opening to the left" mainly stemmed from satisfaction with the present state of affairs and with traditional suspicion of Socialism.

A booming economy and an increasingly high standard of living which benefited primarily the propertied classes accounted for their acceptance of a state which they knew to be weak and lacking in authority. The continuation of a system whose laxity in fiscal and administrative matters allowed them to carry on activities on the fringe of the law, such as speculation in real estate, tax evasion, etc., was in their interest.

Distrust of Socialism was deeply rooted in both the ancient and more recent past. The Socialist conversion from its maximalist positions to the principles of parliamentary democracy appeared to them to have taken place too suddenly to be genuine. Many of these people thought that its new attitude concealed a menace, and that the PSI would prove to be a Trojan horse, which would attempt to introduce its former Communist ally into the citadel of the government.

The opposition to the "opening to the left" was thus extremely diversified as it defended the interests of various social classes and political groups. Although a joint effort of the extremes seemed unthinkable, their opposition represented neverthless a major obstacle which the parties of the center left coalition had to overcome.

CHAPTER 2

THE GOVERNMENTS AND THE PARTIES

THE SECOND FANFANI CABINET

After the elections of May 25, 1958, a cabinet headed by Amintore Fanfani followed immediately on the Zoli Government. It was constituted by Demo-Christians and Social Democrats and appeared to represent a transition to a government of the "opening to the left." The life of this cabinet was short and troubled.

A financial scandal, the so-called Giuffré case, which revealed a story of fantastic speculations of which parish priests and Catholic associations had been among the beneficiaries, put the relations between the two parties in the government to a severe test. In October a split within the DC in Sicily occurred. A local leader, Silvio Milazzo, leading a group of DC representatives in the regional Parliament of Sicily, formed a new political group, around which Milazzo was able to build a new, if heterogeneous, majority which ran the regional government for some time. Finally Milazzo and his followers were ousted from their positions and soon disappeared from the political scene, but the Milazzo case revealed how strong were the dissensions within the DC, and how difficult it was for the central organs of the DC to maintain the different currents and groups in line with the party national policy.

The opposition of the Liberals, Monarchists and neo-

Fascist right to this government was violent and contributed to the rapid downfall of Fanfani's Cabinet. Fanfani, however, received the *coup de grace* from his own party, some groups of which were opposed to the "opening" and viewed with great concern, for the internal equilibrium within the DC, the increase of Fanfani's personal power derived from the combination of the two highest and most powerful offices of Prime Minister and secretary of the party. These groups organized a party rebellion against him which manifested itself in Parliament through the action of the "snipers". That was the term given to Demo-Christian deputies of conservative orientation, who, breaking party discipline, voted in several instances against the government. The action of the "snipers", which threatened to cause a split within the DC, made it impossible for the government to follow its own program and compelled Fanfani to hand in his resignation both as chief of government and as secretary of the party.

Fanfani's retirement marked a pause in the way toward the center-left coalition. The Demo-Christian leader, who was the most convinced supporter of the "opening" in his own party, appeared ready to abandon the struggle; his current, the "Democratic Initiative," was left without a leader and was losing ground to the other currents. But Fanfani's retirement soon emerged as a tactical expedient, designed to permit the anti-"opening" forces within the DC to exhaust themselves. Time thus worked in favor of the "opening", by accentuating the absence of any alternative solutions.

SEGNI AGAIN

After Fanfani's resignation, the formation of the government was entrusted to Antonio Segni who was generally recognized as the man able to deal with difficult situations. Segni was in fact given the task of forming a government whose moderate inclination would assuage the grave tensions caused by the action of the "snipers".

Segni's Cabinet, although composed exclusively of De-mo-Christians (monocolor) gained parliamentary support of the Liberals, Monarchists and neo-Fascists. It was thus called "pendular" because it was in line with the recurrent tendency of a cabinet oriented to the right to follow a cabinet oriented to the left.

Throughout the year 1959, in the shadow of the Segni "pendular" "monocolor" government "of waiting", the internal struggle in the DC and the conflicts between the currents in favor and opposed to the "opening", continued. Replacing Fanfani as secretary of the DC was Aldo Moro, a university professor from Bari, a new man almost unknown to the public. Because of his prudent policies and his mediating abilities, he soon acquired a position of great influence inside the party. He succeeded in solving the crisis, which had apparently reached the point of rupture, and of convincing the center currents of the inevitability of the "opening". The center currents were headed by the "notables"; in opposition to Fanfani they had achieved a certain unity and had created a new current, called the *Dorotei* (Dorotheans).[1]

Thus the party, which had rejected the "opening to the left" under Fanfani's leadership, who was accused of being oriented too much to the left and of wanting to destroy the delicate balance which had been established between the various currents of the DC by increasing his personal power, decided to accept it, along with the guarantees offered by the more moderate Moro.

The Demo-Christian congress held in Florence, at the end of October 1959, officially confirmed this decision. By then, the great majority of the party seemed determined to proceed, though with caution, toward the overtures to the Socialists. The diehard opposition groups, from the extreme right (Pella and Andreotti), as well as the group headed by Mario Scelba, a staunch defender of the quadripartite

---

[1] Called after the Convent of St. Dorothy in Rome, where they held their meetings.

formula, were compelled to accept the orientation of the majority; the fear of a split, which for many months had weighed on the party, was thus dispelled. The congress of Florence concluded with a compromise between the two major currents, the *Dorotei*, headed by the new party secretary Moro, and the current headed by Fanfani. On the eve of the congress, Fanfani abandoned his wait-and-see tactics and, after a short but intensive reorganization of his group, he reassumed his position inside the party, although it was by then conditioned by Moro's prestige and power. The compromise consisted in Moro's commitment to reject right-wing parliamentary support for any future government formation. Since the impossibility of reconstituting the quadripartite alliance had by then been amply demonstrated, Moro's commitment was tantamount to an acceptance of the "opening" and a promise to carry it out as soon as possible.

The significance of the compromise reached at the DC congress was immediately apparent and provoked an immediate reaction on the part of the Liberals who continued to support the Segni government. It was by then obvious that the majority party was preparing an "opening to the left," behind the convenient screen of a right-wing government. For that reason the Liberals decided to undercut the game of the DC leadership and withdrew their support of Segni, thus provoking a government crisis.

THE TAMBRONI CABINET AND THE JULY EVENTS

The move of the Liberals opened a crisis that lasted over two months. Despite the results of the DC congress, the moment was not yet judged ripe for a center-left government; the agreements between the DC and the Socialists still had to be worked out in specific detail and the program had to be established. The formation of a new government, first entrusted to Segni and then to Fanfani, failed. Finally, in April, in order to terminate the crisis, a government headed by Ferdinando Tambroni, a "notable" with close ties with the President of the Republic, was formed. It was another in the long succession of transition governments, constituted in order to meet the normal administrative deadlines, and in order to provide more time for the negotiations for the "opening". In addition to the DC, the MSI also voted in favor of the Tambroni government. The majority was determined by neo-Fascist votes and thus was in open conflict with Moro's recent commitment at the Florence congress to reject the parliamentary support of the extreme right. It was again considered exclusively a measure required by the emergency situation, and as such it was accepted although unwillingly by the DC left.

It appeared that the Tambroni Government would have little impact since it was formed in order to end the embarassing absence of a government administration while more important solutions were being considered. Despite these limitations and the government's temporary character, however, the policies of the Prime Minister in two months provoked one of the most serious crises of the post-war period.

A few weeks following the formation of the new government it appeared obvious that Tambroni would attempt to consolidate his own power to prolong his government much beyond the limits which had been imposed on him by the party. In order to win popularity in the country, he energetically pursued a policy of lowering prices (gasoline, sugar, meat), which, intelligently exploited by publicity in the conservative press, won him the sympathies and approval of moderate opinion which preferred a policy of visible benefits carried out from day to day to a program of reforms.

Toward the end of May and the beginning of June a number of popular manifestations and strikes took place; the first one was organized in Bologna and Ravenna by the PCI against the installation of American missiles, to which Italy was committed in conformity with its membership in the Atlantic Pact; others were inspired by wage questions. In the circumstances Tambroni attempted to dis-

326

tinguish himself from his predecessors. The police intervened against the manifestations by direct order of the Prime Minister, with an exceptional violence: in Ravenna and in Bologna, and mainly in Palermo, many demonstrators were left injured on the ground after the charges of the police. These events, while they won the Prime Minister the reputation of being an energetic man, willing to use force, approved in particular by the right, created a dangerous state of tension, especially among the working classes. The situation was suddenly aggravated when the government, disregarding the widespread agitation in the country. gave the authorization to the MSI to hold its own national congress in Genoa during the first week of July.

Despite the protests of the anti-Fascist parties and organizations of former partisans, echoed by a good part of the press, the government's authorization was upheld, partly in order to recompense the neo-Fascists for their support in Parliament and partly to give the country a new proof of the government's strength and authority.

The MSI's decision to ignore these protests, and the reinforcement that this party had received from the government, were interpreted by anti-Fascist opinion as an unmistakable collusion between the neo-Fascist right and the Prime Minister. The old solidarity between the anti-Fascist parties was revived and without any agreement having been reached beforehand, an anti-governmental bloc was formed that encompassed the extreme left to the DC. The Communist Party, which in recent years had experienced increasing isolation, due to the gradual but evident detachment of the Socialists, did not miss this unexpected chance to exploit the situation and became one of the most zealous champions of the anti-Fascist bloc.

In protest against the neo-Fascist congress, on June 30th, July 1st and 2nd there were skirmishes with the police in Genoa, a city that had suffered severely in 1944 and 1945 from German and Fascist action and where an anti-Fascist spirit was particularly strong. Soon the encounters of the demonstrators with the police took the form of a genuine revolt. The violence of the demonstrators, some of whom were armed, was such that the police was in a weak position and suffered a number of casualties and the destruction of some of its equipment. The Genoa protest soon extended to most major Italian cities in the form of strikes and manifestations; in Rome they were particularly violent with dozens of demonstrators injured. The explosive atmosphere in the streets was soon communicated to Parliament. In both the Chamber and Senate there were clashes between the extreme right and the extreme left which ended in violence. This was not the first time that physical fights had occurred among members of Parliament, but in the tense situation created by the Genoa riots, such clashes not only discredited these institutions but also threatened to aggravate the tension and to provoke new acts of violence throughout the country. At this point, Cesare Merzagora, President of the Senate, an independent and a man of great personal prestige, proposed a "truce" that would permit a pacification of feelings and a calmer examination of the situation by the parties.

The truce did not succeed, however, in saving the Tambroni Government. The Genoa events had clearly demonstrated how alive the traditions of the Resistance and anti-Fascist sentiments still were. They gave a clear indication that the majority of the country rejected any governmental action that depended on reactionary forces and that aimed at the reversal of the tendency, by now obvious, of a progressive and democratic policy. The Tambroni Government had attempted to increase its own strength by seeking the support of an anti-democratic party and a sector of the public which was anti-democratic by mental habit. It emerged from the July events on the brink of a crisis.

Tambroni was accused by some of an outright attempt at a coup d'état. He was charged with having provoked the disorders in order to justify direct intervention, to restrict political liberties and to prolong the life of the government on the pretense that it was an emergency situation. This improbable accusation has up to now not been verified, but it is indicative of the gravity of the situation which had developed and the responsibilities involved.

THE THIRD FANFANI CABINET

Disavowed by his own party, the DC, Tambroni resigned on July 19th and retired to a kind of political limbo. Meanwhile, as a result of the truce proposed by Merzagora, the political crisis was moving toward a solution. All parties recognized that in order to pacify the spirits after the stormy events a united effort was necessary. For that reason a coalition, comprising the PSDI, PRI and PLI with the object of supporting a monocolor Demo-Christian government, was formed.

Fanfani was entrusted with the formation of the new cabinet in which all of the DC currents were represented through their most authoritative leaders. The cabinet was presented to Parliament on August 2nd; its program was oriented mainly toward the normalization of the political situation and the passage of measures, which had been left in suspense by preceding governments (programs for education, for the development of agriculture, anti-monopoly legislation).

The Fanfani Government received a large majority in accordance with the prior agreement reached among the parties. Both in the Chamber and the Senate the DC, PSDI, PRI and PLI voted in favor; the Communists and neo-Fascists voted against, and the Socialists abstained. This was a new and significant event. The alignment of forces in the vote of confidence for the Fanfani Government appeared to be a reconstitution of the quadripartite coalition. In reality, the government was based on a temporary majority; it was justified by the "state of emergency" caused by the July events, but the agreements between the parties had established in advance the length of its duration. In October, after the summer hiatus, during which there is always a standstill in political activities, the temporary Fanfani Government was intended to be transformed into a government of the "opening to the left." This was the significance of the Socialists' abstention in the confidence vote for Fanfani. For the first time since the expulsion of the Social-Communists from the government in 1947, the Socialists assumed an attitude of anticipation, awaiting the overtures of the DC and the government as a prelude to their participation in a future majority.

CHAPTER 3

THE FIRST GOVERNMENT OF THE OPENING TO THE LEFT

NEW DELAYS

New difficulties were encountered in October in achieving the formation of a government of the "opening to the left"; with repeated delays it was to take another fifteen months before it was finally realized. During this period the program of the government was being ironed out between the DC and the Socialists. The Socialists' demands compelled the DC to make a number of concessions, which, in turn, provoked resistance and protests inside the party. This resistance and the desire not to give the public the impression that the DC was bowing to Socialist pressures made for very slow progress. These were merely tactical delays, however, since the orientation toward the "opening" by now was irreversible, as was to be demonstrated by the solution to the problem of the compositions of local governments constituted after the administrative elections of October 1960.

Anticipating, on the local level, the collaboration of the political forces, which in Parliament were to constitute the basis of the center-left government, it was decided that wherever possible center-left local governments would be established. This was not only to better prepare the public for the new government, but also to provide a proving ground for concrete collaboration between Catholics and Socialists. The problem was more difficult to solve than it appeared on the surface, since in many local governments the Socialists formed majorities with the Communists, and the Christian-Democrats formed them with extreme right-wing parties, such as the Monarchists and the neo-Fascists (as was the case in Rome). On the local level as well the negotiations were drawn out for several months, thus depriving some districts of their normal administrative organs.

An agreement was finally reached whereby the DC committed itself to form together with the Socialists a number of local administrations in some of the major Italian cities. The importance of these local governments and the political significance of the agreement served as a guarantee that the DC was willing to proceed, within a short time, to the formation of a national center-left government. On January 21, 1961, the first center-left local junta was formed in Milan, with the participation of the Socialists, Demo-Christians, Radicals, Republicans and Social-Democrats, and in February and March similar governments were formed in Genoa and Florence.

After the hurdle of the "difficult administrations" (as the problem of the center-left local governments was baptized) had been overcome, new difficulties arose to harrass and delay further the formation of the "opening" government; that was the possibility that Parliament might be dissolved before the end of its five-year term. This eventuality was closely linked to the election of the President of the Republic, slated to take place in the spring of 1962.

It was generally known that President Gronchi was seeking reelection, but after the Tambroni episode, for which Gronchi was believed by many to be partially responsible,[1] his possibilities for a second term diminished considerably. There were those who feared that Gronchi might dissolve Parliament, which was opposed to him,[2] and call for new

---

[1] Tambroni was closely associated with the President of the Republic, who had in turn strongly backed Tambroni's candidacy for the premiership.

[2] The President of the Republic is elected by Parliament in a joint session of both chambers.

332

elections in the hope that the newly elected members would be better disposed toward him.

The failure of a new attempt to form a center-left government could have provided the President with the opportunity to justify the dissolution of the chambers. In order to avoid this eventuality, which would have postponed indefinitely the "opening to the left," the parties of the future majority agreed to delay the operation further. The presidential mandate expired in March 1952, and in accordance with a precise Constitutional stipulation, that the President could not dissolve Parliament within the last six months of his mandate,[1] the President would have lost the right to exercise this capacity in October. For that reason the center-left parties agreed to instigate a governmental crisis in November and to launch the center left government immediately following it.

It is difficult to judge whether the fears over the President's attitude were justified or whether this was merely a pretext to postpone the operation, for which the parties did not as yet feel fully prepared. The latter hypothesis appears more likely, inasmuch as the crisis of the Fanfani Government was put off for another three months in anticipation of the yearly congress of the DC to be held at Naples on January 29, 1962.

In his speech at the congress, party secretary Moro reaffirmed the need for an agreement between Socialists and Catholics in order to end the political instability of the past years, and he addressed an open invitation to the PSI to support a government of the "opening to the left." This invitation to the Socialists officially initiated the crisis of the Fanfani Government, which handed in its resignation on February 3rd.

---

[2] Art. 88 of the Italian Constitution provides that the President may dissolve one or both chambers after consultation with their presidents. He may not exercise this right during the last six months of his term of office.

Taking cognizance of the will of the parties, on February 10th the President of the Republic charged Fanfani, who had worked more than any other DC leader for the center-left government, with the task of shaping the new cabinet, which would be composed of Demo-Christians, Social Democrats and Republicans, and supported in Parliament by the Socialists.

After a few days the new government was presented to the chambers for the confidence vote, which by now, after agreement between the parties had been reached, was a mere formality. The government program included the following points:

1) A commitment to consolidate democracy through an ever-increasing participation of the popular masses in the exercise of power, with the aim of characterizing the new government as a government of the whole people and not just the instrument of a class.

2) The unification of a national system for the production of electric power, which in substance meant the nationalization of the power plants. The government was committed to present a law, within three months of the vote of confidence, which was to specify the modes and conditions of this operation.

3) The constitution of a committee to formulate an economic plan, aimed at the integration of private initiative with state initiative.

4) The enactment of the regional institution, as provided for by the Constitution. The government committed itself, in this case, to give precedence to a region with special status, the Friuli-Venezia Giulia region.

5) The carrying out of the so-called "Green Plan"[1] to

---

[1] A program for agricultural development formulated in 1959 in order to inject fresh money into a stagnant agriculture suffocated by the industrial boom and lacking initiative and capital. The plan provides for the expenditure of 550 billion lire over five years. A part of this money is to be invested directly by government agencies, the other part will be granted to private

benefit agriculture, measures to solve the agricultural crisis and to improve living conditions in rural areas.

6) A plan for the development and democratization of the school system.

These were the most important measures to which the government was committed. Others, such as the reform of the Senate and of the state administration, a long-range plan for scientific reform, the increase of pensions, etc., were also part of the program.

In foreign policy the government confirmed its solidarity and active participation in the policies of European and Atlantic integration. It also pledged itself to collaborate with the allied powers in the effort to reach solutions in all the areas of conflict between East and West for the consolidation of world peace.

On the basis of this program the government obtained a confidence vote on March 10th. The vote was as follows:
In the Chamber: 295 votes in favor, 195 against, 83 abstaining.
In the Senate: 122 votes in favor, 58 against.[1]

Communists, Liberals, Monarchists and neo-Fascists voted against. After long discussions within the Socialist Party, the thesis of abstention prevailed over that of open support for the government. Nevertheless, the PSI in fact became part of the majority, pledging to give its vote in support of various proposals of laws that were included in the government program.

Their abstention signified that the PSI looked with approval on the government's intentions, but they wanted proof that these intentions would be borne out by concrete

---

investors to cover from 10 to 50% of the investment costs at a very low interest rate (from 1 to 3%) differentiated in order to help the investments in the underdeveloped areas. All the financing is mainly aimed at the modernization of agriculture and the increase in its productivity. The "Green Plan" was approved by Parliament in June 1961.

[1] The 83 representatives abstaining from the vote in the Chamber belonged to PSI. In the Senate, given the difference in the system of counting the votes, the Socialists, instead of expressing their abstention in the ballot, walked out of the hall.

action. In this sense the Socialists' abstention was psychological, representing last-minute reserves as a consequence of their long opposition.

ONE YEAR OF GOVERNMENT ACTIVITY

The first "opening to the left" government remained in office for little over a year. The elections for the renewal of the chambers (which had been called for April 1963) terminated this first experiment. Despite the short space of time the new majority had had at its disposal, by February 1963, the date of the dissolution of Parliament, its program had been in good part enacted.

The law on the nationalization of the power industries was approved by Parliament on Dec. 6th, 1962. The other basic question of economic policy, that is, the elaboration of a plan, received an important impetus. The National Commission for Economic Planning was established on August 6th, 1962 with the task of preparing a program for a more balanced economic development of the country.[1]

Two other measures, within the framework of the commitments and spirit of the new government, were the approval of a law, in December 1962, establishing a tax on share dividends and one on real estate profits. Both aimed at putting a stop to speculation, especially the widespread speculation that had developed in real estate on the fringes of important towns in a phase of rapid development, which had resulted in artificially increasing prices and in making impossible great projects of low-priced popular housing.

---

[1] On the basis of a report, resulting from preliminary studies recently presented, the future economic plan is to be implemented along two main lines: 1) Suggestions will be made and concrete advantages will be offered to private operators to act in line with the targets of the plan; 2) The investment programs of all the state-controlled industrial corporations (I.R.I., E.N.I.) will be strictly geared to the national plan.

336

The law to do with pensions also assumed a particular importance since it provided for substantial increases for various categories of workers. It was intended to give new buying power to the less prosperous classes.

Finally, the law on the new school organization was passed on January 23, 1963. This law provided for the establishment of a unified medium-grade school compulsory attendance until the age of fourteen years. It resolved the problem of the teaching of Latin, which the Socialists considered as one of the aspects denoting the class character of the Italian school system.[1]

Action on the regional statute, however, was again deferred. The government's pledge to present legislation to Parliament for the implementation of Art. 177 of the Constitution, so that it could be approved by the legislature in office, was continuously delayed or evaded. Quite outside of the complexity of the matter itself, which made rapid passage of the law difficult, reservations were still widely expressed inside the DC as to the usefulness of the policy as such. In particular, because of the lack of any commitment to the contrary on the part of the Socialists, it was feared that they might give way to Communist pressure and form regional governments in coalition with them in areas where left-wing forces were in the majority (Emilia, Tuscany, Marche). In addition, with the elections approaching, the DC feared it would lose the votes of the conservative elements among its electorate, who were opposed to the regional statute.

When direct interventions were made to hold the government to its prior commitments and failed, the PSI decided to renounce the agreement upon which the "opening" program had been based and declared that the party no longer considered itself bound by it. This policy

---

[1] The question, which had caused a long and bitter debate, was solved with a rather dubious compromise, from the educational point of view. It established the first year of high school without Latin, the second with optional Latin, and the third year with compulsory Latin.

decision was taken a few weeks before the elections and ended the first phase of the "opening to the left" experiment. It was, however, only a temporary crisis of the majority coalition that had been formed on the basis of the center-left program. It was a tactical move on the part of the PSI to counter Communist accusations of weakness and defeatism, which were then being leveled against the Socialists in a broad attack on the center-left. It was also because of the coming electoral campaign, in which the majority parties had decided they would present themselves as not being tied to any agreements.

None the less, the pledge to continue the "opening to the left" experiment was reaffirmed just prior to the start of the electoral campaign. Republicans and Social Democrats, in fact, announced that they would not participate in any government other than one based on a center-left majority, while the Socialists proposed to the DC an all-encompassing program of collaboration in the future legislature. The PSI proposal was favorably received by the left-wing currents of the DC, but was not endorsed by the party secretariat as part of campaign tactics; it nevertheless appeared evident that the DC by now considered the policy of the "opening" to be irreversible.

THE ELECTORAL CAMPAIGN

The electoral campaign found the parties of the center-left in a delicate position. In spite of the fact that the government had on the whole acted with speed and several important points of its program had been implemented, the basic structural problems of the state and the economy had not yet been tackled. The one-year period that the government had at its disposal from its formation to the election was obviously too short for any fundamental change to be put into effect, but in spite of its dynamism the government had not succeeded in deeply impressing the country with its determination and with the unity of purpose of the coalition parties. The two most important members of the new majority, the DC and PSI, not only failed in explaining to the country their political program in terms of its immediate and long-range significance, but also showed how numerous the misunderstandings among them still were, and the depth of the internal divisions within each party. Moreover the "opening to the left" was realized in a moment in which a profound economic and social evolution was deeply affecting the country's structures. For the tremendous political and psychological effect it had, the center-left government action was inevitably bound to collide with the forces which were behind the process of evolution. On the one hand, the "opening to the left" with its long-range perspective of increased economic controls acted as a break on the expansion of the economy; on the other it did not have enough time to provide effective measures to affect the profound disequilibrium and injustices that the disorderly growth had created.

This situation provided an ideal breeding ground for the electoral campaign of both extremes. The right endeavoured to exploit the discontent of the middle class, which felt itself threatened by the continuous increase of prices, one of the consequences of the economic boom and of increased government spending. This had set in motion an inflationary spiral by which many saw their own affluence of the past years endangered. The Communist offensive, aimed at undermining the Socialist electorate, was addressed to the masses who, due to the process of industrialization, had moved from rural areas to the cities, and who were acquiring a new awareness of political problems. Communist propaganda attempted to demonstrate the inadequacy of the center-left policies. The Communists accused the government of having narrowed down the scope of the original program and of pursuing a policy of discrimination against those workers represented by the Communist Party without whose collaboration, according to the Communists, there could be no government action that would benefit the working classes.

These were the two most important lines of the electoral campaign which the opponents of the center-left on both sides conducted tirelessly and with the use of considerable financial means. Contributing to these attacks were a number of major scandals in the administration which broke out just on the eve of the electoral campaign and were quickly exploited both by right and left: the right accused the government of following a policy that would lead to the disintegration of the state and its administrative structures, while the Communists denounced the political corruption that fed largely on the monopoly of power held by the DC.

The parties of the majority were unable to counteract effectively this onslaught, which engaged them on two fronts. Their electoral campaign was conducted almost entirely on the defensive. The only party not to be hurt by or involved in the charges and counter charges of this campaign was the Social Democratic party. Due to a shrewd policy and the able leadership of Saragat, it succeeded in convincing those in favor of the "opening" but with some reservations about it that the Social Democratic Party represented a moderating element within the coalition favoring the experiment but proceeding gradually and with caution.

THE RESULTS

The elections held on April 28th had the following results:

Elections to the House of Representatives

Parties	Votes polled	Seats
PCI	7,767,601	166
PSI	4,255,836	87
PSDI	1,876,271	33
PRI	420,213	6
DC	11,773,182	260
PLI	2,144,270	39
PDIUM	536,948	8
MSI	1,570,282	27
Others	407,999	4

The shifts that had taken place between the 1958 and the 1963 elections in overall terms were notable. The DC lost about 750,000 votes, the PLI and the PCI each won about one million votes and the Social Democrats half a million; the Monarchists lost 900,000 and the MSI gained 150,000; the vote for the Socialist and the Republican parties varied only slightly.

For a more precise evaluation of the results, however, one must consider that since the previous elections (1958) there had been an increase of about 1,200,000 valid votes resulting from the growth of the electoral body. These votes should be taken into account in the percentage increase or decrease. It emerges then that the greatest increase was realized by the PLI, with about 3.5 per cent, followed by the Communists with about 2.6 per cent and the PSDI with 1.5 per cent. The DC sustained the most important losses, 4.1 per cent, followed by the Monarchists with 3.2 per cent. With regard to the other parties, the MSI showed a slight increase (0.3 per cent), the PSI a slight drop (—0.4 per cent) and the Republicans remained stationary.

These results differed significantly from the forecasts made on the eve of the elections. While the success of the Liberals and Social Democrats had been predicted, the disintegration of the Monarchists, the maintenance of the Socialist position and the losses sustained by the DC surpassed all expectations. The most striking success of the elections was the progress achieved by the Communists, which on the eve of the election was not expected, even by the organs of the party itself; others had even prognosticated some regression.

AN EVALUATION OF THE RESULTS

The analysis of the results and the evaluation of the causes that had produced them would lead to the following general conclusions.

23.

The votes lost by the DC were the votes of conservatives who had supported the majority party so long as it promised to protect their interests. These votes were transferred to the Liberal Party, which had been, among the right-wing opposition, because of the uniformity of its policies and the ability of its leadership, by far the most effective and convincing. The fading away of the Monarchist Party would indicate the political weakening of its position and hence its electorate. A part of the Monarchist voters, from bourgeois milieu, may have given their votes to the Liberals; while that part of the southern population which had favored the Monarchists because of an ancient attachment to the monarchy, out of ignorance of its own political interests may even have given its votes to the PCI. It also appeared at the time that a great number of votes of migratory workers from the South, particularly in the industrial triangle Genoa-Turin-Milan, and primarily in the two latter cities, went to the PCI. These people, emerging from the isolation of their home areas, had come into contact with a more socially and politically progressive environment, which shook them out of the fatalistic frame of mind that is characteristic of the poorest areas of the South. The southern rural inhabitant, as he was transformed into an industrial worker, under the impact of shrewdly devised propaganda, voted for the Communist Party in protest against a social system that had compelled him to leave his home yet did not enable him to integrate completely into his new environment. The increase of Communist votes was a reflection further of a protest among part of the Socialist electorate, who were dissatisfied with the program of the center-left, expressing a demand for a policy more committed to the reform of structures. The losses of the PSI on the left, however, were almost entirely compensated for by its gains on the right, representing the votes of those who supported the center-left, and who in, recognition of the democratic evolution of the PSI, voted for this party for the first time.

In conclusion, outside of the individual variations in the vote, the center-left parties, as a whole, managed to maintain their strength. It appeared possible that the losses sustained by the DC might be regained in the next elections, in view of the fact that the unexpected increase in Communist votes produced considerable apprehension among the moderate electorate. It was hence conceivable that there would be a reflux of Liberal votes back to the DC which has traditionally benefited from the fear of Communism. The other conclusion which clearly emerged from the elections was the absence of any kind of political alternative to the center-left. The political events of the following years were to demonstrate that this assumption was correct.

CHAPTER 4

THE ECONOMIC MIRACLE

In the ten years between 1952-1962 Italy made more progress in the economic field than in the entire preceding span of the twentieth century. To support this statement it is enough to compare the data on national income. In fifty years, that is, between 1901 and 1950, the per capita income in Italy increased 62 per cent; the increase registered in the ten years 1950-1960 was 47 per cent; while the global revenue over the same years almost doubled.[1]

This evolution, the basis of which was a high general increase in production, became especially intensive during the third legislature. The rate of overall increase, which between 1950 and 1958 had oscillated around 5 per cent, rose, between 1958 and 1962, to 6 and 7 per cent. These figures also bear out the contention that in these recent years the country changed more than in the fifteen preceding years. A development of a magnitude such as that which

---

[1] In spite of the remarkable increase in the national income recorded over the last years, per capita income in Italy is still considerably below that in the most important Western European countries:

Italy	$ 580
United Kingdom	$1245
France	$1167
Western Germany	$1142

In 1960, the year to which the data are referred, the per capita income of the United States was $2539.

344

took place in Italy between 1958 and 1962 could not have failed to produce deep changes in the structures of society and in social habits.

This transformation, which could be observed in the many facets of everyday life, much more so than might be evident from production figures, is at the heart of what has been called the "Italian miracle." The miracle was first of all economic, since it was based on the exceptional results achieved in the field of production, but it was also a social miracle since its effects were felt, though not in equal proportion, by the whole society.

Of the two aspects of the "miracle", the economic one can be more easily evaluated; statistics show the extent of the increase of income, production and investments, etc. The "social miracle" can also be evaluated quantitatively in some of its aspects, such as the increase in the standard of living, the level of consumption and the movement of the population. But its qualitative elements remain outside even approximate evaluation, either because of the lack of appropriate instruments of measurement or because the natural dynamics of these phenomena manifest themselves only within a long period of time.

Only the most important aspects of this dual phenomenon need be stressed here, along with a necessarily general evaluation of the possible political consequences.

The basic characteristic of this economic growth has been a progressive divergence between the rythm of industrial and agricultural development. In the last decade the yearly increase in agricultural production has been modest, around 3 per cent, while the yearly increase of industrial production has been about 9 per cent, and more recently it went as high as 13.6 per cent (1960).

In some sectors of production industrial development reached a record output. As occurs in most expanding economies, the increase was most marked in production goods as opposed to consumer goods and greater in durable consumer goods. Major progress was realized in metallurgy, the automobile industry and the chemical industry.

	1959	1960	1961	1962
Steel	6,761,799	8,229,068	9,124,286	9,490,320
Automobiles	470,661	595,907	693,672	877,811

If the figures relating to employment are considered by sector, the discrepancy between agricultural and industrial activity appears even greater. While in industry and in the services there was a considerable increase in manpower units both in the absolute and relative sense, in agriculture a general decrease was evident beginning from 1955.

The following figures are for the working population by economic sectors in the years between 1952 and 1962:

	Agriculture	*Industry*	*Tertiary*
1952	7,663,000	5,728,000	4,681,000
1962	5,430,000	7,991,000	6,368,000

In percentages, the agricultural working population receded from 39.6 per cent to 26.2 per cent, while in industry and in the tertiary activities the increase was, respectively, from 29.6 to 38.6 per cent and from 24.2 to 30.8 per cent. Hence in the ten years under examination, a complete reversal of positions took place; while in 1952 agricultural activities engaged the highest percentage of the working population, in 1962 the agricultural population had been clearly outnumbered by both industrial and tertiary population.

This reversal resulted not only from a greater absorption of the unemployed and new manpower by industry and the services, but above all also from a massive displacement of manpower from agriculture to industry.

This is perhaps the most evident and most characteristic aspect of the "Italian miracle." The transfers from agricultural to industrial activity occurred everywhere, as may be deduced from the reduction in the number of agricultural laborers in the North and of tenant farmers in Central Italy. But the phenomenon occurred on an even larger scale in the southern areas. It was not just a local transfer from agricultural to industrial activities corresponding to a local

346

industrial expansion; it was a genuine migration cutting across regional and geographic boundaries, whose momentum was still unbroken by 1963, from the Calabrian and Sicilian agricultural areas to the great industrial cities of the North in general, and the industrial triangle Turin-Genoa-Milan[1] in particular.

It has been claimed that the "economic miracle" was made possible by the manpower resources of the South, without which the "boom", which got its major impetus from the northern industries, would not have been possible. If one considers the incessant flow of migratory workers up the peninsula every month, accompanied by tens of thousands of families, to the extent of emptying the southern rural areas, one cannot but conclude that this movement, although perhaps not the decisive factor, was still an essential factor of the "miracle". The importance of the availability of manpower is confirmed by the preoccupation with the possibility of having to limit the process of expansion in the not-so-distant future, precisely because of a shortage in manpower reserves. The scarcity of specialized workers, in particular, which the northern industries have already experienced for some time has induced various enterprises to offer advantageous inducements to Italian workers who have emigrated abroad to return and train while on the job. Hence the ancient and painful movement of emigration, which year after year compelled thousands of workers to become expatriates, has slackened in Italy. A contrary trend is now evident, that of a gradual repatriation of many emigrants from abroad back to their home regions.

	Emigration of workers to foreign countries	Returns of workers to Italy
1957	341,733	163,277
1958	255,459	139,038
1959	268,490	156,121
1960	383,908	192,235
1961	371,611	207,132

---

[1] It is estimated that every year more than 100,000 persons, most from the South, emigrate to Milan.

Another change of fundamental importance in the field
of labor resulting from the exceptional growth of production
is the clear decrease in unemployment registered from 1956
on, even though unemployment and underemployment are
still problems to be dealt with. The training and instruction
of unemployed manpower and the adoption of better organizational techniques in all sectors of economic and administrative life appears as the most effective means to cope
with the phenomenon. The solution to the overall problem
which has been the most serious of all facing the country
since Italian unity, however, is now in sight. The attainment
of full employment is expected in 1970-1971, if the situation
will continue to develop favorably.

Unemployed (in thousands)

1956	1,867
1957	1,662
1958	1,340
1959	1,120
1960	846
1961	720
1962	623

NEW TRENDS IN ITALIAN SOCIETY

The effects of the "Italian miracle" by now permeate
every aspect of the country's economic life and have a decided impact on the living habits of the Italian people.

The employment of capital and investments has increased. Foreign trade has increased as well as foreign investments in Italy. The productivity of labor has likewise
gone up about 25 per cent between 1957 and 1962. Wages
and consumption have also increased and important changes
are evident in the distribution of goods.

Gross investment: 1958-1962 (in billion lire)

1953	2,284
1958	3,576
1959	3,935
1960	4,746
1961	5,358

Expenses for consumer goods[1] (in billion lire)

1953	8,532
1958	11,294
1959	11,810
1960	12,777
1961	13,800

With regard to individual consumption, the percentage expended for food has decreased from 52 per cent (1951) to 44 per cent (1960), while the consumption per capita of industrial products, clothing, electrical appliances, housing, amusements, travel and books has increased. The economic expansion of the last ten years and the growth in the standard of living have diminished considerably the distance in the major social and economic indices between Italy and the economically more advanced countries. Until a few years ago Italy was one of the group of European underveloped countries along with Spain, Greece and Portugal. It is now preparing to join the major industrial powers.

An economic revolution such as the one that has taken place in Italy during the last ten years obviously has profound repercussions on the social and political life of the country. It has brought into the open, and even exasperated the profound structural disequilibrium of the state and of Italian society. The very continuation of this process of development therefore and its best utilization presupposes the solution of problems that are primarily political and social in nature.

The economic boom happened unexpectedly and the forces and energies that it liberated have been restricted and hampered by the structures of a state which is passing through a profound crisis of authority and organization.

Some of the problems provoked by the process of industrialization and the massive internal emigration in cojunction with it are illustrative. In the South entire villages have lost the better part of their population within a few

---

[1] Including: food and beverages, tobacco, clothing, housing, health, transportation, communication, culture and recreation.

years; the depopulation of vast areas has rendered a series of already completed, or about to be completed, reform projects unusable. Thousands of peasant properties abandoned all along the peninsula have caused a further aggravation of the situation of agriculture, not only reducing its income but causing a crisis in its structural system traditionally based on the agricultural laborer and the sharecropper. In view of these facts it is imperative to stop the process of depopulation of the rural areas. This involves not only areas in the South but also in the center along the Appenines and in some of the mountainous regions of the North. Such measures should correspond both to the requirements of modern techniques (mechanization of agriculture) and to the demands for social progress urgently manifest in the genuine rebellion of the peasants against the condition of social and economic inferiority in which they were held for centuries.

	Agricultural Income	National Income (in billion lire at the current prices.)
1953	2,678	10,193
1958	3,011	14,718
1959	3,033	15,777
1960	2,993	17,132
1961	3,297	18,905

In the areas most affected by the emigration of the southern masses, with their primitive living habits and low standard of education, all the phenomena typical of rural to urban migration are manifest, such as an enormous rise in the value of usable real estate, exploited by speculation; a crisis in transport and public services; delinquency; an increase in social stratification and the creation of privilege within the same social class; and tensions and conflicts between the immigrants and their new environment.

The administrative problems caused by these new situations are of first magnitude. From the political standpoint the position of inferiority of the immigrants made them vulnerable to demagogic exploitation by extremist parties. The elections of 1963 demonstrated with what facility the Communist Party succeeded in turning this situation to its own advantage.

On the administrative level the situation is rendered extremely difficult because of the scant possibilities the communal and provincial administrations have to intervene. The action of local organs is limited in reality both by the lack of adequate financial means, and by an administrative system which subjects local initiative to the most minute controls by the central organs. The latter in fact have never before demonstrated their inefficiency more than in recent years.

Furthermore, the rapidity with which the process of development had taken place rendered solutions obsolete which had been approved on the political level. It is now evident, for instance, that in the light of the economic and social consequences of the "miracle", the problem of the South poses itself in a radically different way from what it was a few years ago. Although the process of industrialization has also penetrated the South, the cleavage between North and South has increased instead of diminished. Although around some of the areas of industrial development, the standard of living has risen considerably, in agricultural zones it has fallen as a result of the massive emigration. Faced with the flight from the land, the continuation of such programs as the land reform would be an unnecessary dissipation of means and time.

In the era of the "miracle", the southern problem cannot be dealt with as an isolated phenomenon, solvable by specific local measures, as formerly. On the contrary, a solution to the problem of the South now appears as an integral part of a solution to the over-riding national problem of the disequilibrium between economic sectors (industry and agriculture) and between regions (the North and the South). The elimination of this unbalance is the necessary prelude to a better distribution of the national income, which has been the basic aim of Italian politics since 1945.

In the course of 1963 an excessive increase in consumption, resulting from the higher purchasing power accumulated during the years of the boom, arrested the process of economic expansion and ushered in a period of recession.[1]

The Italian economic boom had been sustained largely by a steady increase in exports, made possible by the expansion of international trade and in particular by the growth of the European Common Market, in which Italy has been one of the most active participants.[2] From 1957 until 1961 the balance of payments remained quite favorable, thereby helping to establish the lira as one of the most solid currencies in the world. Beginning in 1962, the tendency was suddenly reversed. In the period from October 1962 to March 1964, due to an exceptional increase in the import of consumer goods, the balance of payments showed a deficit of about 1,855 million dollars. The stability of the lira was seriously threatened at the same time that a rapid increase in prices initiated an inflationary spiral. In order to avoid a devaluation, which would have had serious economic and social consequences, the Italian goverment was compelled to embark on a policy of strict credit limitations, intended to reduce consumption as well as productive investments. The initial financial crisis was then trasformed into a general economic recession, accompanied by a slowdown in productive activity, which was especially acute in certain sectors. In the building trade industry, which in the years 1961 and 1962 had attracted small investors who were favored by a policy of small and medium long-term loans, the crisis developed into one of major proportions.

The recession, or *congiuntura* as it became widely known,

---

[1] In 1963, the total amount of private spending exceeded 17,500 billion lire out of a total net income of 24,200 billion lire.

[2] From 1959, the year in which the Common Market countries agreed on the first 10% decrease in customs tariffs, Italian trade with the community increased at a much faster rate than the country's trade with the rest of the world.

352

was determined largely by political factors, as well as by strictly economic causes. As on previous occasions in the course of the country's history, past and present, the reformist aims of the government provoked a strong adverse reaction in the business community. The nationalization of electric energy, although it had been carried out under particularly favorable conditions for the expropriated firms, and the projected law on urban-planning (a measure that has been periodically announced but that has not as yet been enacted), which envisages a massive expropriation of construction real estate at 1958 rates, and other reform measures, discouraged and antagonized private entrepreneurs. Believing their own interests threatened by center-left policies and fearing the adoption of even more radical measures in the future, they tended to whittle down their own production and to suspend their programs of investment. A typical example of outright panic, which occurred among the less responsible circles of private industry, was the "flight of capital". It is estimated that in the last months of 1963 and the first months of 1964 more than 100 billion lire were transferred clandestinely to Swiss banks by those who feared new nationalizations and who anticipated that the results of the center-left policies would be catastrophic. Another phenomenon tending to heighten lack of confidence and pessimism among capital investors was a substantial increase in labor costs, which under the pressure of the trade unions were steadily rising. In the vast sector of the manufacturing industries, it is estimated that for the year 1963 average salaries increased by 15.9%, corresponding to an increase in productivity of only 5.6%. The falling off of competition among Italian industries, as a result, and a drammatic reduction in profits were further factors that weighed negatively on the decisions of businessmen.

These economic, political and psychological factors combined to make a solution to the problems of the economic recession extremely difficult. They were bound to influence profoundly the orientation of the center-left governments, which succeded each other in office after the April 1963 elections.

CHAPTER 5

THE OPENING TO THE LEFT: SECOND PHASE

THE FIRST AND SECOND MORO CABINETS

The uncertainty of the electorate with regard to the center-left formula, made manifest by the election results of 1963, and the economic recession, forced the center-left coalition to abandon for the time being its programmatic realizations. Within the DC in particular, the substantial loss of votes to the right-wing Liberals encouraged the opposition of moderate and conservative currents, which continued to regard the collaboration with the Socialists with reserve. On the other hand, the electoral results, although not entirely satisfactory to the center-left parties, provided no other avenue to a solution. Any possibility of a return to the former centrism being excluded, no other path remained but to continue on the one that had been taken, giving consideration to the trends indicated by the electoral results. These not only appeared to suggest a moderation of the center-left program, but also indicated a need to clarify the relationship between the government parties and the Socialist Party, which, although part of the government majority, had demonstrated that it was not yet prepared to share the responsibilities of government. The PSI's persistence in this position, more akin to that of a critic than of a participant, not only risked ultimately weakening the center-left formula but in the long run also seriously jeopardizing the PSI itself, which was caught between two fires: the Communists, who accused it of betraying the working class, and the conservative forces, which doubted its democratic conversion.

Following the elections, Prime Minister Amintore Fanfani, as was customary, presented his resignation to the government. The Tuscan politician, who headed the strongest left-wing current of the Christian Democracy Party, and who had a reputation as a radical and a "difficult man," was not in accord with the new tendencies, which favored a moderate re-edition, or as it was called, a "clean-up" of the center left. The most fitting candidate to quiet the fears of the DC and its electorate, as well as to negotiate with the Socialists from a position of authority was the secretary of the DC, Aldo Moro. After receiving the commission from President Segni to form the government, Moro first made certain of the collaboration of the Repubblicans and Social Democrats before tackling the more important negotiations with the Socialists. Despite the fact that Pietro Nenni and several of his lieutenants had accepted the idea of direct participation in the government, the strength of the currents in opposition, headed by Riccardo Lombardi and Tullio Vecchietti, and the disillusion within the party over its losses at the polls, persuaded Nenni to postpone Socialist entry into the government. Once again the negotiations were limited to the question of external participation of the Socialists in the majority. Agreement was reached after three weeks of intensive and arduous negotiations, interrupted first by the illness and then by the death of Pope John XXIII, which profoundly stirred the country and placed the problem of the ministerial crisis in the background. Hewever, the agreed-upon program, which followed the lines of the proceding Fanfani Government but was oriented much more toward the center, was roundly rejected by the Socialist Central Committee at its meeting on June 17th.

Confronted with the intransigence of the PSI left wing, the only course open was to bid for time in the expectation that the situation would evolve and that the disposition of forces within the PSI would be altered at the Socialist national congress scheduled to take place in the fall. In this situation the only alternative to tide the country over the crisis was to constitute a new monocolor interim government. On June 19th, the mandate was given to the Christian Democrat, Giovanni Leone, president of the Chamber and a personality above party currents. His business government, composed exclusively of Christian Democrats, was charged with expediting pending business such as the vote on the budget, and with governing the country until the political situation had been clarified. The political truce assured by the Leone Government bore fruit. While opposition to the center-left formula diminished within the DC, due to an evident lack of alternatives, the Nenni current in the PSI gained ground. At the Socialist congress, which took place on October 25-29, Nenni's position prevailed, although he had difficulty in winning over the group headed by Riccardo Lombardi. Nenni's victory opened the way to the formation of a new government of the center left. On November 5th, Prime Minister Leone handed in his resignation, and following almost a month of further negotiations, Aldo Moro, the politician most indicated to carry out this delicate operation, formed the first coalition government composed of sixteen Christian Democrats, six Socialists, three Social Democrats and one Republican.

The historic Socialist decision to return to the government after more than sixteen years of absence was, however, to have adverse consequences for the unity of the party. On December 17th, during the vote of confidence on the Moro Government, twenty-five deputies and thirteen senators belonging to the PSI decided to abstain in protest against the decision of the Socialist majority. The direction of the PSI referred the rebel deputies to the party's committee of control, which acted to suspend them from all political activity for one year. This measure, although not unusually severe, provided the representatives of the Socialist left wing with the pretext to leave the party. On January 11th, the secessionists gathered in Rome and announced their break from the party. They founded a new socialist party under the name of Socialist Party of Proletarian Unity (PSIUP), electing Tullio Vecchietti as political secretary. The Socialist Party lost more than one-fourth of its deputies to the new party,[1] but a much lower percentage of its membership. The PSIUP became the extreme left wing of the Italian political spectrum, taking an even more radical line, especially in matters of foreign policy, than the PCI.[2]

The Moro Government, which received one of the largest majorities in ten years (350 votes in favor to 233 opposed in the Chamber; 175 in favor to 111 opposed in the Senate), presented a program which, while it retained some parts of the original center-left program (the establishment of regional administrations, the projected law to regulate urban-planning, the formulation of an economic plan that would respect private initiative), explicitly excluded new nationalizations, and put major stress upon an economic policy designed to maintain the stability of the lira and to fight inflation.

These were assurances the country required in the face of the worsening economic situation, which in the first months of 1964 entered its most critical phase. At the end of February, in order to reverse the unfavorable trend in the balance of payments and to arrest the continuous increase in prices, the Council of Ministers decided upon a series of measures tending to limit consumption.[3] These measures were followed a few weeks later by an international financial operation, according to which credit facilities were extended to Italy by the U.S. Treasury and the International Monetary Fund for one billion 250 million dollars. It was valuable aid, which expressed confidence in an Italian recovery and helped to save the lira. At the same time, the government

---

[1] Twelve out of 44 senators and 26 out of 87 deputies joined the PSIUP.

[2] The congress of the PSIUP, held in Rome in December 1965, concluded with a manifestation of open sympathy for the Chinese ideological line.

[3] These consisted of a special purchase tax on cars, an increase in the price of gasoline, and greater discipline in installment-plan buying (which had developed increasingly in recent years). Subsequently, a special 20% tax was imposed on luxury goods and a 20% increase for three years was made in the general turnover tax.

initiated a program to boost Italian exports abroad, a move that met with immediate success, literally reversing, in the course of a few months, the unfavorable balance of payments.[1]

Despite the rapid improvement in the financial situation in the first semester of 1964, the problem of economic stagnation continued, characterized by a reduction in industrial production in some sectors (textiles, the mechanical industries) and an increase in the number of unemployed. This prompted the government to moderate further its reform measures, already considerably watered down in the program of the Moro Government. It adopted a traditional economic policy, considered more likely to resolve rapidly the imbalances that had become manifest in various sectors of production, as well as to calm the fears of businessmen on whom recovery in large measure depended. This policy aroused protest and resistance among the most intransigent Socialist elements and in particular the Lombardi group, which was represented in the government by Antonio Giolitti, Minister of the Budget. Disappointed in the expectation that they would be able to expedite structural reforms, on the basis of which they had agreed to participate in the government, they were frankly looking for a pretext to cause a government crisis, hoping to prepare the way for more radical policies.

The occasion arose in June 1964 during the debate over the budget for public instruction, which envisaged a small increase (149 million lire) in the state contributions to private intermediary schools. These are in major part administered by the Catholic Church. Taking advantage of the traditional anti-clerical position of the party, the Lombardi group succeeded in persuading the Socialist deputies to abstain; the Social Democrats and Republicans followed their example, in order not to leave the impression that the Socialists alone were the defenders of the state schools.

---

[1] In the 12 months between April and March 1965 the Italian balance of payments showed a surplus of 1,282 million dollars.

The vote on the projected bill, on June 25th, was 228 against, 225 in favor and 56 abstentions, placing the government in the minority. The Prime Minister, acknowledging that underlying the pretext of state contributions to private schools was a difference of much vaster scope, handed in his resignation. Lombardi's aim of creating a government oriented further to the left, which would be open to the Communists, not only failed, however, but produced the contrary results. Once again, Moro, who represented the moderate center left, received the commission to form a new government. It was constituted at the end of July with a program which was not only directed almost exclusively toward combatting the economic recession, but which also modified still further the urban planning bill measure, the last surviving aspect of the original center-left program.[1]

The second Moro Government, again a coalition of the Socialists (representing the majority current, which had once more succeeded in neutralizing the Lombardi group), the Social Democrats and the Republicans, was to be one of the longest-lived of the post-war period, remaining in office until January 1966.

EPILOGUE

After one and half years the Moro Government had not tackled any of the basic problems that the center-left program had proposed to solve. On the other hand, it had been formed with the primary objective of reversing the economic trend and of placing the national economy back on the road toward expansion and development. At the end of 1965, despite the fact that the government had not always acted with the necessary energy and speed, there could be no doubt that its aim had been largely, although

---

[1] The general expropriation, envisaged by the original project of the law, was limited to centers in which "particular local plans" existed and to zones of "recognized urbanization".

not entirely, realized. The economic balance-sheet at the end of the year showed a general gain.[1] Signs of crisis persisted in some sectors and the number of unemployed was still over one million, but the prospects for the immediate future were more favorable than they had been at the beginning of the second semester of 1964. The political achievement of the Moro Government, in effecting a working relationship between the two major parties of the coalition, the DC and the PSI, was no less important. Although there had been difficult moments, their collaboration appeared to have become sufficiently consolidated to give rise to the hope for a long period of political stability. The exercise of power in a particularly difficult moment for the working class and the necessity to underwrite unpopular decisions produced in the PSI a new consciousness of its own political responsibilities. Having abandoned the sterile, traditional, maximalist positions of its long and historic past, the Socialist Party was in the process of orienting toward a more concrete and modern conception of political struggle.

Two important events occurred in the second half of 1964 which pointed to new directions in the evolution of the nation's political forces. The first was the death of the Communist leader, Palmiro Togliatti,[2] which took place in August at Yalta (Crimea) where the Communist leader was for a period of rest, and the second, the election to the presidency of the Republic of Giuseppe Saragat, former leader of the Social Democrats.

A man of indisputable prestige and ability, Togliatti had

---

[1] The industrial production has increased by 4,2, national income by 3,4 but for 1966 national income is expected to grow to a 4,5%.

[2] Palmiro Togliatti left, as a sort of spiritual testament, a document later disseminated under the title of Yalta memoir. In it, the leader of the PCI declared himself opposed to the condemnation of Chinese communism which was the ostensible objective of the Communist summit meeting scheduled to convene in Moscow. It contained a number of frank criticisms of the Soviet Communist political line on the subjects of de-Stalinization and the relationships between Communist Parties. For the latter it demanded greater autonomy. The Yalta memoir was widely used in support of their views by groups favoring a greater liberalization within the PCI.

succeeded in maintaining party unity and even safeguarding it through the difficult tests of 1956. His death touched off a struggle over his succession. Luigi Longo was elected to his post as secretary of the party; he was an old and authoritative militant, but he lacked Togliatti's culture and political finesse. Following Longo in the party hierarchy were two young leaders, Giovanni Amendola and Pietro Ingrao. They had reached political maturity during the anti-fascist struggle and in the immediate post-war years, and they were far removed from the influence of international or Russian communism. Both tried to promote the so-called "Italian road to socialism," which Togliatti had already cautiously indicated. But the opposing directions they advocated competitively, and certain manifestations of revisionism difficult to reconcile with the ideological orthodoxy of the party, ended up by creating confusion and disarray within the party and by dividing it into two opposed currents. The Socialist alignment with the parties of the democratic left and the stabilization of the center-laft formula completed the already considerable isolation of the Italian Communist Party. The ideological ferment within the last two years has made it incapable of taking any precise political course, and the open division following Togliatti's death have placed it in a position of immobility and crisis. Nonetheless, the PCI continues to maintain its position as the second largest party, as confirmed by the results of the last elections,[1] due to its impressive grassroots organization and its influence on the masses.

The election of a new President of the Republic in the final days of 1964 was necessitated by the illness of Antonio Segni. Segni, who had been elected to the presidency in May 1962, was obliged to resign following an interim period of three months, in the course of which the presidential func-

---

[1] The elections for the renewal of local administrative organs held on November 22, 1964, produced the following results (in percentages: DC, 37.36; PCI, 26.02; PSI, 11.30; PLI, 7.95; PSDI, 6.60; MSI, 5.0; PSIUP, 2.90; PRI, 1.2; PDIUM (Monarchist Party) 0.9.

tions were carried out by Cesare Merzagora, President of the Senate. The election of Giuseppe Saragat to the highest office of the state came about as the result of the irreconcilable positions assumed by two tendencies, within the DC, each supporting its own candidate: Giovanni Leone for the center-right current and Amintore Fanfani for the center-left. The intransigency of the two factions ended by neutralizing both and opened the way, after twenty ballots (one of which was held on Christmas day), for the election of the Social Democratic leader, who received 646 preferential votes out of 937, with 10 abstentions and 150 blank votes [1]

The profound crisis within the DC, which became evident on this occasion, compelled its secretary, Mariano Rumor, to take energetic action to restore party unity. He pressed for the dissolution of the organizations of the currents within the party, and the reestablishment of greater authority in the hands of the secretariat and of the organs of the central direction.

The election of Saragat, a strong personality with whom the PSDI had been identified for many years, and the increased integration of the PSI in the government majority, brought to the fore once again the question of "socialist unification", which Saragat himself had tried to re-initiate in the spring of 1964.[2] The possibility of a fusion between the PSI and the PSDI into a mass party of socialist democracy acquired greater actuality in the second half of 1965. Following the national congress of the two parties (November 1965 for the PSI and January 1966 for the PSDI), it entered the first cautious phase toward realization. If the unification should be achieved, as now seems likely, it could have important and far-reaching effects on the Italian political alignment. Outside of guaranteeing greater political stability

---

[1] Saragat received the votes of the Communists, Socialists, Social-Democrats and Republicans, and of at least two thirds of the Christian Democrats. The PSIUP and the remaning third of the DC voted blank ballot. Neofascists and Liberals voted for their own candidates: Augusto De Marsanich and Gaetano Martino.

[2] For the attempts at socialist unification, see page 296.

and consolidating the center-left platform, the unification could make a valuable contribution to that process of concentration of political forces that is an essential condition for a politically mature democratic society. But the basic political value of the move consists in the promotion of a strong progressive force, which, leaving aside the traditional ideological positions that have proved inadequate in the face of the recent evolution of Italian society, would lean toward a concept of political struggle that would better correspond to the real and concrete requirements of a society engaged in the process of peaceful development. In this sense socialist unification could provide an effective pole of attraction for the broad masses, whose present domination by the Communist Party constitutes a major obstacle to the formation of a well-integrated political society.

This could happen, however, only if the unified party posed new solutions to the problems of Italian society. The experience of three years of the center-left has demonstrated that before nationalizations or the threat of nationalizations, genuine structural reforms are necessary to create the preconditions for a more efficient functioning of society and its institutions and for a better utilization of those powers that are vested in the state. This is particularly true in a country such as Italy, where for historical and economic reasons the state has arrogated to itself broad functions in all fields, from the economy to education.

The crisis of the state, which in recent years has been blatantly and sometimes dramatically manifest in scandals, obvious shortcomings, and conflicts of power over what are its basic functions, from the administration of justice to education, make the need for energetic reforms especially urgent. Instruments such as those of economic planning through which future governments would control the development of the national economy and assure a more equitable redistribution of wealth, would lose their entire usefulness if the administrative organs of the state were to remain at the level of their present inefficiency. For this reason we do not think it unrealistic to affirm that, outside of the more or less messianic and integralistic aims that have traditionally influenced the positions of the Italian parties, the political struggle in the future will be engaged over such subjects as administrative reform, the functioning of justice, the modernization of the educational system, and the reorganization of social security. The future of Italian society will depend on the extent to which these problems are met and solved.

BIBLIOGRAPHY

GENERAL

CATALANO, Franco, *L'Italia dalla dittatura alla democrazia (1918-1948)*, Milano, Lerici Editore, 1962.

CHABOD, Federico, *A History of Italian Fascism*, London, Weidenfeld & Nicolson, 1963.

GRINDROD, Muriel, *The Rebuilding of Italy*, London, Royal Institute of International Affairs, 1955.

HUGHES, H. Stuart, *The United States and Italy*, Cambridge, Mass., Harvard University Press, 1953.

JEMOLO, A. Carlo, *Chiesa e stato in Italia negli ultimi cento anni*, Torino, Einaudi, 1952.

MACK SMITH, Dennis, *Italy. A Modern History*, Ann Arbor, The University of Michigan Press, 1959.

SALVATORELLI L., and MIRA F., *Storia d'Italia nel periodo fascista*, Torino, Einaudi, 1956.

WISKEMAN, Elizabeth, *Italy*, London, Oxford University Press, 1947.

THE WAR 1939-1945 AND THE END OF FASCISM

BADOGLIO, Pietro, *Italy in the Second World War*, London, Oxford University Press, 1948.

BARTOLI, Domenico, *Vittorio Emanuele III*, Milano, Mondadori, 1946.

BATTAGLIA, Roberto, *Storia della Resistenza Italiana*, Torino, Einaudi, 1953.

BIANCHI, Gianfranco, *25 luglio, crollo di un regime*, Milano, Mursia, 1963.

BIANCO, D. Livio, *Guerra partigiana*, Torino, Einaudi, 1954.

BONOMI, Ivanoe, *Diario di un anno: 2 giugno 1943 - 10 giugno 1944*, Milano, Garzanti 1947.

CHURCHILL, S. Winston, *The Second World War*, vol. 5: *Closing the Ring*, Boston, Houghton Mifflin Co., 1951.

CIANO, Galeazzo, *The Ciano Diaries 1939-1943*, New York, Doubleday, 1945.

CLARK, W. Mark, *Calculated Risk*, New York, Harper, 1950.

CROCE, Benedetto, *Quando l'Italia era tagliata in due (settembre 1943 - giugno 1944)*, Bari, Laterza, 1946.

DEAKIN, F. William, *The Brutal Friendship*, New York, Harper & Row, 1962.

FAVAGROSSA, Carlo, *Perché perdemmo la guerra*, Milano, Rizzoli, 1946.

FRANCOVICH, Carlo, *La Resistenza a Firenze*, Firenze, La Nuova Italia, 1962.

GOBETTI, Piero, *La Rivoluzione Liberale*, Torino, Einaudi, 1950.

GRAMSCI, Antonio, *Lettere dal Carcere*, Torino, Einaudi, 1947.

GRINDROD, Muriel, *The New Italy: Transition from War to Peace*, London, Royal Institute of International Affairs, 1947.

HILTON-YOUNG, W., *The Italian Left: A Short History of Political Socialism in Italy*, London, Longmans, 1949.

Istituto Nazionale per la Storia del Movimento di Liberaz. in Italia, *La Resistenza Europea e gli Alleati*, Milano, Lerici, 1962.

KOGAN, Norman, *Italy and the Allies*, Cambridge, Mass., Harvard University Press, 1956.

MONELLI, Paolo, *Roma 1943*, Roma, Migliaresi, 1944.

MUSSOLINI, Benito, *Memoirs 1942-1943*, London, Weidenfeld & Nicolson, 1949.

PISCHEL, Giuliano, *Che cosa è il Partito d'Azione*, Milano, Tarantola, 1945.

SALVADORI, Max, *Brief History of the Patriot Movement in Italy (1943-1945)*, Chicago, Clemente & Sons, 1954.

SECCHIA, Pietro, *I comunisti e l'insurrezione (1943-1945)*, Roma, Cultura Sociale, 1954.

WEBSTER, Richard, *Christian Democracy in Italy, 1860-1960*, London, Hollis & Carter, 1961.

WISKEMANN, Elizabeth, *The Rome-Berlin Axis*, New York, Oxford University Press, 1949.

THE CRUCIAL YEARS: 1945-1948

ADAMS J.C. & BARILE P., *The Government of Republican Italy*, Boston, Houghton Mifflin Co, 1961.

Banco di Roma, *Review of the Economic Conditions in Italy* (1947-1956), Roma, Banco di Roma, 1957.

CALAMANDREI P. & LEVI P., *Commentario sistematico alla Costituzione Italiana*, Barbera, Firenze, 1950.

Comitato Interministeriale per la Ricostruz., *The Development of Italy's Economic System within the Framework of European Recovery and Cooperation*, Roma, Poligrafico dello Stato, 1952.

COMPAGNA F. & DE CAPRARIIS V., *Geografia delle elezioni italiane dal 1946 al 1953*, Bologna, Il Mulino, 1954.

Confederazione Generale dell'Industria Italiana, *Labour Management Councils in Italy*, Roma, The Confederation, 1951.

CONTI, Giovanni, *La Costituente*, Roma, La Voce, 1956.

CORBINO, Epicarmo, *Limiti e scelta della ricostruzione economica*, Scritti e discorsi, Roma, 1946.

De Castro, Diego, *Il problema di Trieste*, Bologna, Cappelli, 1953.
De Maria, Giovanni, *Problemi economici e sociali del dopoguerra*, Milano, Malfasi, 1951.
Di Maggio, Michele, *Cronache senza Regime (1944-1952)*, Bologna, Cappelli, 1953.
Einaudi, Mario, *Communism in Western Europe*, Ithaca, Cornell University Press, 1951.
Ferrara, Marcella and Ferrara, Maurizio, *Cronache di vita italiana (1944-1958)*, Roma, Editori Riuniti, 1960.
Manzocchi, Bruzio, *Lineamenti di politica economica in Italia (1945-1959)*, Roma, Editori Riuniti, 1960.
Maranini, Giuseppe, *Miti e realtà della democrazia*, Milano, Comunità, 1958.
Pella, Giuseppe, *General Report on Italy's Economic Situation*, Roma, Poligrafico dello Stato, 1951.
Romita, Giuseppe, *Dalla Monarchia alla Repubblica*, Pisa, Nistri-Lischi, 1959.
Rossi, Ernesto, *Settimo: non rubare*, Bari, Laterza, 1952.
Scoccimarro, Mauro, *Il Secondo Dopoguerra*, Roma, Editori Riuniti, 1956.
Sforza, Carlo, *Cinque anni a Palazzo Chigi: La politica estera italiana dal 1947 al 1951*, Roma, Atlante, 1952.
Sturzo, Luigi, *Politica di questi anni. Consensi e critiche. Dal settembre 1946 all'aprile 1948*, Bologna, Zanichelli, 1954.
UNRRA, Italian Mission, *Survey of Italy's Economy*, Roma, UNRRA, June 1947.
U. S. Dept. of State, *Paris Peace Conference, 1946, Selected Documents*, Washington, Government Printing Office, 1947.
Valiani, Leo, *L'avvento di De Gasperi. Tre anni di Politica Italiana*, Torino, De Silva, 1949.

THE YEARS OF QUADRIPARTITE, 1948-1953

Andreotti, Giulio, *De Gasperi e il suo tempo*, Milano, Mondadori, 1956.
Atti della Commissione Parlamentare d'Inchiesta sulla Disoccupazione (16 volumes), Roma, 1954.
Atti della Commissione d'Inchiesta sulla Miseria in Italia e sui mezzi per combatterla (15 volumes), Roma, 1958.
Centro di Documentazione Presidenza del Consiglio, *Italy Today*, Roma, Istituto Poligrafico dello Stato, 1955.
Compagna, Francesco, *La lotta politica italiana nel secondo dopoguerra e il Mezzogiorno*, Bari, Laterza, 1950.
De Gasperi, Alcide, *Discorsi politici*, Roma, Ediz. Cinque Lune, 1956 (2 voll.).
Dieci anni dopo 1945-1955, Bari, Laterza, 1955.
Einaudi, Luigi, *Lo scrittoio del presidente*, Torino, Einaudi, 1956.
Falconi, Carlo, *La chiesa e le organizzazioni cattoliche in Italia, 1945-1955*, Torino, Einaudi, 1956.

367

GALLI, Giorgio, *La Sinistra Italiana nel dopoguerra*, Bologna, Mulino, 1958.

— — *Storia del Partito Comunista Italiano*, Milano, Schwarz, 1958.

GALLI G. & FACCHI P., *La Sinistra Democristiana*, Milano, Feltrinelli, 1962.

JEMOLO, C. Arturo, *Italia tormentata (1946-1951)*, Bari, Laterza, 1951.

LAPALOMBARA, Joseph, *The Italian Labor Movement. Problems and Prospects*, Ithaca, Cornell University Press, 1957.

LA PIRA, Giorgio, *Per una architettura cristiana dello Stato*, Firenze, Libreria Editrice Fiorentina, 1954.

L'Integrazione Europea, edited by Grove Haines, Bologna, Mulino, 1957.

LUZZATTO FEGIZ, Pierpaolo, *Il volto sconosciuto dell'Italia*, Milano, Giuffré, 1956.

MARANINI, GENTILE, TREMELLONI, CIASCA, MOSCA, *Aspetti di vita contemporanea Italiana*, Bologna, Cappelli, 1957.

NEUFELD, Maurice F., *Italy: School for Awakening Countries*, New York, State School of Industrial and Labor Relations, 1961.

Problemi sullo sviluppo delle aree arretrate, Bologna, Mulino, 1960.

RODANÒ, Carlo, *Mezzogiorno e sviluppo economico*, Bari, Laterza, 1954.

ROSSI, Ernesto, *I padroni del vapore*, Bari, Laterza, 1955.

ROSSI, D. Manlio, *Riforma Agraria ed Azione Meridionalista*, Bologna, Edizioni Agricole, 1948.

— — *Dieci Anni di Politica Agraria nel Mezzogiorno*, Bari, Laterza, 1958.

SALVEMINI, Gaetano, *Scritti sulla Questione Meridionale 1896-1955*, Torino, Einaudi, 1955.

SCOCCIMARRO, Mauro, *Il secondo Dopoguerra*, Roma, Editori Riuniti, 1956.

SCOTELLARO, Rocco, *Contadini del Sud*, Bari, Laterza, 1954.

SPINELLI, Altiero, *L'Europa non cade dal cielo*, Bologna, Mulino, 1960.

TARCHIANI, Alberto, *Dieci anni tra Roma e Washington*, Milano, Mondadori, 1955.

VANONI, Ezio, *Discorsi sul programma di sviluppo economico*, Roma, Poligrafico dello Stato, 1956.

VINCIGUERRA, Mario, *I partiti politici italiani dal 1948 al 1955*, Roma, Edizioni Centro Editoriale dell'Osservatore, 1955.

FROM THE FOUR-PARTY COALITION
TO THE OPENING TO THE LEFT, 1953-1958

Atti del Convegno Economico dell'Istituto Gramsci. Marzo 23-25, Roma, Editori Riuniti, 1962.

Atti del I Convegno di Studio della D. C., S. Pellegrino Terme 13-16 Settembre 1961, Roma, Cinque Lune, 1962.

Atti e Documenti della Democrazia Cristiana, 1943-1959, Roma, Cinque Lune, 1959.

BIONDI, Pompeo, *Un'esperienza democratica*, Firenze, Sansoni, 1958.

Centro di Ricerca e Documentazione, *Annuario Politico Italiano 1963*, Milano, Comunità, 1963.

Comitato Internazionale per la Ricostruzione, *Politica di sviluppo. Cinque anni di lavoro*, Roma, Poligrafico dello Stato, 1958.

FANFANI, Amintore, *Anni difficili ma non sterili*, Bologna, Cappelli, 1958.

— — *Da Napoli a Firenze*, Milano, Garzanti, 1959.

— — *Dopo Firenze*, Milano, Garzanti, 1961.

FALCONI, Carlo, *Il Pentagono Vaticano*, Bari, Laterza, 1958.

GIORDANO, Renato, *Il Mercato Comune e i suoi problemi*, Roma, Opere Nuove, 1958.

GONELLA, Guido, *L'Attuazione della Costituzione nel triennio 1955-58*, Roma, Società Nuova, 1958.

GRIECO, Ruggero, *La crisi agraria e i monopoli*, Roma, Ecs, 1957.

GRONCHI, Giovanni, *Discorsi d'America*, Milano, Garzanti, 1956.

LA MALFA, Ugo, *La Crisi del Comunismo e la via della Democrazia*, Bologna, Mulino, 1957.

La propaganda politica in Italia, Bologna, Mulino, 1960.

LENTI, Libero, *Problemi economici d'oggi*, Milano, Garzanti, 1958.

NENNI, Pietro, *Dialogo con la Sinistra Cattolica*, Milano-Roma, Avanti, 1954.

— — *Una legislatura fallita: 1953-1958*, Milano-Roma, Ediz. Avanti, 1958.

— — *Where the Italian Socialists stand*, Foreign Affairs, January, 1962 (p. 221).

ROSSI, Ernesto, *Il Malgoverno*, Bari, Laterza, 1954.

ROSSI, Nerino, *Cinque anni difficili*, Bologna, Cappelli, 1958.

SCALFARI, Eugenio, Convegno (IX) degli "Amici del Mondo", Roma, 1960. *Le Baronie elettriche*, Bari, Laterza, 1960.

SPREAFICO A. & LAPALOMBARA J., *Elezioni e comportamento politico in Italia*, Milano, Comunità, 1963.

TAGLIAMONTE, Francesco, *Questo è il Mercato Comune*, Bologna, Cappelli, 1959.

TREMELLONI, Roberto, *Le strade del benessere in uno stato efficente*, Milano, Istituto Lombardo di Studi Sociali, 1958.

THE OPENING TO THE LEFT 1958-1963

BOCCA, Giorgio, *I giovani leoni del Neo-capitalismo*, Bari, Laterza, 1963.

CARLYLE, Margaret, *The Awakening of Southern Italy*, London, Oxford University Press, 1962.

CLOUGH, Shepard B., *The Economic History of Modern Italy*, New York, Columbia University Press, 1964.

Conferenza Nazionale del P.C.I., Atti e Risoluzioni, Roma, Editori Riuniti, 1964.

Falconi, Carlo, *La Chiesa e le Organizzazioni Cattoliche in Europa*, Milano, Comunità, 1960.

Fanfani, Amintore, *Centro-Sinistra 1962*, Milano, Garzanti, 1963.

Gorresio, Vittorio, *L'Italia a sinistra.* Milano, Rizzoli, 1963.

Hughes, Stuart H., *The United States and Italy, (revised edition)*, Cambridge, Harvard University Press, 1965.

Kogan, Norman, *The Politics of Italian Foreign Policy*, New York, Praeger, 1963.

La Malfa, Ugo, *La Politica Economica in Italia 1946-1962*, Milano, Ediz. di Comunità, 1963.

Lapalombara, Joseph, *Interests Groups in Italian Politics*, Princeton, Princeton University Press, 1964.

Lutz, Vera, *A Study in Economic Development*, London, New York, Toronto, Oxford University Press, 1962.

Nenni, Pietro, *La battaglia Socialista per la svolta a sinistra nella terza Legislatura, 1958-1963*, Milano, Avanti, 1963.

Pesenti, A., Vitello, V., *Tendenze del Capitalismo Italiano*, Roma, Editori Riuniti, 1962.

Saraceno, Pasquale, *L'Italia verso la piena occupazione*, Milano, Feltrinelli, 1963.

Sartori, G., Somogyi, S., Lotti, L., Predieri, A., *Il Parlamento Italiano*, Napoli, ESI, 1963.

Togliatti, Palmiro, *Nella Democrazia e nella Pace verso il Socialismo*, Roma, Editori Riuniti, 1963.

STATISTICS

Istituto Centrale di Statistica, *Annuario Statistico Italiano*, Roma, Poligrafico dello Stato, (yearly publication).

Istituto Centrale di Statistica, *Bollettino Mensile di Statistica*, Roma, Poligrafico dello Stato, (monthly publication).

Monthly Bulletin of Statistics, United Nations, New York.

Presidenza del Consiglio dei Ministri, *Le elezioni politiche 1946, 1948, 1953*, Roma, 1958.

— — *La Terza Legislatura*, Roma, 1963.

Svimez, *Statistiche sul Mezzogiorno d'Italia 1861-1953*, Roma, Svimez, 1954.

INDEX

Scoccimarro, Mauro, 75, 78
Segni, Antonio, 263, 264, 274, 283, 284, 299, 301, 304, 305, 323, 324, 355, 361
Senise, Carmine, 17
Sforza, Count Carlo, 64, 73, 238
Sicilian Separatist Movement, 59
Sicily, 14, 23, 26, 59, 182, 229
Sila, and Reform, 219
Socialdemocratic Party (PSLI, later PSDI), its origin, 140; third De Gasperi cabinet, 142; and tripartite, 188-189; 1948 elections, 194-195; 196; and quadripartite, 201-207, 241; 1953 elections, 250, 254, 255; 256-257; and Scelba cabinet, 271; 299; Zoli government, 305-306; 1958 elections, 309-311; 322, 329, 334; 1963 elections, 340-341; 1964 elections, 361
Socialist Party (PSIUP, later PSI), 37; before World War II, 38, 41-46; conflicts within CLN, 75; non-participation in the second Bonomi cabinet, 79; and post-war problems, 88, 90-91, 93, 95, 96; 1946 e-lections, 108, 115-118; 129; financial problems of Reconstruction, 131; second De Gasperi Government, 134; the party splits, 138-140; article seven, 144; its exclusion from the government, 146-147, 150, 152-153, 157, 158; in the Popular Front, 189-190; 1948 elections, 194-196; situation after 1948 elections, 213, 216; 1953 elections, 249, 251, 253-257; 258; and Scelba cabinet, 272; its relations with DC, 280-281; autonomist tendency within the party, 287-292; Hungarian revolution, 296, 298; 1958 elections, 299, 309, 311; the opening to the left, 315-318, 320, 321, 324, 330-332, 335; 1963 elections, 338-43; 1964 elections, 361
Socialist Party of Proletarian Unity (PSIUP), its foundation, 356; political line, 357; 1964 elections, 361
Socialist Unification, 362

Socialist Unified Party (PSU), 205
Somalia, 171, 172
Sorel, Georges, 34
Spaak, Henri, 238
Spanish Civil War, 5, 46, 48
Sottogoverno, 244
Squadristi, 44-45.
Stalin, 262, 295, 301
Stalingrad, 9
Steel Pact, 4
Stevenson, Adlai, 64
Stone, Ellery, 113, 159
Stralcio Law, 219, 220
Sturzo, Don Luigi, 51, 52-54
Südtiroler Volkspartei, 169
Suez, 294

Tambroni, Ferdinando, 325-329
Tangiers, 22
Tenda, 170
Terre Irredente, 43
Tito, Marshal, 26, 267, 268
Togliatti, Palmiro, 47, 67, 69, 78, 97, 214, 293, 360
Toniolo, Giuseppe, 51
Torino, strikes, March 1943, 8, 48; cradle of Communist party, 47; PSI Congress, 281; 293
Trentino-Alto Adige, Region, 168-169, 182, 186
Trento, 162, 169
Treves, Claudio, 46
Trieste, 162-166; 173, 266-268
Truman, President, 145
Tunisia, campaign, 5, 14
Turati, Filippo, 46

UIL (*Unione Italiana del Lavoro*), 215
Umberto, Crown Prince (later Umberto II), 62, 63, 66, 68, 72, 112, 115
Unità, communist daily, 114, 294
Unità Popolare, 252, 255
Unity of Action Pact, see: *Patto d'Unità d'Azione*
UNRRA, 74, 107, 124, 125, 141
Uomo Qualunque, origin, 99, 108-109; 1946 elections, 116-117; 138, 149, 152; its disintegration, 154; 1948 elections, 189, 194; 245